OFFICIAL COPY.

[Issued with Army Orders for June, 1924.

Crown Copyright Reserved.

SMALL ARMS TRAINING.

VOLUME I.

40
W.O.
8986

1924.

LONDON:
PUBLISHED BY HIS MAJESTY'S STATIONERY OFFICE.

To be purchased directly from H.M. STATIONERY OFFICE at the following addresses
Imperial House, Kingsway, London. W.C. 2; 28, Abingdon Street, London, S.W. 1;
York Street Manchester; 1, St. Andrew's Crescent, Cardiff;
120, George Street. Edinburgh;
or through any Bookseller.

1924.

Price 1s. *Net.*

Issued by Command of the Army Council.

THE WAR OFFICE,
June, 1924.

CONTENTS.

CHAPTER I.

INSTRUCTIONS APPLICABLE TO ALL SMALL ARM WEAPONS.

WEAPONS, GROUND AND FORMATIONS.

THE SMALL ARMS SCHOOL, HYTHE.

CHAPTER II.

THE RIFLE AND BAYONET.

TESTS OF ELEMENTARY TRAINING.

EXERCISING THE TRAINED SOLDIER.

MINIATURE AND 30-YARDS RANGES.

CHAPTER III.
LEWIS GUN TRAINING.

GENERAL INSTRUCTIONS ON TRAINING.

CHAPTER IV.

·303-INCH HOTCHKISS GUN TRAINING.

HOTCHKISS GUN HANDLING.

SMALL ARMS TRAINING.

VOLUME 1

1924.

CHAPTER I.

INSTRUCTIONS APPLICABLE TO ALL SMALL ARM WEAPONS.

PRINCIPLES AND MACHINERY OF TRAINING.

1. *General.*

1. This manual lays down the system of training in the use of the following weapons :—

(*a*) The rifle and bayonet. (Vol. I.)
(*b*) The light machine gun (·303 Lewis and ·303 Hotchkiss).* (Vol. I.)
(*c*) The grenade and rifle grenade. (Vol. II.)
(*d*) The revolver. (Vol. II.)

---

* The Vickers machine gun is dealt with in Machine Gun Training. The term "Light Automatic(s)" is used to refer to either or both of these weapons collectively or generally, according to the context.

2. *Object of small arms or weapon training.*—The purpose of small arms or weapon training is :—

    (*a*) To render the individual soldier proficient in the use of his weapons in battle, to make him acquainted with the capabilities of the weapon with which he is armed, and to give him confidence in its use, power and accuracy.

    (*b*) To ensure that leaders shall be capable (so far as the use of the weapon is concerned) of directing and controlling their commands in war, and of instructing them in peace.

3. A high standard of skill with every weapon with which he is armed is highly desirable in the soldier, but skill at arms must not be regarded as the sole end of weapon training. The most skilfully planned tactical dispositions in war will fail if the men are unable to use their weapons with effect when manœuvre has placed them in a position to do so and conversely, skill at arms by the individual will lose most of its effect in the fight unless skilled leadership directs the weapon to the position most suitable for its employment.

Training will not, therefore, be confined to the training of the soldier to handle the weapon, but will also aim at producing leaders skilled in directing the employment of the weapon in battle, that is to say, in minor tactics.

4. The three concrete fundamentals of minor tactics are :—

    (*a*) The use of weapons.

    (*b*) The use of ground.

    (*c*) The use of formations.

Even during the initial or elementary stages of training, training in (*b*) and (*c*) should run concurrently with weapon training, and during the more advanced stages training in the use of the weapon will invariably be combined with the use of ground and formations. Neither in theory nor in practice can these three be separated—they are inseparable.

2. *Responsibility for training.*

1. The training, and exercise, of the soldier in the use of his weapons is not a specialist subject : it is the normal duty of the leader, *i.e.*, the section and platoon commander.

2. Normally, the machinery of weapon training corresponds with infantry or cavalry organization and chain of command as laid down in the establishments and training manuals of these arms. Thus, in the case of the infantry soldier, the section commander will exercise and train the soldier ; the platoon commander will control and assist such training; the company and battalion commander will direct the training and supervise it, so far as is necessary.

During the individual training season, however, circumstances may render necessary the adoption of some measure of centralization, and where this requires a special training staff, whether in a unit or a depot, the Small Arms School is responsible for assisting in the training of the officers and N.C.Os. required for this special duty.

Furthermore, all officers of regular infantry and cavalry, and a proportion of officers of the other arms will qualify at a Small Arms School. (*See* Secs. **33-37**.)

3. *Guiding rules for weapon training.*

The following guiding rules for weapon training are applicable to all the weapons with which the soldier is armed and with which this manual deals :—

1. Not more than eight men should be instructed by one instructor, or the instruction will suffer.

2. An elementary lesson in one particular subject should not last more than three quarters of an hour.

3. Training should be progressive. Progression is ensured only when a definite programme is thought out before training begins. This applies equally in the case of a lesson lasting half an hour or of a course lasting six weeks.

4. Monotony kills interest, and must be avoided at all costs. Too much repetition leads to monotony.

5. Teaching should be **by reason rather than memory**.

6. Competition is the spice of training in peace time. During all stages of training in every weapon the spirit of competition should be fostered by the instructor.

7. Standard tests, giving a definite aim, goal, or degree of efficiency to be reached by the individual or the unit, are a great incentive towards efficiency. The conditions of existing standard tests should be explained by the instructor. Such procedure leads to increased effort towards skill and efficiency.

8. The sporting spirit and desire to play for his side, or team, or regiment is inherent in every individual of the British race. This should be fostered and made use of by the instructor.

4. *The instructor.*

1. So far as the instructor is concerned, training in the use of weapons may be divided approximately into three stages :—

> (a) Training the recruit ; or the tyro ; *i.e.*, the man with no knowledge of a particular weapon.

(b) Refreshing or exercising the trained soldier, *i.e.*, practising him in knowledge already imparted.

(c) Training the officer, non-commissioned officer or soldier in the duties of the fire unit leader.

2. The qualified instructor should be capable of undertaking all three stages.

5. *System of instruction.*

1. The two main organs of instruction are the eye and the ear. The usual tendency, a wrong one, is to train too much by the ear and not enough by the eye, because talking requires less effort than action. The brain, however, grasps more readily and retains more firmly what it sees with the eye than what it hears with the ear. The instructor must, therefore, utilise his men's eyes, even more than their hearing, and for this purpose, instruction should follow a definite sequence :—

Explanation.—Instruction by the ear.

Demonstration.—Instruction by the eye.

Execution.—Testing the results of the instruction and correcting mistakes.

Repetition.—Practice to gain improvement.

This actual sequence, though advisable, need not be invariably followed.

2. At all times the reasoning powers of those under instruction should constantly be called into play. This ensures that the brain is working. It is especially necessary in the case of automatic weapons. Men should be called upon to reason and work out for themselves the " whys and wherefores " of all action—whether tactical or technical—that they are instructed to carry out.

Instructors should recognize that the surest and quickest road to success is to call upon and develop the brain power of those under instruction.

6. *Demonstration as a means of instruction.*

1. The system of teaching by demonstration will be employed during every stage of instruction, of the recruit, the tyro, the soldier, and the leader. This applies on the manœuvre ground, the range (battle firing and classification), the barrack square, and the barrack room. Training by demonstration requires forethought, preparation and rehearsal.

2. The allotment of live practice ammunition for all weapons in peace time is necessarily limited. It is therefore important, when demonstrations are given involving the use of live ammunition, especially tracer, that the numbers attending should be as large as practicable, provided that they comprise only those likely to benefit from the demonstration and are not too many to follow it adequately. In other words, it is necessary to balance economy of ammunition with instructional efficiency.

3. The following rules should be borne in mind by commanders and others when carrying out demonstrations where considerable numbers of spectators are present :—

 (*a*) The audience, whether officers, non-commissioned officers or men, should be well under control, divided up into parties, each under a leader. The latter should be made responsible throughout the demonstration for explaining the objects and lessons which the demonstration is intended to show.

(b) Care should be taken that all the audience are in a position throughout to see the demonstration and hear the explanation. In this respect any view points or halting places selected must be carefully chosen and the direction of the wind must be taken into account.

(c) Discussion should follow the demonstration and any criticisms or views expressed should be heard by all.

(d) Careful rehearsal by the individuals or units giving the demonstration is essential.

7. *Anti-gas defence.*

1. Gas defensive measures will be frequently incorporated into all exercises involving the use of the weapon. This applies to all weapons without exception. In framing competitions for weapon training on service lines the importance of efficiency in gas defensive measures combined with the use of the weapon should be taken into account.

8. *Safety precautions during training.*

1. At the beginning of all weapon training parades, arms, dummy cartridges, pouches, &c., will be carefully examined.

2. The detailed safety precautions necessary during training, and especially when ammunition is used, are laid down in other chapters of this manual.

3. Any building which contains explosives should be considered as an explosive store and be dealt with as far as possible under the Magazine Regulations.

Experiments, tests, &c., with explosives, tubes, fuzes, grenades or detonators are in no case to take place inside any building. They will be carried out in the open with the greatest care and only by individuals who have received expert training and are qualified to do so.

4. The use of dummy ammunition during training is necessary to efficiency, but the consequent risk of accident must be recognised by all commanders.

5. Dummy ammunition is employed during training in the case of all weapons dealt with in this manual. Unless the regulations for its use are strictly carried out accidents are almost certain to occur either sooner or later.

The best preventive of accident is discipline.

6. When dummy cartridges are used for setting up stoppages with light automatics on the range, officers conducting the practice will personally supervise the issue and subsequent collection of the dummy cartridges.

9. *Weapon training year.*

1. For purposes of firing annual courses and accounting for practice ammunition the weapon training period will be divided into years beginning as under, to accord with local climatic conditions.

At Home (Regulars, Militia, Channel
    Islands Militia, and Territorial Army)   1st November.

Gibraltar   ...   .⎫
Mauritius ...   .⎬1st January.
North China   ...   .⎭

Ceylon	...	...	...	...	} 1st February.
Cyprus	...	...	...	...	
Bermuda	...	...	...	...	
Egypt and Sudan ...		...	...	...	
Jamaica	...	...	...	...	} 1st April.
Malta	...	...	...	...	
Malaya	...	...	...	...	
South China		...	...	...	...	1st September.
West Africa		...	...	...	...	1st October.

2. In interim garrisons abroad the weapon training year will begin on the following dates :—

Palestine	...	...	...	...	...	1st March.
Iraq	...	...	...	...	} 1st April.
Rhine	...	...	...	...	

3. In India the weapon training year will begin on 1st April except in the case of the Baluchistan District, where for climatic reasons it will begin on 1st January.

10. *Special instructions.*

1. The words " Battalion " and " Company " throughout this manual will be read, when necessary, to mean " Regiment," and " Squadron or Battery."

2. General Officers Commanding-in-Chief will correspond direct with the Commandant, Small Arms School, Hythe, on weapon training questions.

The Theory of Small Arms Fire.

In order to obtain the full fire effect from the weapons with which their men are armed it is necessary for officers and fire unit leaders to have a working knowledge of the theory of small arms fire.

11. *Definitions.*

The *axis of the barrel* is an imaginary line following the centre of the bore from breech to muzzle.

The *line of departure* is the direction which the bullet takes on leaving the muzzle, *i.e.*, prolonging the axis of the barrel.

The *line of fire* is an imaginary line from the muzzle of the rifle to the target.

The *line of sight* is a straight line from the firer's eye, through the sights, to the point aimed at.

The *trajectory* is the actual curved path of the bullet.

The *culminating point* is the greatest height above the line of sight to which the bullet rises in its flight ; this is reached at a point a little beyond half the distance to which the bullet travels.

The *first catch* is that point where the bullet has descended sufficiently to strike the head of a man whether mounted, standing, kneeling, lying, &c.

The *first graze* is the point where the bullet, if not interfered with, will first strike the ground.

The *dangerous space* for any particular range is the distance between the *first catch* and the *first graze.*

PLATE 1.

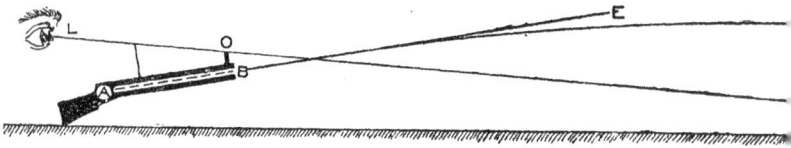

DEFINITIONS :—

A B	=	Axis of Barrel
B E	=	Line of Departure
B S	=	Line of fire (not drawn in diagram)

L O S	=	Line of Sight
B P S	=	Trajectory
P	=	Culminating Po

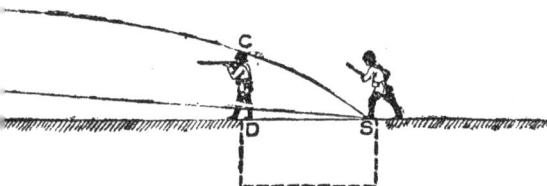

C	=	First Catch
S	=	First Graze
D S	=	Dangerous Space

The *cone of fire* is the figure formed in the air by the several trajectories of the bullets fired.

12. *Factors affecting the bullet before it leaves the muzzle.*

1. *Rifling.*—A *barrel* is said to be rifled when it has spiral *grooves* cut down the *bore*. Rifling a *barrel* enables an elongated bullet to be used ; the advantage of this form of bullet is that it has great weight in proportion to the surface directly opposed to the air ; it has therefore great power of overcoming the resistance of the air, and thus keeping up its velocity. When the charge is fired, the bullet is forced into, and follows, the *grooves* up the *barrel*, thus leaving the *muzzle* with rotation on its longer axis, *i.e.*, spinning sideways but with nose foremost. This tends to keep its nose foremost and therefore to ensure accuracy of flight.

2. *Force of explosion.*—On firing a round of ammunition, the gases formed cause the bullet to move from *lead* to *muzzle*, leaving the latter at a speed of 2,440 feet per second, in the case of Mark VII ammunition.

3. *Jump.*—On the weapon being fired, a vibratory or wavy motion is set up in the *barrel*, and at the moment the bullet leaves the *bore* the *muzzle* is usually deflected from its original axis both vertically and laterally.

This deviation is known as " jump."

Vertical jump may be either positive (upwards) or negative (downwards). It is compensated for by the use of varying heights of *foresight*.

Lateral jump is allowed for by lateral adjustment of the *foresight*.

Varying strengths of charges causing changes in *muzzle* velocity will affect the jump.

The stocking up, *i.e.*, fitting of S.M.L.E. rifle, is most carefully adjusted at the factory, but any warping of the fore end, loosening of screws, etc., may affect the jump.

PLATE 2.

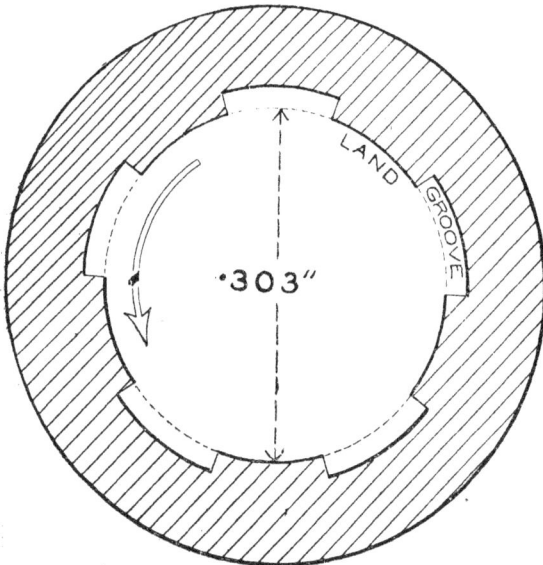

ENFIELD RIFLING.
Left handed, one complete turn in 10″.
Depth of grooves ·0065″.

4. *Effect of firing with the bayonet fixed.*—The weight of the bayonet affects the jump and the shooting of the rifle (*see* Plate 3).

Normally with Mk. VII ammunition the jump is positive and allowance has to be made as in the following table :—

Range.				Elevation required.
600	...	...	...	450
500	...	...	...	350
400	...	...	...	200
300	...	...	...	200 and aim down 2 feet.
200	...	...	...	Aim down 1½ feet.

No two rifles shoot exactly alike.

In every case the man must know the requirements of his own rifle.

5. *Resting the rifle.*—The rifle should be rested near the point of balance. If the rifle is properly rested the jump is not affected.

6. *Heated barrel.*—The *bore* expands and hence the bullet fits less tightly. Thus, after prolonged rapid fire, bullets tend to fall short.

7. *Oily barrel.*—The first shot or two may be erratic until the oil is burnt up.

13. *Factors affecting the bullet after it leaves the muzzle.*

1. *Resistance of the air.*—Resistance of the air causes the velocity of the bullet to decrease rapidly. The Mk. VII bullet leaves the *muzzle* travelling at the rate of about 800 yards per second. The resistance of the air allows it to travel only about 600 yards in first second, about 400 yards in second second, about 300 yards in third second.

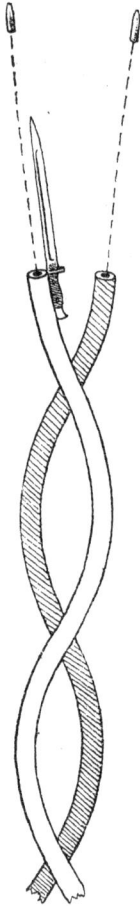

PLATE 3.

JUMP.

S.M.L.E. M'k. VII. Ammunition.

In the above diagram the barrel B shews the effect of firing with bayonet fixed.

14

2. *Gravity.*—Gravity acts on the bullet immediately it leaves the *muzzle*, drawing it downwards with ever-increasing velocity. Thus the path of the bullet (known as the *trajectory*) is curved instead of straight.

3. *Elevation.*—In order to allow for the fall of the bullet it is necessary to direct the line of departure as much above the object to be hit as the bullet will fall below it if the axis of the *barrel* is pointed at the target. This raising of the *barrel* to allow for the curve of the trajectory is termed *giving elevation.* (*See* Plate 4.)

As the target must be kept in view, the weapon is provided with sights which permit the firer to give the elevation required whilst keeping his eye fixed on the mark.

4. *Light.*—In bad light the foresight is less distinctly seen than in good light, and more of it is unconsciously taken into the line of sight. This factor naturally affects the elevation used, less being required on a dull than on a bright day.

5. *Sighting of* ·303″ *weapons.*—In the sighting of ·303″ weapons a " mean," or average, graduation for each range has been adopted. In this way a high general standard of accuracy sufficient for all practical purposes is obtained. Each weapon is carefully tested before issue, and is sighted so as to hit the point aimed at, but it must be understood that no two behave in an exactly similar manner. Even if compensation could be made for every error in the sighting before issue, wear of parts and loosening or tightening of screws, etc., would bring about faults from time to time. It is therefore necessary that every man should study the shooting of his own weapon and find out if there is any error at the shorter ranges, *i.e.*, below 500 or 600 yards, in the graduations marked on the backsight.

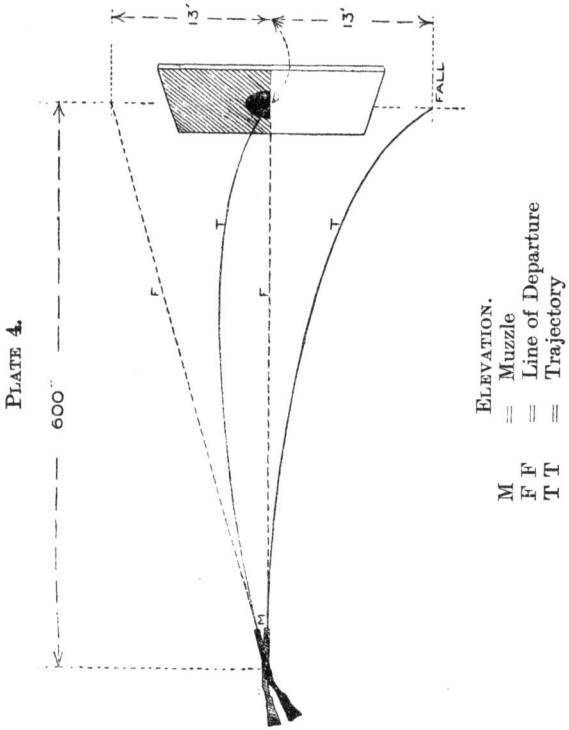

PLATE 4.

ELEVATION.

M   = Muzzle
F F = Line of Departure
T T = Trajectory

Thus he will be able to give his weapon the correct elevation for the estimated, or ascertained, range of the target.

At the longer ranges the backsight elevation may be regarded as the best possible guide under all conditions.

6. *Drift.*—Drift is the term used to express the lateral deviation of the bullet after it has left the barrel. This deviation, which is considerably less than that caused by jump, is brought about by the rotation of the bullet and the position which it assumes in its flight. The left-handed rifling of the service rifle and Hotchkiss gun causes the bullet to rotate from right over to the left, and, owing to gyroscopic action, the point works over slightly to the left. The consequent increased air pressure on the right side of the bullet, therefore, forces it to the left.

The rifling of the Lewis gun being right-handed, the bullet deviates to the right.

The deflection due to drift at distances below 1,000 yards is negligible. At 1,500 yards it may be regarded as about 7 feet.

Drifting is not allowed for in the sighting of ·303″ weapons.

7. *Wind.*—The effect of wind on the path of the bullet is considerable, especially at the longer ranges. The direction and strength of the wind can be judged by watching trees, grass, &c., and by personal sensation.

Men must study the effect of wind blowing at 10, 20 and 30 miles per hour, and know the necessary allowances to make at the different ranges. (*See Wind Tables, Secs.* **48** *and* **49.**)

Head and rear winds.—Up to 1,500 yards no allowance is necessary.

For strong winds at 1,500 yards add on 50 for a head wind.
     ,,   ,,   2,000 ,, deduct 50 ,, rear ,,

8. *Atmospheric conditions.*—The rifle is sighted at the factory with

    (*a*) Horizontal line of sight.
    (*b*) Barometer 30″ (sea level).
    (*c*) Thermometer 60° Fahr.

Allowance for barometric pressure need not be made except when firing at considerable altitudes. Going up hill the air becomes rarer, and there being less pressure, the barometer falls, and as the air offers less resistance less elevation is required.

Only extreme changes of temperature require consideration : thermometer rising, air becomes rarer, offers less resistance, therefore less elevation is required ; with thermometer falling more elevation is required.

The rules for correction in cases of variations in barometric pressure and changes of temperature are :—

For every inch the barometer rises above or falls below· 30 inches, add, or deduct, 1½ yards for each 100 yards of range.

Note.—Barometer falls about 1 inch for every 1,000 feet of altitude.

For every degree the thermometer rises above or falls below 60° Fahr. deduct, or add, 1/10th yard for each 100 yards of range.

Example : On the frontier in India a range-taker gives 1,600 yards to the object. Barometer reads 24″, thermometer reads 90°.

    Barometer : 6 × 1½ × 16   =   144 Deduct.
    Thermometer : 30 × 1/10th × 16 =   48 Deduct.
    Correct backsight elevation   = 1,400.

14. *Dangerous space.*

1. The extent of the dangerous space depends on :—
   (*a*) The range.   (*See* Plate 5 (*a*).)
   (*b*) The firer's position and the consequent height of his
         weapon above the ground.   (*See* Plate 5 (*b*).)
   (*c*) The height of the object fired at.   (*See* Plate 5 (*c*).)
   (*d*) The flatness of the trajectory.   (*See* Plate 5 (*d*).)
   (*e*) The conformation of the ground.   (*See* Plate 5 (*e*).)

2. *The dangerous space—*

   Decreases :—
         As the range increases, owing to the steeper angles
         of descent of the bullet at the longer ranges.   (*See*
         Plate 5 (*a*).)

   Increases :—
      (*a*) The nearer the weapon is to the ground (*see*
            Plate 5 (*b*).),
      (*b*) The higher the object fired at (*see* Plate 5 (*c*).),
      (*c*) The flatter the trajectory (*see* Plate 5 (*d*)),
      (*d*) The more nearly the slope of the ground conforms
            to the angle at which the bullet falls (*see*
            Plate 5 (*e*).)

15. *Angles of descent.*

1. A general knowledge of the angle of fall of the bullet
in the last 100 yards of its flight, at all ranges, is essential
as a guide in deciding when individual fire may be opened
with effect (*see* Appendix VII. Vol. II.)

2. The longer the range the more abruptly does the bullet
fall ; consequently, the greater the distance the more accurately must the range be ascertained.

PLATE 5 (*a*).

DANGEROUS SPACE.

This diagram shews height increased 6 times.

Range = 600×.
Slope of fall = 1 in 90.
∴ Dangerous space for prone man (1′ high) is 30 × (approx.).

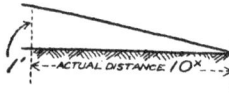

Range = 1,000×
Slope = 1 in 30.
Dangerous space is 10× (approx.).

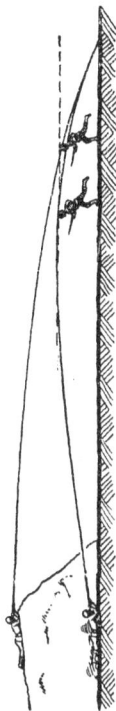

PLATE 5 (b).

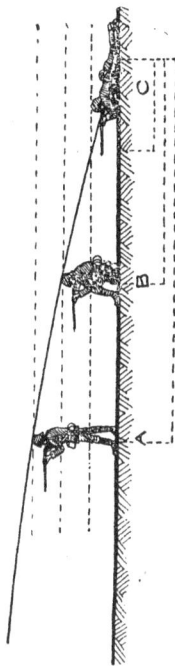

PLATE 5 (c).

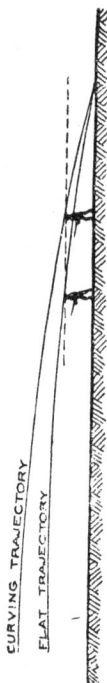

PLATE 5 (d).

CURVING TRAJECTORY

FLAT TRAJECTORY

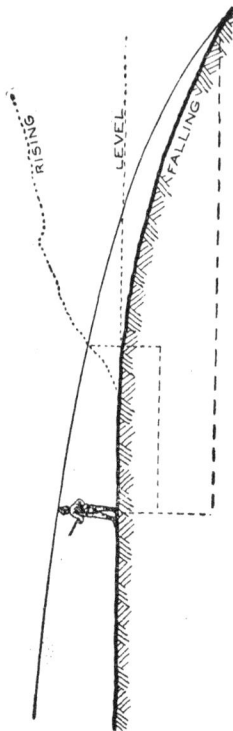

PLATE 5 (e).

RISING

LEVEL

FALLING

3. Hence the effective limits of individual rifle fire are to a great extent governed by the curve of the trajectory and the power of correctly estimating ranges, and unless the strike of the bullet can be observed, the effect of individual rifle fire at long ranges must be largely a matter of chance.

16. *Ricochets.*

1. Bullets which rebound after striking the ground or any other obstacle and continue their flight are said to ricochet.

2. Ricochets may occur from any surface, and bullets may ricochet two or even three times before their flight is finally arrested. Bullets are less likely to ricochet from soft ground than from hard, smooth surfaces.

17. *Firing up and down hill.*

1. When a shot is fired at a target placed on the same level as the firer, the forces acting on the bullet cause it to travel in its greatest curve, and the greatest elevation for any given distance must, therefore, be given to the weapon.

2. If a shot is fired perpendicularly upwards or downwards, no elevation is required, for the bullet will travel in an approximately straight line until its impetus is exhausted.

3. Hence it follows that when shooting up or down hill, less e'evation is necessary than when the object is on the same level.

4. Only steep slopes such as are found in mountainous regions need be taken into account.

5. The following is a rough guide. (*See* Plate 6.)

For slopes of 20° deduct $\frac{1}{8}$th of range.
,, ,, 40° deduct $\frac{1}{4}$,,
,, ,, 60° deduct $\frac{1}{2}$,,

PLATE 6.

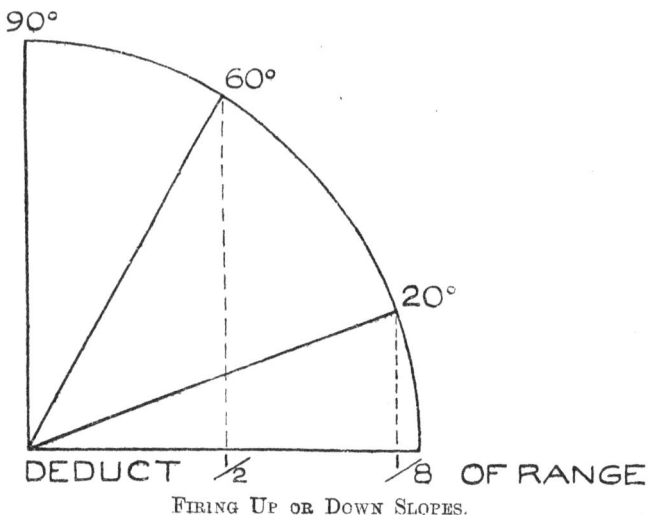

FIRING UP OR DOWN SLOPES.

18. *Collective fire.*

1. *At the longer ranges* collective rifle fire or automatic fire, rather than individual rifle fire, are necessary to obtain a good effect under service conditions.

2. Individual marksmanship is greatly affected by such causes as the condition of the firer, the atmosphere, heat, light, imperfection of ammunition, uncertainty in estimation

of the range, the difficulty of aiming at a small or indistinct object, the steepness of the fall of the bullet being rapidly accentuated as the range increases.

3. The diagram represents a large target fired at by an individual, without alteration of elevation or point of aim. (*See* Plate 7.)

The following points should be noted :—

(*a*) All the shots are not in the same place.

(*b*) The shot holes are more numerous in the centre.

(*c*) Approximately half the shots are above the centre horizontal line, the other half below.

(*d*) Approximately half the shots are on the right of the centre vertical line, the other half on the left.

(*e*) The distance between the topmost shot and the lowest one is greater than that between the extreme right and left shots.

The following deductions can be made :—

(*a*) Since the shots are not in the same place, it follows that the trajectories of all the bullets do not coincide. The figure thus formed is known as the " *cone of fire.*"

(*b*) Since the shot holes are more numerous in the centre, it is evident that the cone of fire is denser in the centre than on the outside.

(*c*) (*d*) and (*e*) show that the cone of fire is not circular but oblong in section, and that its density decreases uniformly from the centre to the outside.

PLATE 7.

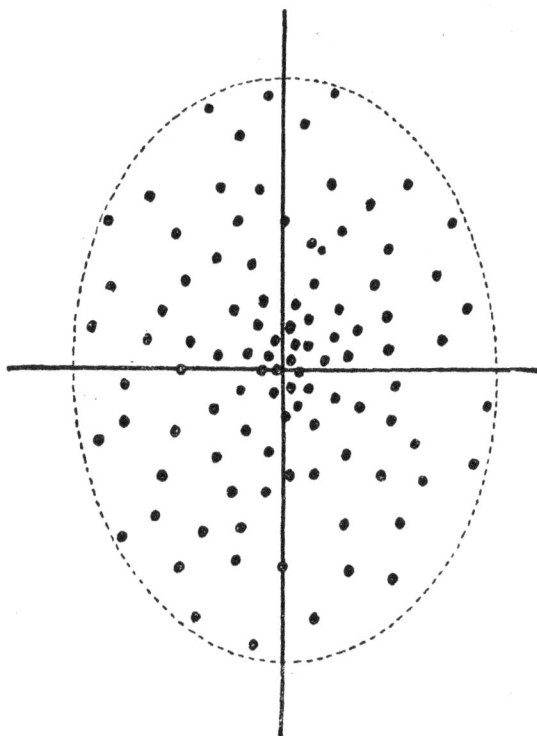

CONE OF FIRE OF RIFLE, VERTICAL SECTION.
100 shots.

19. *The cone of fire.*

1. The cone of fire from a number of rifles is larger than that from one, since skill and eyesight vary. The size of the cone will be still further increased by such causes as the firers being tired, or the aiming mark being hard to see.

2. Where collective fire is applied to a large vertical target the portion of ground struck by all the shots passing through the target is known as " *the Beaten Zone.*"

3. If three rings are then drawn on the target as shown in Plate 8, that portion of ground struck by shots passing through the centre ring is known as " *The Nucleus of the Beaten Zone.*"

4. That portion struck by bullets passing through the centre and second rings is known as " *The Zone of Effective Fire or Effective Beaten Zone.*"

5. *The Nucleus* contains 50 per cent. of shots fired.

6. *The Effective Beaten Zone* contains 75 per cent. of shots fired.

7. The part of the Beaten Zone outside the Effective Beaten Zone contains the remainder.

8. Useful results can only be expected if the target is included within the *Effective Beaten Zone* for any range.

9. Experiments have shown that as the range increases the size of the *Effective Beaten Zone* (E.B.Z.) decreases. (*See* Plate 9.) This is due to the increased angle of descent of the bullet. Beyond 1,500 yards the E.B.Z. increases again, especially laterally, owing to the increased effects of errors in aiming and their causes.

10. Under favourable peace conditions it has been found that the size of the E.B.Z. varies little in the case of different units.

PLATE 8.

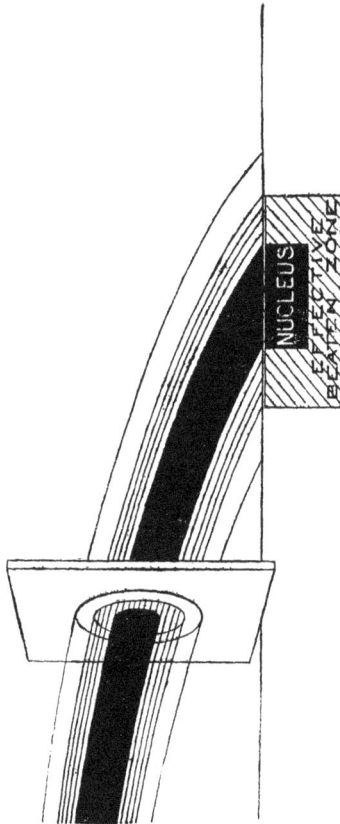

NUCLEUS

EFFECTIVE BEATEN ZONE

Plate 9.

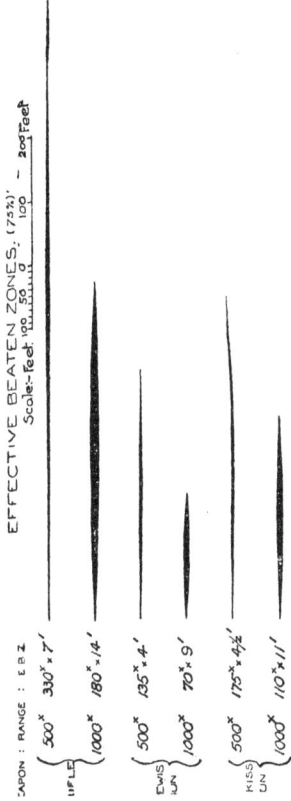

EFFECTIVE BEATEN ZONES. (75%).
Scale–Feet 100 50 0 100 200 Feet

WEAPON : RANGE : E B Z
RIFLE { 500ˣ 330ˣ x 7'
1000ˣ 180ˣ x 14'
LEWIS GUN { 500ˣ 135ˣ x 4'
1000ˣ 70ˣ x 9'
VICKERS GUN { 500ˣ 175ˣ x 4½'
1000ˣ 110ˣ x 11'

11. The size of the E.B.Z. on level ground is as follows :—
Rifle—

      500 yards ...   ... 330 yards long by 7 ft. wide
   1,000 yards ...   ... 180 yards long by 14 ft. wide
   1,500 yards ...   ... 150 yards long by 28 ft. wide

Lewis Gun—

      500 yards ...   ... 135 yards long by 4 ft. wide
   1,000 yards ...   ...   70 yards long by 9 ft. wide

Hotchkiss—

      500 yards ...   ... 175 yards long by $4\frac{1}{2}$ ft. wide
   1,000 yards ...   ... 110 yards long by 11 ft. wide

20. *The permissible error in ranging.*

1. By this term is meant the error which can be made in estimating the range while still keeping the target within the E.B.Z.

PLATE 10.

PERMISSIBLE   ERROR = $\frac{1}{2}$ E B Z

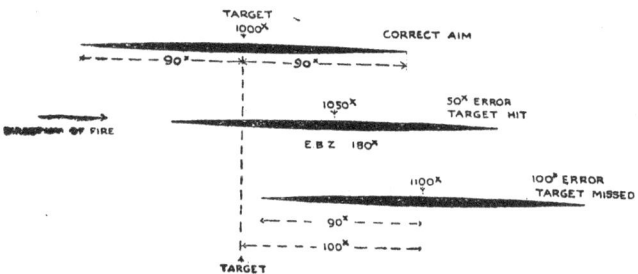

2. The permissible error in ranging is equal to half the depth of the E.B.Z. for any particular range. (*See* Plate 10.)

For example, assume target to be 1,000 yards distant.

E.B.Z. of the rifle is 180 yards.

If the range is obtained absolutely correct, half the E.B.Z. will be on one side of target and half on the other.

If an error of over 90 yards is made (*i.e.*, half E.B.Z.), the whole of the E.B.Z. will miss the target.

21. *Fire effect in relation to ground.*

1. " Cones of Fire," " Beaten Zones," and " Dangerous Spaces " have already been explained. It is necessary, however, to consider them in relation to various forms of ground.

2. For example, a cone of fire striking a steep hillside will cover a very small area of ground—A B.

FIG. 1.

3. The same cone of fire striking a gentler slope will cover a slightly larger area of ground—B C.

FIG. 2.

4. In similar proportion—*see* D E.

FIG. 3.

5. The greatest area swept by bullets will be in the case where the fall of the ground is parallel to the trajectory of the bullets, in which case the whole area F G is a danger zone, of which H F is the beaten zone.

FIG. 4.

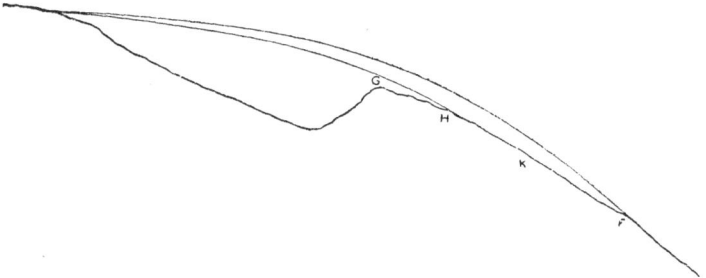

Troops, even though under cover from the enemy's view at K, would be in danger from unaimed fire.

6. The above considerations indicate that it is more difficult to get fire effect against rising ground, than against ground which is flat or falling away. Conversely, this knowledge is a guide to the probable danger incurred by troops crossing various kinds of ground, and is of assistance in selecting sites for defence posts and larger localities for defence.

7. Troops advancing in depth should therefore adopt formations suitable to the occasion.

22. *Observation of fire.*

1. Observation of fire is of great importance, and every opportunity of practising this should be made use of during battle practices. The possibilities of observing fire will depend largely on the nature of the surface of the ground.

2. If observation can be obtained, it is the best method of obtaining the correct sighting elevation, since the error of the day is automatically overcome.

3. Automatic weapons, owing to their close grouping, are a valuable means of obtaining the correct sighting elevation, since even if the strike of one bullet only is observed, it follows that the remainder of the " Beaten Zone " is in the vicinity. This is not quite the case with rifle fire, since the strike of one bullet may bear no relation to the position of the fall of the majority of the bullets of the men firing.

(For further details of theory, see *Text Book of Small Arms.*)

WEAPONS, GROUND AND FORMATIONS.

23. *General considerations.*

1. The principles governing fire direction, fire control, fire discipline, fire and formations, fire and movement, and the use of ground are set out in Infantry Training, Vol. II (1921), Chapter I.

2. Secs. **23–32** deal with the system of training both the leader and the man in these subjects.

3. The aim of the system of training will be to build up by progressive stages the individual knowledge required to give collective effect to these principles.

4. The individual requirements include the following :—

(a) In the leader—

    i. Ability to estimate range and to give clear concise fire orders suitable for all occasions and targets, and to exercise proper fire control over his unit.

    ii. Ability to study ground in relation to fire effect so as to select fire positions quickly and be able to take advantage of good lines of approach that afford cover.

    iii. Ability to manœuvre his unit in the formation most suitable to prevailing conditions and to vary the formation of his unit accordingly.

    iv. Ability to give practical effect to the principles which govern the application of infantry fire in battle.

(*b*) In the man—

    i. Ability to use his weapon to produce accurate fire of the required volume.

    ii. Ability to recognise aiming points indicated by the leader.

    iii. Ability to give immediate effect to the detailed instructions included in the fire order of the leader.

    iv. Ability to adapt his firing position to make the best use of the ground within the fire position selected by the leader.

    v. Ability to reconnoitre ground and report to the leader points suitable for fire positions and the existence of good lines of approach.

    vi. Knowledge of his individual position in any type of formation ordered by the leader.

    vii. Ability to carry on the fight and use his weapons effectively when control by the leader is no longer possible.

5. The progressive stages of individual training leading up to these requirements include the following subjects, which are dealt with in this chapter as being generally applicable to all small arm weapons :—

    (*a*) Visual training,
    (*b*) Judging distance.
    (*c*) Fire control.
    (*d*) Training in the use of ground.
    (*e*) Training in the use of formations

24. *Visual training.*

1. Exercises framed to stimulate the soldier's powers of discernment and recognition should commence early in his training and continue throughout his service.

2. Visual training will include the study of ground, impressions of size, recognition of targets and ground features, and observation of fire. Training will begin with questions framed to develop the recruit's powers of discerning objects and describing what he sees. Any ordinary objects will be counted, and figures of different colours will be placed sometimes in the open and sometimes under partial cover in front of various backgrounds. Men will be employed to perform the firing motions in order to show how motion catches the eye and exposes the firer's position. Blank ammunition will be used to give practice to the ear in locating an enemy by sound.

3. As progress is made, these exercises will be carried out under stricter conditions, the observer lying down or behind cover. Special attention will be given to recognising features of ground such as fire positions, dead ground, &c. The use of field glasses will be practised, distant objects being examined and described both with and without the aid of glasses. Leaders will be constantly practised in searching ground with glasses.

4. In connection with visual training, men will be familiarised with all terms applied to features of ground, colours, shapes, and military objects generally, so that their powers of description and recognition may be improved.

5. A Military Vocabulary is appended, which every soldier should know :—

1. *Features, Artificial.*

Footpath.	Obstacles.	Chimney.
Ride.	Viaduct.	Chimney Stack
Track.	Culvert.	Factory.
Cross Roads.	Cutting.	Crane.
Road Junction.	Embankment.	Gasometer
Fenced.	Canal.	Gable-end.
Unfenced.	Lock.	Thatch.
Post and Rail ⎫	Ferry.	Tiled.
Wire ⎬ Fences.	Ford.	Slate.
Iron ⎭	Moat.	
Hurdles.	Windmill.	

2. *Colours.*

White.	Yellow.	Green.	Brown
Black.	Blue.	Red.	

3. *Features, Natural.*

Fir.	Copse.	Grass.	River.
Poplar.	Bush.	Stubble.	Stream.
Bushy-topped	Gorse.	Ricks.	Pond.
(Trees).	Corn Field.	Stacks.	Lake.
Hedgerow.	Plough.	Stooks.	
Wood.			

4. *Topographical.*

Valley.	Knoll.	Concave.	Nullah.
Defile.	Saddle.	Convex.	Donga.
Ridge.	Fold.	Cliff.	Clearing.
Crest-line.	Slopes, forward	Gorge.	Salient.
Horizon.	and reverse.	Ravine.	Sector of Ground
Spur.	Dead Ground.	Quarry.	

5. *Field engineering.*

Trench.	Dug-out.	Redoubt.	Circular.
Parapet.	Shell-hole.	Observation	Vertical.
Parados.	Defence post	Post.	Horizontal.
Fire Step.	(held by section	Blockhouse.	Oblique.
Revetment.	or small group).	Sangar.	Enfilade.
Traverse.	Centre of resist-	Right Angle.	Direct.
Breastwork.	ance (held by	Square.	Indirect.
Barricade.	larger body).	Triangle.	

6. *Formations.*

Column of Route.	Deployed in Section Columns.		Fours.
Mass.	,, Platoon Columns.		Arrow Head.
Line.	,, Company Columns.		File.
Extended Line.	Diamond.		Single File.
	Square.		

7. *Aeroplanes.*

Tractor	Triplane.	Fuselage.	Rudder.
Pusher.	Biplane.	Plane.	Strut.
Identification	Monoplane.	Wing.	Cockpit.
rings.	Motor.	Tail.	Under-carriage.
Streamers.	Propeller.		

8. *Airships.*   •

Envelope.	Nacelle (or car).	Elevators.	Rudder.

9. *Kite Balloons.*

Stabilisers.	Basket.	Parachute.

6. In the elementary stages of Visual Training and while the Military Vocabulary is being taught the objects to be seen or recognized may be indicated by descriptions or by the instructor aiming a rifle at the object and those under

instruction looking along the sights. The instructor then explains to the men what they have been looking at, using the Military Vocabulary.

7. Instruction in visual training should be progressive. The following stages, during which the Military Vocabulary should be practised, indicate a progressive sequence of instruction.

INSTRUCTOR'S NOTES.

1st Stage.   TAUGHT IN OR NEAR BARRACKS.

The recruit should be taught to recognize his immediate surroundings, *i.e.*, his eyes must be trained to convey what they see to the brain and to discern detail.   For example, does he know all badges of rank which he sees daily, and can he describe what they comprise ?   Does he know the names of familiar objects round him, such as " A roof with a gable end," " A church with a ' tower ' as opposed to one with a ' spire,' " and so on ?   Keeping (in this stage) to elementary terms in Military Vocabulary.

Kit required.—Either use objects seen from the barrack square or landscape targets.   One rifle and aiming rest.

2nd Stage.   ·   OPEN COUNTRY.

(Or in wet weather on landscape targets with small improvised figures, &c.)

Object.—To teach men to locate service targets up to 800 yards.

(*a*) *Silhouette targets* of different sizes, shapes and colours, arranged against various backgrounds.   The areas in which the targets are, should have their limits clearly marked and should be described.

    i. Targets counted.

    ii. Their characteristics and positions described.

    iii. Reasons for difference in their visibility brought out.

Kit required.—Silhouette targets Nos. 2, 3, 4 and 5. Flag, and a man.

    (*b*) *Men employed* instead of targets.

      i. Movement quickly detected.

      ii. Blank ammunition used to train the ear to locate sound.

This exercise requires careful preparation on the part of the officer or non-commissioned officer who is going to conduct it :—

    (*a*) Targets not too difficult in one sector.

    (*b*) Targets more difficult in another sector.

    (*c*) Men in normal firing positions.

These arrangements should be made only a short time before the exercise begins. Unless this is done the light may change and the value of the exercise will then be lost.

    Kit required.—Flag, and men with rifles and blank ammunition.

3rd Stage.   Examination of Ground.

    (On landscape targets, or open country.)

Object.—To enable men to make clear reports, to understand instructions, and to recognize features of military importance.

    (*a*) *Definite line* in landscape. Described in detail.

    (*b*) *Areas of ground.*—Clearly defined boundaries. Description of general shape. Natural and artificial features. Trees, fences, fields, &c. Features of military importance brought to notice by questions. Military Vocabulary largely increased.

As progress is made.—The section examines the ground and gives a description. A limited time will be given for the examination by the section, which is then turned about to give its description. Large areas should be divided into sectors : foreground, middle distance, and background.

(c) *Road work.*—Cultivate an eye for country by making men observe what they pass on the march. Question them after a given interval.

SPECIAL NOTE.

The recruit should be taught on such lines as under :—

(*a*) Difference between a hedgerow and a fence.
Difference between a tree and a bush.

(*b*) Various agricultural terms.

(*c*) Features, natural and artificial.

(*d*) Topographical terms.

(*e*) Colours.

(*f*) Any other terms of Military Vocabulary not taught in the 1st Stage.

Kit required.—If working indoors, a landscape target.

4th Stage. RECOGNITION WITHOUT AIDS.

Object.—To train the firer to recognize targets described and to understand the exact point at which his commander wishes him to aim.

In all lessons on Recognition, accuracy of aim will be insisted on, however indistinct the point indicated may appear.

In this stage the Instructor indicates various targets without aids (Direct Method). The men recognize and lay aims. Plenty of practice is necessary.

Kit required.—One aiming rest per man.

5th Stage. RECOGNITION WITH AIDS.

In this stage, the Instructor explains to the men the various aids used in indicating targets in fire orders, and describes difficult targets using aids.

The men recognize, and lay aims.

Kit required.—One aiming rest per man.

NOTE.—After the recruit has been thoroughly trained in the above five stages of Recognition, he will be given practice in receiving complete Fire Orders.

25. *Training of the leader in indication.*

1. It is estimated that 75 per cent. of shots are probably wasted owing to bad indication and recognition.

2. In teaching Indication, a reference point, or points, with ranges to each will always be given.

3. Aiming points will be described whenever possible by the direct method, *e.g.*, without aids. If aids are used the reference point will always be named before the description of the aiming point.

4. To ensure uniformity, one system of Indication is imperative throughout the army.

5. Supplementary methods, known respectively as the Vertical Clock Ray and Degree methods, may be used in connection with reference points.

INSTRUCTOR'S NOTES.

Taught in Stages.

1st Stage.

Description of aiming points, without aids. "Direct," or normal method, using (*a*) or (*b*) as required :—

    (*a*) Indication by description of any obvious target.

    (*b*) Indication by direction, *e.g.*, slightly, quarter, half, three-quarter, right or left from either—

      i. Last target, or

      ii. General direction in which men are moving or facing, ending up with description of target in each case.

Kit required.—One aiming rest for each leader.

2nd Stage.

Indication of aiming points, using aids. **Aids should only be used when absolutely necessary.**

Various Aids.

1. *Reference points.*—Prominent objects—about 20° apart—Reasonably distant—Of different kinds. Names by which they are known must be made clear to all.

2. *Vertical Clock Ray.*—Shows the direction of an object from a " reference point." The lowest part of the reference point is taken to be the centre of the face of a clock hanging vertically. The direction of the target right or left of the reference point is given by the Clock Ray.

Example : Windmill—4 o'clock—two bushes. (Plate 11.)

3. *Degree Method*, the angular distance being measured by graticuled field glasses, by the use of the hand or by any convenient appliance such as the *foresight* or *backsight* of the rifle, or the *foresight* of the Lewis gun. This method shows

approximately the angular distance of the target from the reference point and can also be used to denote, in the case of a distributed fire order, the lateral width of distribution required to cover the target.

PLATE 11.

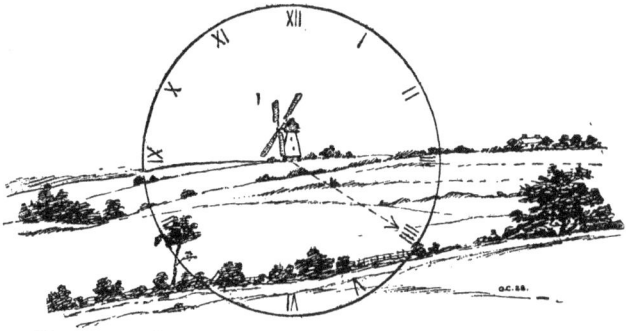

Example : Windmill—4 o'clock—2°—small bush. (Plate 12.)

i. All officers, non-commissioned officers and men should know what angles are subtended by the various parts of their own hands when held at arm's length or by the *sights* of the rifle when held in the aiming position.

NOTE.—The degrees shewn in Plate 13 are only approximate ; each man must test for himself.

ii. For purposes of instruction a degree scale (calculated for a given distance, say 20 yards) should be painted on a wall in barracks.

PLATE 12.

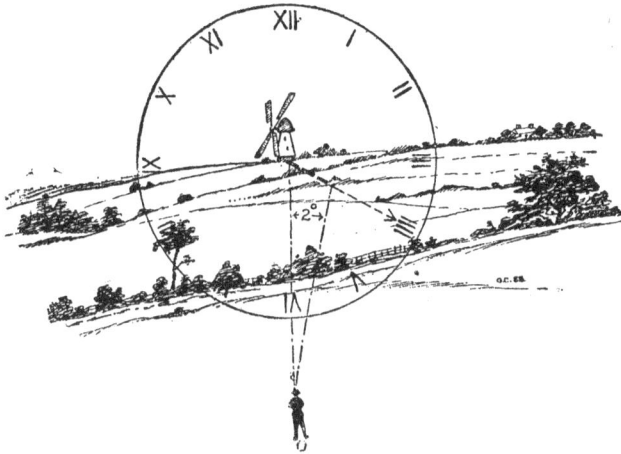

PLATE 13.

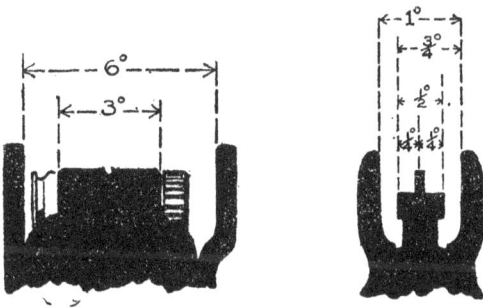

iii. The angles subtended may vary slightly with each person It is therefore necessary for each individual to memorize the angles as seen by him.

iv. The indication should end in each case with a description of the aiming point.

Example of the use of both the Clock Ray and Degrees to indicate a target and the amount of distribution required :—
Windmill—4 o'clock—2°—small bush—right 5°. (Plate 14.)

PLATE 14.

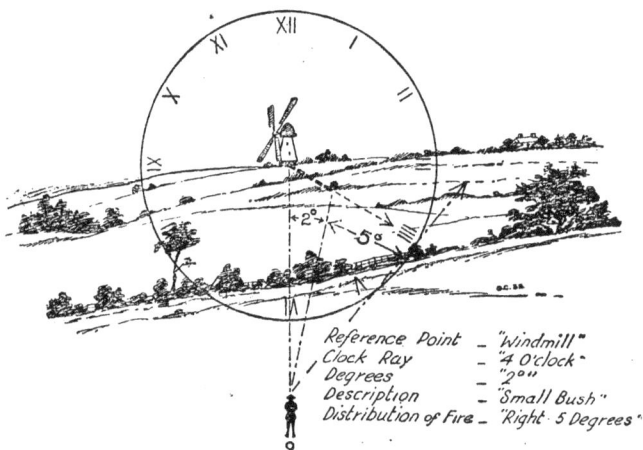

Reference Point	_	"Windmill"
Clock Ray	_	"4 O'clock"
Degrees	_	"2°"
Description	_	"Small Bush"
Distribution of Fire	_	"Right 5 Degrees"

NOTE.—Combined Clock Ray and degrees make a lengthy fire order and are seldom necessary.

Practice in indication.—A rifle is laid on the point or points to be indicated (or pins can be used on miniature landscape targets) ; the leader under instruction indicates the target by the methods described above. The remainder of the class recognize it.

4.— *Horizontal Clock Code. This code is used to describe targets to an observer at a distance and when the target cannot be accurately located by co-ordinates on a squared map.*

i. All officers and senior N.C.Os. down to platoon serjeants will be instructed in this method, as it enables infantry to indicate the approximate positions of targets to artillery, machine guns, &c.

ii. In this method the " reference point " is taken to be the centre of a clock lying flat on the ground with 12 o'clock pointing approximately due North.

iii. The position of the target is indicated by using a clock ray combined with the distance between the reference point and the target, *estimated in yards.*

N.B.—For estimating a lateral distance in yards, *see* Lateral Judging Distance, Section 27).

iv. In Plate 15 an infantry observer has seen a gun firing behind some rising ground South of Staple Church, and sends back the following message :—

" Reference Map, HAZEBROUCK 5 A. Can see enemy gun firing. Six o'clock. 800 yards from STAPLE CHURCH. Time 1430."

v. An advantage of this method is that the receiver of the message need not know the sender's position.

PLATE 15.

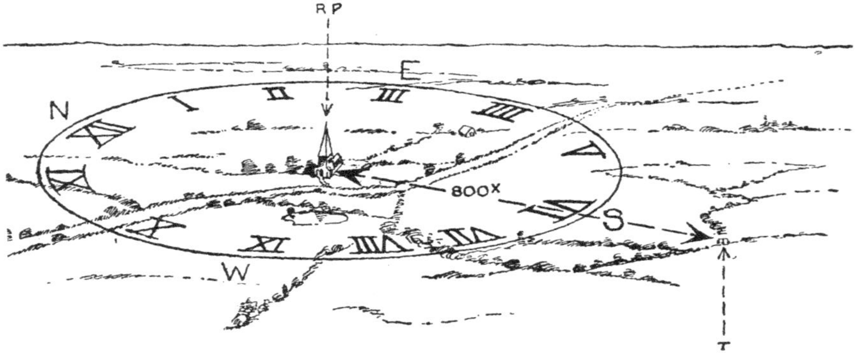

HORIZONTAL CLOCK.

R P = Reference Point.

T = Target.

vi. *Reporting observation of artillery fire.*—The Horizontal
Clock Code can also be used when reporting the
fall of rounds fired by the artillery. In this case
the target is taken as the centre of the horizontal
clock with 12 o'clock pointing approximately
true North.

As each round falls, its direction from the target is reported
with reference to the clock face, and its distance from the
target is estimated in yards (*e.g.*, 3 o'clock, 200 yards;
9 o'clock, 50 yards).

Whenever possible the place or places from which the
target can be seen should be stated, or information given as
to where a guide can be procured to lead the artillery observing
officer to a point whence he can see the target. This gives the
artillery observing officer a chance of having the target
definitely pointed out to him.

26. *Judging distance.*

1. Distances may be judged :—

   (*a*) By measuring the intervening ground with the eye
   in terms of some familiar unit such as 100 yards.

   (*b*) By objects of known size ; by the visibility of the
   object as affected by light, atmospheric conditions,
   background, &c.

   (*c*) By bracketing.

   (*d*) By halving.

   (*e*) By use of key ranges and maps.

   (*f*) By the mean (or average) of the estimates of several
   individuals.

2. All methods will be practised until it is found that distances can be approximately judged from the general impression conveyed to the eye.   The observer must, however, bear in mind that his judgment may be influenced by certain conditions of ground, light, &c., which are mentioned below

(*a*) *Objects are overestimated*—

When kneeling or lying.

When both background and object are of a similar colour.

On broken ground.

When looking over a valley or undulating ground in dull or foggy weather.

(*b*) *Objects are underestimated*—

When the sun is behind the observer.

In bright light or clear atmosphere.

When both background and object are of different colours.

When the intervening ground is level or covered with snow.

When looking upwards or downwards.

When the object is large.

3. The best means of obtaining the range is by observation of fire.   Especially is this the case with automatic weapons.

4. *Recruits and Trained soldiers* will be taught to judge up to 800 yards.

5. *Officers, N.C.Os. and selected men* will be taught to judge up to 1,400 yards.

6. *Practice.*—Constant practice is necessary under all conditions, both in peace and war, as serious errors will otherwise occur in action.

INSTRUCTOR'S NOTES.

The following is the sequence and the various methods of judging distance which should be taught.

A SEQUENCE OF INSTRUCTION.

I. *Unit of measure.*—Some familiar distance is used as a unit; 100 yards is a convenient unit; the section place themselves independently at what they think is 100 yards from an object; the distance between the farthest and nearest man of the section is paced; 100 yards is measured accurately from the object; the section is shown the correct unit. This method can only be used when the whole of the ground to be measured is visible; examples are shown to which this method cannot be, or can only be partly, applied. The section practises on figures put out at varying distances up to 400 yards.

II. *Appearance.*—The appearance of men in different positions, and of objects of known size, is studied and noted, at various distances and under all conditions of light, background, &c.

The following points should be noted :—

(*a*) The apparent height of the object.
(*b*) Appearance of the heads and shoulders of men.
(*c*) Distinctness of outline.
(*d*) Distinctness of the face, hands, rifle and head-dress.
(*e*) Movements when loading and firing.

Appearance varies with the eyesight of individuals; a classification range is suitable for the early lessons.

Opportunities for revising the impressions of the appearance of men at various distances should be given.

Although it is recognized that no hard-and-fast rules can be laid down, owing to the varying strength of men's eyesight, rapid progress has been made by normal-sighted men when acting upon the following rules :—

   i. At 200 yards. All parts of the body are distinctly seen.

  ii. At 300 yards. The outline of the face is slightly confused. The buttons resemble a stripe.

 iii. At 400 yards. Outline of body remains normal : but the face is not seen except under favourable circumstances.

  iv. At 500 yards. The body begins to taper slightly from the shoulders. Movements of the limbs are discernible.

   v. At 600 yards. The head appears a mere dot, details are no longer distinguishable; tapering of the body very noticeable.

  vi. It is useful to know that when the rifle is held in the aiming position the *blade* of the *foresight* covers a man standing at 400 yards and a man kneeling at 250 yards.

Fig. 5.

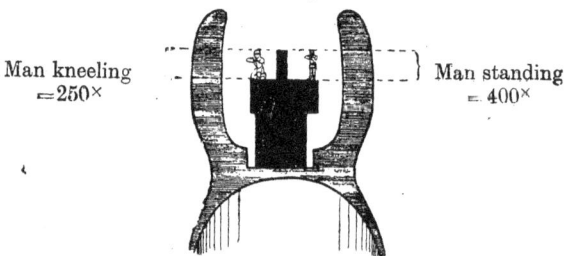

Man kneeling ⇌ 250×   Man standing ⇌ 400×

III.   *Bracketing.*—Decide on the longest distance the object can be ; decide on the shortest distance the object can be ; take the mean.

IV.   *Halving.*—Judge the distance to a point considered to be half way and double this estimate.

V.   *Key ranges.*—Judging by the aid of some known distance or with the assistance of range cards or maps.

VI.   *The mean (or average).*—Add together the distances estimated by the various men judging ; divide the result by the number judging.   Ignore obviously incorrect estimates.

Note.—As progress is made the time allowed for judging distances should be limited, but guessing is never to be allowed. Reasons for estimates and the method used will always be given.

27. *Lateral judging distance.*

1. All officers, non-commissioned officers and scouts should know some measurement which will cover laterally one-tenth of a forward distance ; measurement can be obtained by covering 10 yards at 100 yards, then applying at longer distances.

2. With the rifle held in the aiming position the *back sight protectors* of the rifle approximately give this measurement.

28. *Quarterly judging distance test.*

1. This will be carried out by all Cavalry, Royal Engineer Field Units and Infantry.

2. The regulations and method of carrying out the test are as follows :—

(*a*) *Distances.*—Recruits and trained soldiers will judge up to 800 yards ; subaltern and non-commissioned officers and men in possession of J.D. badges up to 1,400 yards.

(b) *Ground.*—An unfamiliar piece of ground will be selected for the test and the distances selected should be such as to approximate closely some multiple of 50 yards.

(c) *Aids.*—No assistance from maps or other means will be allowed.

(d) *Objects to be judged on :—*

Four objects will be judged on.

Two will be natural objects, such as likely hostile fire positions.

Two will be men who will show themselves and fire three rounds of blank ammunition when called up by signal.

(e) *Estimates, how given :—*

Always in multiples of 50 yards.

Officers write down their estimates.

Other ranks adjust their sights to the estimated distance.

(f) *Time limits.*—Half a minute will be allowed for each estimate. The time will be taken from the end of the verbal indication in the case of each of the two natural objects, and from the sound of the third shot fired in the case of each of the two objects represented by men firing blank. At the conclusion of the time limits a whistle will be blown, when those judging distance will stand to attention, and no further writing or adjustment of sights will be permitted.

(*g*) The register keeper will then examine each paper and the sights of each rifle, and record the estimates in the register (A.F. B 186).

On return to barracks the mean percentage of error will be worked out for each individual who took part in the test, and entered up in the register, which will be preserved for record.

(*h*) *Standard of efficiency.*—In order to qualify, the mean percentage of error of an individual must not exceed 20 per cent.

(*j*) All ranks whose mean error exceeds 20 per cent., or who have attended less than two tests in the year, will be regarded as inefficient and will be given extra instruction in this subject.

29. *Range cards.*

1. These are of two kinds :—

(*a*) For use in the attack.
(*b*) For use in the defence.

Any available method such as range finding instruments, maps, information from Lewis or Vickers Machine gunners, field artillery, &c., should be made use of for obtaining the correct ranges.

2. *Attack range card.*—The successive steps are as follows :—

(*a*) Ranges to be taken in *direct* line of advance.
(*b*) Draw two parallel lines and fill in *Starting Point* and *Objective.*
(*c*) Take or estimate range to the *objective* and write in right-hand column.

(B 27/7)Q

C

Fig. 6.

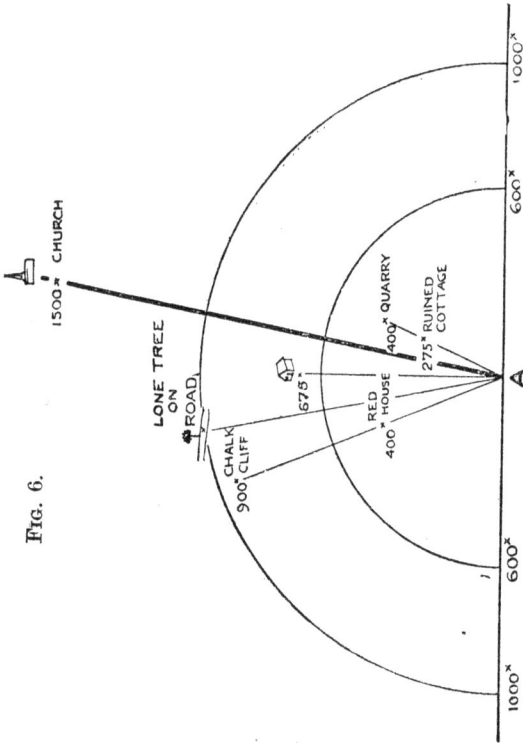

RANGE CARD IN DEFENCE.

"A" Taken from right end of York Trench. By B. & S. Rangefinder.
Made out by Sjt. Brown. 21/3/17.

CHURCH 1500ˣ

LONE TREE ON ROAD

CHALK CLIFF 900ˣ

675ˣ

RED HOUSE 400ˣ

QUARRY 400ˣ

RUINED COTTAGE 275ˣ

A

1000ˣ   600ˣ   600ˣ   1000ˣ

(d) Select some object about half way to the *objective* and enter its range in right-hand column. Select and take ranges to other intermediate objects, choosing those which will be easily recognised when reached and which appear to be near a probable fire position.

(e) A simple subtraction sum will give the range from each successive object to the *objective*. Enter the ranges so obtained in left-hand column and strike out those in the right-hand column.

0	Objective (described)	1700
100	Small Wood	1600
700	Ruined Farm	1000
900	Mound, Bush on Top	800
1300	Line of Poplars	400
1700	Starting Point (described)	0

3. *Defence range card.*—The successive steps are as follows:—

(a) Mark off on the card the position from which the ranges are taken.

(b) Describe position accurately.

(c) Select an unmistakable object and draw a *thick* setting ray to it.

(d) Draw two semicircles representing 600 and 1,000 yards respectively.

(e) Select objects to range on, *e.g.*, positions which the enemy may occupy or have to pass ; obstacles ; a bridge ; a gap in a thick hedge ; barbed-wire fences.

(*f*) Keeping the card set on the setting ray, *draw* rays to show the direction of objects and of lengths corresponding to the distances.

(*g*) Write short descriptions in horizontal block lettering or draw representations.

(*h*) Write the distance to each object against the description.

Notes.—i. Avoid too many rays, which are apt to become confusing.

    ii. When possible make one ray do for more than one object.

4. Fig. 6 shows an example of a range card made for use in defence. The ranges in this case are supposed to be taken from the point A. The direction line from A to the church is drawn thicker than the other lines to facilitate " setting " the range card in the same manner in which a map is set. When the card is set for the point from which the ranges are taken—which is noted on the card—by pointing the thick direction line on the church, the other direction lines will indicate the direction and the ranges of the other points marked on the card.

5. The point from which the ranges are taken should always be described clearly on the card to facilitate setting it.

30. *Application of fire.*

1. " *Fire Organization* " is arranged by the higher command to secure co-operation in the fire of various arms and units.

2. " *Fire Direction* is the term applied to instructions, given by an officer or non-commissioned officer commanding

more than one fire unit to their fire unit leaders, as to how
the fire of units is to be applied.

3. " *Fire Control* " *orders* are given by fire unit leaders
to their men.

4. As laid down in Infantry Training, Vol. II, (1921) Chapter
I, the normal infantry fire unit is the section. In battle,
whether in attack or defence, fire will be controlled by the
section leader as long as possible.

5. In modern battle, conditions will frequently exist
where control by the section commander is difficult or impossible—casualties amongst leaders will occur, situations will
arise where no fire orders or only the briefest instructions
may be possible, or it may be obvious to all that fire is
required, *e.g.*, to beat down a counter-attack. Under such
circumstances it is necessary that every man of the section
should understand and should have been trained how to
apply fire to the best advantage. A normal system of fire
application is required.

6. The following simple system of fire application for the
section will be instilled into all ranks :—

The fire of the men of the section may be applied in two
ways—(*a*) concentrated or (*b*) distributed.

(*a*) Concentrated fire by the men of a section implies that
every man of the section applies his fire to the same point.

(*b*) When distributed fire (*i.e.*, against a linear target
such as a line of men or an occupied area) is either called for
obviously by the situation, or ordered by the section commander, the men of the section will apply fire in the following
manner :—

**The limits between which fire is to be distributed
having been named or being obvious, each rifleman of**

the section will fire at the approximate point between these limits which corresponds to his actual position in the section. Each Lewis gun will fire in groups of short bursts at irregular intervals within these limits.

7. This normal system, which is explained (diagrammatically only) in Plate **16,** has the following special advantages :—

(*a*) It ensures that the fire of each section is distributed over the whole of the target.

(*b*) It allows any section commander to switch his fire against any other target that the situation may demand whilst the whole of the original target remains under the fire of the other sections.

(*c*) It allows of movement by one section taking place whilst fire is still applied to the whole target by another or other sections.

8. Although this system of fire application is the normal one, the section commander is in no way prohibited from seizing every opportunity that may be offered of directing his fire to the best advantage.

31. *Instruction of leaders in fire control orders.*

1. Fire control orders may be of three different kinds: —

i. Normal.
ii. Brief.
iii. Anticipatory.

An example of each is given below.

2. **Normal fire orders.**—A full and complete fire order containing :—

i. Designation of unit, *e.g.,* " No. 5 Section."
ii. Range, *e.g.,* " Five hundred."

PLATE 16.

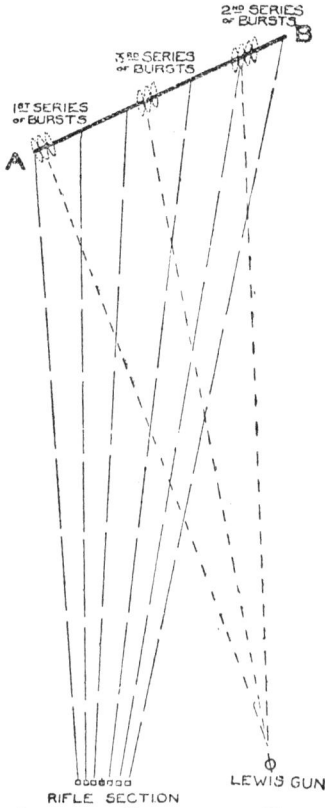

2ND SERIES
or BURSTS

3RD SERIES
or BURSTS

1ST SERIES
or BURSTS

A

B

RIFLE SECTION

LEWIS GUN

SYSTEM OF DISTRIBUTING FIRE.

A—B = Limits indicated by fire unit commander.

    iii. Indication, *e.g.*, " Quarter left—gateway—one width
right."

    iv. Number of rounds, *e.g.*, " Five rounds."

    v. Kind of fire, *e.g.*, " Fire," or " Rapid—Fire."

Reasons for the above method :—

    i. To make it clear to whom the order is addressed.

    ii. The range is given next so that once the men have
adjusted their *sights* they can concentrate their whole attention on recognising the target.   Knowledge of the range
also limits the area in which they need search for the target.

    iii. The indication of the target is given third and includes
the direction and description of the target (as already explained in the Section on Visual Training).

    Indication for concentrated fire.—The point of aim must be
given ; this may either be part of the actual target or an
auxiliary aiming point.   When no special part of the target
or auxiliary aiming point is mentioned, the centre of the
lowest visible part is intended.

    Indication for distributed fire.—The limits between which
fire is to be distributed will be named.   Each section will
distribute within the limits indicated as already explained in
Sec. **30,** 6 (*b*).

    iv. The number of rounds (normally 5) is named in order
to control the expenditure of ammunition and to ensure a
lull in the firing during which fresh orders can be given if
necessary.

    v. The kind of fire ordered should be that which the
target and the situation at the moment demand.

3. **Brief fire orders** are used when the target is an obvious one and when time does not admit of a full fire order being given, *e.g.*, " Quarter left, Rapid—Fire " ; or " 300, Half Right, Rapid—Fire."

4. **Anticipatory fire orders** are used in both attack and defence, anticipating either the movements of our own troops or those of the enemy.

Examples.—

    (a) *Attack.*—" No. 5 Section—Four Hundred—Hedge in front of Farm House ; No. 6 Section is moving up that covered approach on our right. We must cover their advance while they cross the bit of open ground—Await my order to fire."

    (b) *Defence*—" No. 3 Section—Five Hundred—Quarter right—Small Wood—When the enemy comes out into the open, open Rapid Fire on my order."

From the above it will be seen that all preparations for opening fire have been made, but the actual opening of fire is withheld until it is required.

5. **Fire orders, general.**—Fire orders should be given :—

    (a) i. As orders.
        ii. With decision.
       iii. Calmly.
       iv. Loudly.
        v. With pauses (to allow each part to be understood and acted on).
       vi. Every word must be important.
      vii. Avoid conversational tone and manner, and unnecessary or confusing detail.

(b) The order **Stop** means reload and wait for orders. The whistle may be used to draw attention.

(c) *Sighting* best changed by " Up (or Down)—100," &c.

(d) *Mutual understanding* between commanders and their men simplifies fire orders.

(e) *Rapid fire* is normally used to gain the maximum effect in the minimum time ; to obtain surprise effect on a vulnerable target ; to cover the movement of a neighbouring section or sections across an exposed piece of ground. Hence the aim must be to achieve a practically simultaneous opening of fire. In giving an order for " Rapid —fire," a pause should be made after the word " Rapid " to allow the men to come to the aim ; then on the word " Fire," each man will press his trigger when he has got a good aim. Rapid fire is aimed fire, and no attempt should be made to obtain a " Volley."

6. Lewis Gun Section " Fire Control Orders ".—

(a) Unless otherwise stated, a fire control order given to a Lewis Gun Section implies that the gun only will fire.

(b) If the leader wants to use his rifle fire at the same target as his gun, he will mention " Gun and Rifles."

c) If the gun is temporarily out of action, or the leader wishes to engage a target with rifle fire (whether the gun is in action against another target or not) the fire order will be preceded by the word " riflemen."

(d) The rate of fire to be used with the gun will be controlled as follows :—

> If the fire order is :—
>
>> FIRE—The firer will fire at the rate of 5 bursts a minute.
>>
>> RAPID—FIRE—The firer will fire in short bursts with just sufficient pauses between bursts to observe the fire and relay aim.

(e) The duration of the fire can be controlled in two ways, either by—

>> i. Stating the number of bursts before the order " Fire " or " Rapid—Fire " ; or,
>>
>> ii. Not mentioning any definite number of bursts, but merely giving the order " Fire " or " Rapid—Fire," followed by the command " Stop."

NOTES FOR INSTRUCTORS.

Methods of practising fire orders.

1. *Preliminary.*—When practising leaders in fire orders, those under instruction should sometimes be made to write down their orders, so that they can afterwards be discussed by the instructor.

2. When exercising leaders and their fire units in fire orders, either landscape targets or open country can be used.

I.—**Key rifles may be used as follows :—**

The instructor has two rifles in aiming rests and uses either one or both as required, *e.g., one* when a concentrated fire order is required and *both* for a distributed fire order, one rifle being laid on each end of the target to show the limits of distribution.

A selected fire unit leader then looks along the key rifle or rifles and gives his fire order.

The class (also using their rifles in aiming rests or some improvised rests) lay their rifles on what they recognise to be the target, and then stand clear.

The instructor then looks along each rifle in turn and discusses—

    i. The fire order given ; and

    ii. The fire effect that would have been obtained by the class.

II.—A second method of practising fire orders, using rests, is as follows :—

Concealed men are called up individually and fire blank—meanwhile the class, except the commander, have their backs turned. The men again conceal themselves ; the class turn about. The commander gives his fire orders—the class adjust *sights* and lay rifles from rests on the point at which they would have fired. The men are again called up, aims and sights are checked. The fire orders and probable effect of fire are then discussed. As progress is made, two men may be called up at a time and orders given for distribution between the points which they mark.

III.—A more advanced exercise in fire orders can be carried out as follows. (In this exercise neither key rifles nor aiming rests will be used) :—

The class will occupy a fire position under service conditions, and men equipped with pole targets will represent an enemy platoon in various formations advancing to attack the section in position.

The movements of the men representing the enemy with pole targets can be controlled by whistle and signal by the instructor carrying out the exercise, a previous rehearsal having been carried out to ensure the correct appearances and movements of the target bearers.

SPECIAL NOTES.

1. The above are not tactical exercises, but are framed in order to practise leaders in fire orders. The suitability or otherwise of the orders should be discussed with reference to the nature of the targets, and the following method of discussion is suggested :—

> When it is found that no fire effect would have been obtained, the fire order should be analysed and the poor result traced either to the class or the faultiness of the fire order, e.g., was the range given approximately correct ? If so, the class have no excuse for looking for the target at any other distance. Was the indication clear and short, or was there room for doubt ? Were aids used when there was no necessity for them ? Was the volume and rate of fire ordered suitable to the target ?

2. In all the above exercises, absolute accuracy of aim on the part of the class must be insisted on.

32. *Training in the use of ground and the use of formations.*

1. During firing instruction with the rifle and advanced handling with the light automatic, the soldier will be taught how to modify his firing positions to suit various forms of ground.

In visual training exercises he will be taught the elementary study of ground.

2. Owing to the fact that no two areas of ground are alike and also that no area of ground is so ideal as to present no disadvantages, skilful use of ground can only be secured by a combination of :—

(a) Knowledge of the military uses of ground.
(b) Recognition of features favourable or unfavourable to requirements.
(c) Power of instinctively weighing in the balance the advantages and disadvantages, and of making quick decisions.

These qualities can be developed by methodical training and constant practice.

3. By lectures and demonstrations the leader and the soldier will be taught the influence of various ground features in relation to fire effect and movement.

4. By exercises of the nature indicated in the Notes for Instructors below, he will be taught, practically :—

(a) The use of ground.
(b) The combined use of ground and formations.
(c) The combination of fire and movement.

Notes for Instructors.

I.—Exercises to teach the use of ground.

Individual stalk.

Preliminary.—A definite point is selected from 200 to 600 yards away where a sniper or a patrol is supposed to be located, the object being to approach sufficiently close to shoot with the certainty of killing.

Procedure.—The section or party is given a few minutes to study the ground, to decide upon the position from which to shoot, and to consider the best means of getting there. Individuals may then be questioned, and one or more detailed to carry out the practice within a time limit. The instructor and remainder of the party proceed to the objective to view the action of the selected men and will note the good and bad points of execution.

Discussion.—On the conclusion, discussion should take place on the following lines :—
  i. The reasons for the line of approach selected.
  ii. The fire position chosen.
  iii. If risks had to be taken, were they taken early while there was less chance of being seen and hit, or were they taken late ?
  iv. Was full advantage taken of dead ground and cover, both from fire and view ?
  v. Were sky-line, high ground, or unsuitable back-grounds avoided ?

II.—Exercises to teach the combined use of ground and formations.

Note.—Commanders will first exercise their units from a drill point of view only, until simple battle formations, deployments, and changes of direction can be rapidly carried out with precision. (*See* Infantry Training, Vol. I, (1922) Chapter VIII.)

Section stalk.

Preliminary.—As in Exercise 1, a definite objective is pointed out from 200 to 800 yards away.

Procedure.—A few minutes are allowed in which the section leader considers the problem and decides upon the following points :—

    (*a*) The ultimate fire position.
    (*b*) The most concealed line of approach.
    (*c*) The formations to adopt at various stages of the advance.

Discussion.—The following points will be brought out :—
    i. Those mentioned for discussion after Exercise I.
    ii. Leadership, handling and command of the section.
    iii. Suitability of the formations adopted.
    iv. The action of individuals.

SPECIAL NOTE.

It will be found useful for two sections of a platoon to carry out this exercise together, one attacking, the other defending.

III.—**Exercise to teach the combination of fire** and **movement.**

The attack by two sections under battle conditions (limited frontage) :—

Preliminary.—The objective and the limits of the ground that may be used are pointed out.

Procedure.—Leaders will have to consider the following points :—

    (*a*) The amount of cover which the ground affords.
    (*b*) The possibility of advancing without fire, and portions of the ground where the fire of one section may be needed to cover the movement of the other section.

(c) Suitable fire positions and how to approach them.

(d) Formations to use and method of advance.

(e) Suitable fire orders to deal with situations that arise.

Discussion.

   i. Ground and formations as in Exercise II.

  ii. The combination of fire and movement.

 iii. The fire orders of the leaders, and fire discipline of the men, both of the attackers and the defenders.

SPECIAL NOTES.

i. The remaining two sections of the platoon should act as defenders of the position, as in Exercise II.

ii. Coloured flags will be found useful in this stage to denote various volumes of fire which the attackers come under during their advance.

iii. One umpire should be appointed with each attacking section, and also one for the defenders.

GENERAL NOTE REGARDING ALL EXERCISES.

Instructors should guard against these exercises developing into a game of " hide and seek." Boldness should be encouraged. Crawling should be discouraged by fixing a time limit, and should only be allowed for movement over the last two or three yards into a fire position and for concealing movement over stretches of a few yards where exposure would otherwise occur.

The Small Arms School, Hythe.

33. *Objects of the school.*

1. The Small Arms School is established for the following purposes :—

    ι. To qualify officers to conduct weapon training in their units and to train selected warrant and non-commissioned officers to act as instructors in the weapons with which their units are armed, namely, rifle, bayonet, revolver, Lewis or Hotchkiss guns, hand, rifle and smoke grenades.

    ii. To study and to teach by demonstration and otherwise the correct technical and tactical handling of these weapons on the battlefield.

    iii. To arrange, carry out and report on such trials of weapons and ammunition as the Army Council may require in order to advance the knowledge of Small Arms generally, and especially to test the suitability or the reverse of any Small Arms or ammunition for use by men of average training under service conditions.

    iv. To advise and report to the Army Council on ranges and training material suitable and necessary for Weapon Training.

    v. To study and keep in touch, as far as training in Small Arms is concerned, with the regulations, methods of training and progress in foreign armies.

34. *The Commandant.*

1. The Commandant is responsible for and will report to the Army Council upon all training and trials carried out at the Small Arms School.

2. He will keep in close touch with Commands at Home and abroad, with India, and the forces of the Oversea Dominions on matters connected with Small Arms Training.

He will submit to the Army Council extracts from the Weapon Training reports of General Officers Commanding-in-Chief, together with any statistics and recommendations that he may consider necessary upon results obtained in the annual weapon training courses by troops serving at Home.

3. He will draw up the annual courses and necessary training tests for all Small Arms, except Vickers' machine guns and Tank Hotchkiss guns, and submit them for approval to the Army Council.

4. He is empowered to visit Commands and will report on the standard of Small Arms training in the Commands, and he will keep touch by visits or otherwise with such training establishments as the Staff College, the Senior Officers' School, the Royal Military College, and the Machine Gun School.

5. He will be an *ex-officio* member of the Small Arms Committee.

35. *Courses of instruction.*

1. The yearly programme of courses of instruction to be held at the Small Arms School, with full details and preliminary instructions for all ranks selected to attend such courses, will be published annually in Army Council Instructions.

2. Attendance at the Small Arms School is governed by the King's Regulations.

36. *Record of qualifications.*

1. The Commandant will forward to the War Office lists of officers who have attended, showing the results of their examination.

He will also furnish General Officers Commanding-in-Chief and the Deputy Adjutant-General, Royal Marines, with the names of officers, warrant officers and N.C.Os. who have qualified, and with the names of those who have failed.

3. The names of those who have qualified will be published in Command or District Orders and the qualification entered in their records of service. The particular weapons in which qualification has been obtained should be carefully stated.

4. Officer students attending a qualifying course will be classed as :—

> Distinguished.
> Qualified I.
> Qualified II.
> Failed.

5. Warrant Officers and N.C.Os. attending a qualifying course will be classed as :—

> Distinguished.
> Qualified.
> Not suitable as an instructor.

37. *The Corps of the Small Arms and Machine Gun Schools.*

1. The warrant and non-commissioned officer instructional staff employed at the Small Arms School belongs to the Corps of the Small Arms and Machine Gun Schools.

2. Candidates for appointment to this Corps must be serjeants or lance-serjeants, and will be finally approved for transfer only if found suitable after a six months' probation at the School.

3. Full details as to pay, terms of service, qualifications, &c., can be obtained on application to the Commandant of the Small Arms School.

4. A proportion of the personnel of the Corps is employed on instructional duties at the Royal Military College, Sandhurst, and in the Experimental Department of the Director of Artillery and at the Machine Gun School.

CHAPTER II.

THE RIFLE AND BAYONET.

THE CARE AND MECHANISM OF THE RIFLE.

38. *Care of rifle.*

1. Officers commanding platoons are responsible to their company commander for the condition of the arms on their charge, and for instructing their men in the care thereof so that no unnecessary wear of the bore may occur and the arms may be kept in such condition as to be always capable of accurate and rapid shooting.

PLATE 17.

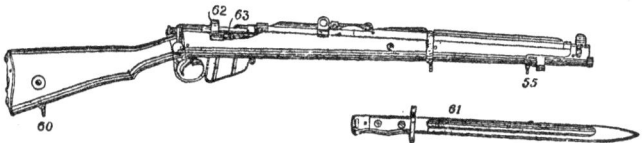

2. **Causes of wear.**—Wear in the *bore* of a rifle is caused by :—

(*a*) Friction of the bullet.
(*b*) Heat due to the explosion.
(*c*) Friction due to the pull-through gauze.

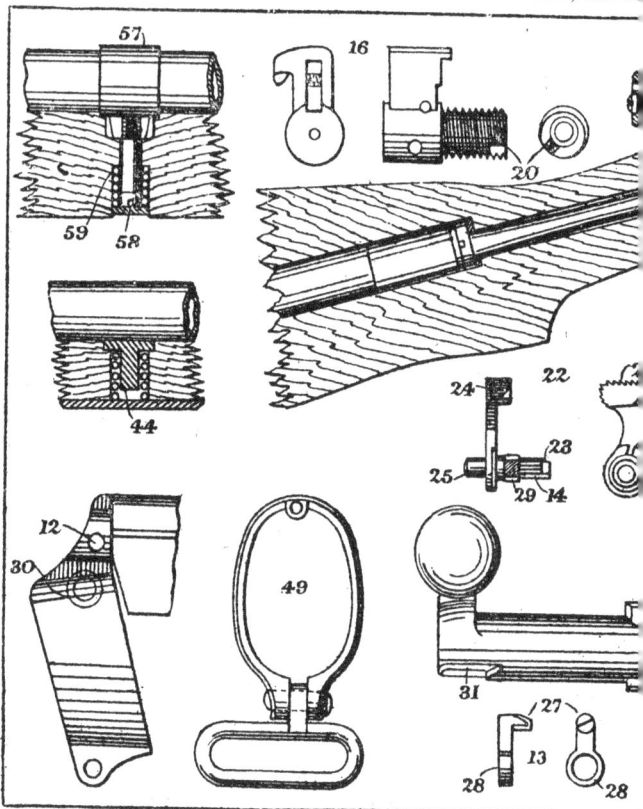

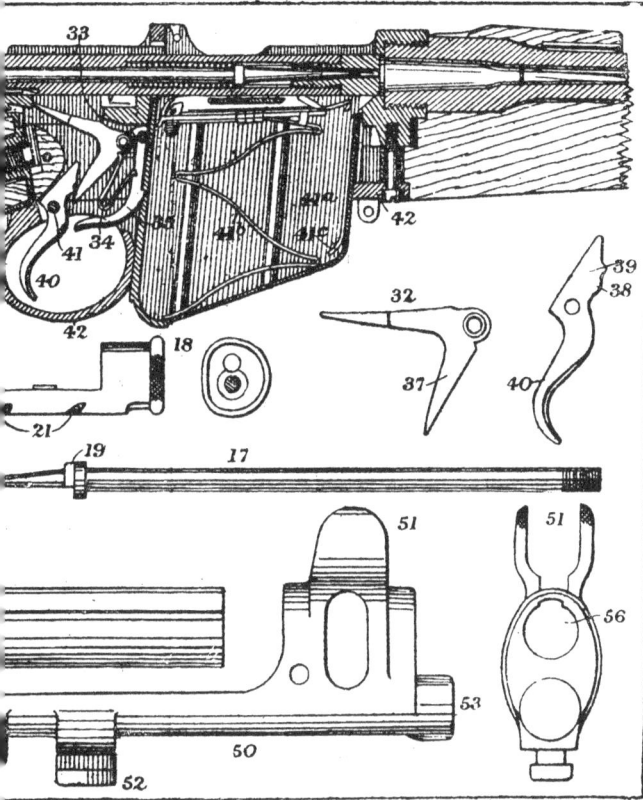

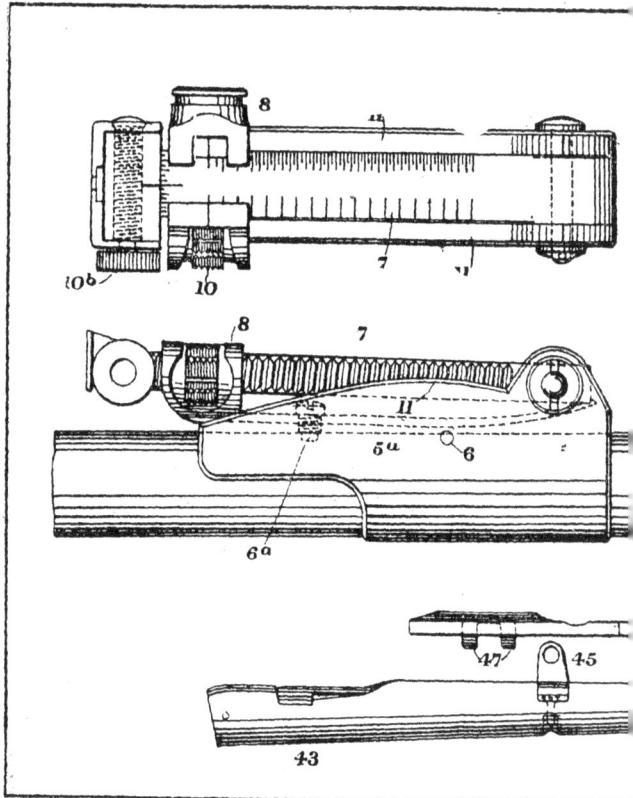

DGAUGE.

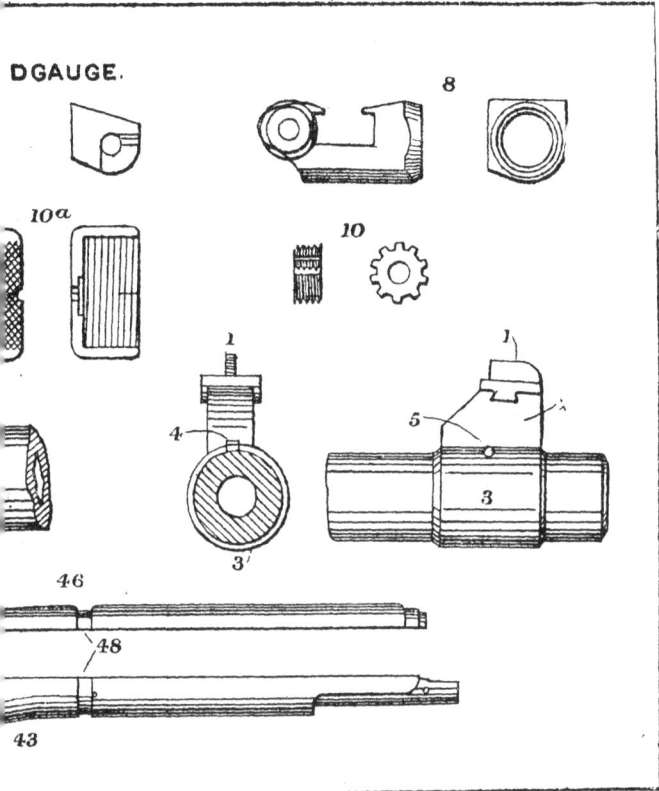

PLATE 20.

NAMES OF THE PARTS OF RIFLE, SHORT M.L.E., MARK III,
REFERRED TO IN PLATES 17 TO 19.

1. Blade foresight.
2. Foresight block.
3. Band foresight block.
4. Key   ,,   ,,
5. Crosspin   ,,   ,,
5A. Backsight bed.
6.   ,,   ,, crosspin.
6A.   ,,   ,, sight spring
      screw.
7. Backsight leaf.
8.   ,,   slide.
9.   ,,   slide catch.
10.   ,,   fine adjustment
      worm wheel.
10A. Windgauge.
10B.   ,,   screw.
11. Backsight ramps.
12. Seating for safety catch.
13. Safety catch.
14. Locking bolt stem.
15. Bolt.
16.   ,, head.
17. Striker.
18. Cocking-piece.
19. Striker collar with stud.
20. Bolt head tenon.
21. Cocking-piece locking recesses.
22. Locking bolt.
23.   ,,   ,, flat.
24.   ,,   ,, thumb-piece.
25.   ,,   ,, aperture sight
      stem.
26. Locking bolt stop pin recesses.
27.   ,,   ,, safety catch stem.
28.   ,,   ,,   ,,   ,, arm.
29.   ,,   ,, screw threads.
30.   ,,   ,, seating.
31. Bolt cam grooves.

32. Sear.
33.   ,, seating.
34.   ,, spring.
35. Magazine catch.
36. Full bent of cocking-piece.
37. Short arm of sear.
38.   ⎫
39.   ⎬ Trigger ribs.
40. Trigger.
41.   ,, axis pin.
41A. Magazine case.
41B.   ,, platform spring.
41C.   ,, auxiliary   ,,
42. Guard trigger.
43. Stock fore-end.
44. Spring and stud fore-end.
45. Protector backsight.
46. Handguard, front and rear.
47. Spring handguard, rear.
48. Lower band groove.
49. Lower band.
50. Nosecap.
51. Protector foresight.
52. Sword bar.
53. Boss for ring of sword bayonet
      crosspiece.
54. Swivel seating.
55.   ,, piling.
56. Nosecap barrel opening.
57. Inner band.
58.   ,,   ,, screw.
59.   ,,   ,,   ,, spring.
60. Butt sling swivel.
61. Sword bayonet, pattern '07.
      Modified.
62. Bridge charger guide.
63 Cut-off.

When properly cared for, 5,000 to 6,000 rounds can be fired from a rifle before it becomes unserviceable. To prevent unnecessary wear caused by too frequent use of the gauze the " Instructions for Cleaning " will be strictly adhered to.

No cutting or gritty material, such as emery powder or bath brick, will be used for cleaning any part of the rifle.

Although it may sometimes be found necessary to modify the instructions for cleaning to suit local climatic conditions, the guiding principles must not be departed from.

In dusty climates the *action* will be kept dry and a cover made of khaki, or other suitable material, will be used to protect the *muzzle* and *bolt*. Anything in the nature of a plug for the *bore* is, however, forbidden.

3. **Fouling.**—In order that the Instructions for Cleaning may be understood it is essential that the causes of fouling are explained to the soldier.

Fouling may be of three kinds :—

(1) **Internal,** caused by gas or other harmful matter being forced into the pores of the steel.

(2) **Superficial,** caused by the deposit in the *bore* of the solid products of the charge and of the cap composition.

(3) **Metallic** (nickelling), caused by a portion of the cupro-nickel of the envelope of the bullet being left on the surface of the *bore*. This appears as a whitish streak on the *lands* or as a slight roughness on the edge of the *grooves*. Metallic fouling causes the rifle to shoot inaccurately. If the rifle shoots badly for no other apparent reason, the presence of metallic fouling should be suspected and looked for. (The gauge-plug may be found

necessary to locate it. No attempt must be made by the soldier to remove this form of fouling ; the rifle should be taken to the armourer.)

(i) Boiling water is an effective method to remove internal fouling. Its action is to open the pores of the steel and allow the harmful matter to be removed by the flannelette on the pull-through. This method should always be used when possible.

(ii) Superficial fouling can be readily removed when the *barrel* is still warm by the use of the flannelette on the *pull-through*.

(iii) If internal or superficial fouling is allowed to remain in the *bore*, it will harden and turn to red rust ; to remove which it may be necessary to use the wire gauze.

(iv) The surest method of preventing rust is to keep the interior of the *bore* covered with a film of oil, which prevents the moisture of the air attacking the steel, and to remove the fouling immediately after firing and before it has time to harden and form rust.

Rust attacks a rough surface more readily than a smooth one and consequently a *bore* that has once become rusty will require more care than one that has been carefully looked after.

Barrels will therefore always be kept slightly oily (see para. 6 of this section) except—

    (*a*) **Immediately before firing ;**
    (*b*) **At inspections in barrack rooms, when dry barrels may be ordered.**

4. Cleaning materials.

(*a*) The *Pull-through*, which will be kept in the *butt trap* of the rifle, is provided with three loops. The first loop (the one nearest the weight) is for the wire gauze, the second for the flannelette, and the third for the purpose of removing the *pull-through* should it break or get jammed in the *bore*.

If a jam occurs the soldier must not attempt to remove the obstruction but the rifle will be taken to the armourer.

   i. The *pull-through* will be drawn through the *barrel* from *breach* to *muzzle* in **one continuous motion**.

   ii. The cord must be drawn straight through and not allowed to rub against the *muzzle* of the *bore*, otherwise it will cause a groove to be worn where it rubs ; this is known as " cordwear " and affects the accuracy of the rifle.

   iii. The *pull-through* will be packed in the *butt trap* as follows :—Hold the *pull-through* (loop end) between the forefinger and thumb, so that the end falls about 2 inches below the third finger ; roll it loosely three times round the fingers. Slip the coil off the fingers, and twist the remainder of the cord tightly round it, leaving sufficient to allow the *weight* to drop easily into the recess made for it in the *butt.* Push the cord into the *trap*, leaving the loop end uppermost, and close the *trap*.

(*b*) **Oil.**—Service oil is carried in the oil bottle, for which a recess in the *butt trap* is provided. No other form of lubricant is to Le allowed to remain in the *bore*. Paraffin, though an effective agent for removing rust, will not prevent it.

(*c*) **Flannelette.**—No other form of material will be used for cleaning the *bore*. For cleaning the *bore* (or for drying it) after firing, a piece of flannelette large enough to fit the *bore* tightly, 4 inches by 2 inches, will be used. It will be placed in the second loop of the *pull-through* and wrapped round the cord.

For oiling the *bore* a slightly smaller piece of flannelette will be used. If the piece used is too big, the oil will be scraped off as it enters the *bore*. The oil should be well rubbed, with the fingers, into the flannelette.

(*d*) **Stick, cleaning chamber,** made of wood about a foot long; at one end a slot is cut, the other end is cut square to allow a grip to be taken and the stick to be turned by hand. A piece of dry flannelette is placed in the slot and wound round the stick (to ensure that the stick is covered). The stick is then passed through the boltway into the *chamber* and turned round several times. This is the only effective method of cleaning the *chamber*.

(*e*) **Wire gauze,** in pieces $2\frac{1}{2}$ inches by $1\frac{1}{2}$ inches, is supplied and, except on active service, should only be used with the permission of an officer for the purpose of removing hard fouling or rust.

In attaching it to the *pull-through* the following method will be adopted :—

    i. Fold the gauze as in diagram, Fig. 7, so that the longer sides take the form of an " S."

    ii. Open the first loop of the *pull-through* and put one side of it in each loop of the " S."

    iii. Then coil each half of the gauze tightly round that portion of the cord over which it is placed until the two rolls, thus formed, meet.

The gauze must be thoroughly oiled before use and care taken to ensure that there are no loose strands of wire which may scratch the *bore*. The gauze will fit the *bore* tightly and will, if necessary, be packed with a small piece of flannelette or other soft material to ensure it so fitting.

The gauze should not be allowed to remain on the *pull-through* except on active service when it will provide the normal means of cleaning the *bore*.

FIG. 7.

WIRE GAUZE FOLDED.

SECTION.

ON PULL-THROUGH.

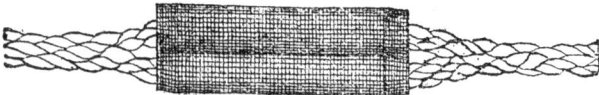

5. **Before cleaning the rifle** the *bolt*, *magazine* and *sling* will be removed from the rifle and placed on a clean spot.

To remove the *bolt* :—

   i. Raise the *knob* as far as it will go.
   ii. Draw back the *bolt head* to the *resisting shoulder*, and release it from the *retaining spring*.
   iii. Raise the *bolt head* as far as possible and remove the *bolt* by drawing it backwards.

To replace the *bolt* :—

    i. Ensure that the number on the *bolt* and on the right of the *body* of the rifle correspond.

    ii. See that the *resisting lug* and the *cocking-piece* are in one straight line and that the *bolt head* is screwed home.

    iii. Place the *bolt* in the *body* with the *extractor* uppermost and press it forward until the *head* is clear of the *resisting shoulder.*

    iv. Press the *bolt head* down until it is caught by the *retaining spring.*

    v. Close the *breech,* ensuring that the *bolt lever* is down, press the *trigger* and apply the *safety catch.*

To remove the *magazine,* depress the *magazine catch* inside the *trigger guard* and withdraw the *magazine.*

To remove the *magazine platform* :—

    i. Depress the rear end of the *platform* as far as possible, at the same time holding up the front end.

    ii. Pull the front end towards the rear end of the *case* until it passes under the *front lips.* The front end of the *platform* should then rise out of the *case.*

    iii. Tilt the rear end of the *platform* sideways, left side uppermost and draw it forward out of the *case.*

To replace the *magazine platform* :—

    i. Insert the rear end of the *platform* in front of the *rear lips* of the *case,* tilting it sideways so that the right side enters first.

ii. Depress the rear end until the front end is below the
level of the *front lips* of the *case*.

iii. Press forward, guiding the front end through the
internal ribs in the *magazine case*.

6.—(*a*) **Daily cleaning**.—The exterior of the rifle will
be cleaned daily and all particles of dirt or dust removed
from the *gas escapes* and crevices. The frictional parts will
be kept slightly oiled. The *bore* will be pulled through with
a piece of flannelette until the rag is clean, and immediately
re-oiled.

(*b*) **Cleaning before firing**.—All traces of oil will be
removed from the *bore*, and the *action* wiped with an oily
rag.

The cartridge and *chamber* will on no account be oiled before
firing, nor will any lubricant be used with a view to facilitate
extraction, as such a procedure is liable to injure the rifle.

(*c*) **Cleaning after firing** :—

i. Remove all fouling and grease from the *bore*.

ii. Pour about 5 or 6 pints of boiling water through
the *bore* from *breech* to *muzzle*, using a funnel.

iii. Thoroughly dry the *bore* and proceed to clean the
rest of the rifle, thus allowing the *bore* to cool.

iv. The *breech* will be cleaned with a stick, cleaning
chamber.

v. Special attention will be paid to the face of the *bolt*,
gas escapes and *bayonet boss*.

vi. If bayonets have been fixed during firing, the
bayonet will be carefully wiped before it is
returned to the scabbard.

vii. All metal parts will be carefully wiped and oiled,
after which the *barrel* will be pulled through with

a piece of oily flannelette. The *bore* will be found to require special care during the three days following firing.

viii. On active service, where boiling water is not normally available, the wire gauze will be used.

ix. Care must be used to prevent the browning from being rubbed off the rifle, as this is a great preventative against rust.

(*d*) **Cleaning after firing blank or ballistite.**—After firing blank ammunition, including ballistite, special care should be taken that the cleaning is thorough. Although in this case there is no friction between bullet and *bore*, and so no internal fouling or " sweating," there is greater accumulation of superficial fouling from blank than ball cartridge, because there is no bullet in blank ammunition to scour the fouling left by the preceding round. The firing also is in most cases more prolonged, and a greater interval must usually elapse before the rifle can be thoroughly cleaned. When blank firing precedes practice with ball, the rifles will be carefully cleaned before ball practice commences.

(*e*) **Cleaning after firing tracer.**—After firing tracer ammunition the rifle must be cleaned similarly as after firing ball.

7. **Cleaning ·22-inch rifles.**—In order to avoid damage to the bore of these rifles when cleaning, and thus preserve the high accuracy necessary for training, the following instructions will be strictly adhered to :—

i. The rod, brush and cleaner will always be inserted from the breech end (the breech bolt having been removed) so that the muzzle end of the bore cannot be damaged by the friction of the rod.

    ii. The bore should be cleaned after firing 60 rounds (*not oftener*) with the rod and cleaner with a strip of flannelette ½-inch wide in the eye.

   iii. On the conclusion of firing, the rod, with brush attached, should be passed up and down the bore a few times ; then remove the brush and attach the cleaner with strip of flannelette ½-inch wide in the eye, this will be passed up and down the bore in a similar manner, the flannelette being replaced until the bore is rag clean. After cleaning, the bore should be lubricated by using a ⅜-inch wide strip of flannelette well soaked in oil. This oil should be removed with dry flannelette before firing is again commenced.

   iv. The brush should be frequently cleaned with " Oil, mineral, burning" (paraffin), to free it from fouling.

Note.—Care should be taken to observe that the rod, brush or cleaner are not bent or allowed to come in contact with dust or grit as carelessness in this respect will cause friction and damage the bore.

    8. **General notes on care of rifle.**—(*a*) When the rifle is not in use, the *leaf* and *slide* of the *backsight* should be lowered.

    (*b*) The *mainspring* should never be allowed to remain compressed except when the rifle is loaded. The position of the *cocking-piece* shows whether the *mainspring* is compressed or not.

    (*c*) The *magazine* must not be removed from the rifle except for cleaning purposes or as laid down in Section **56** (3), and, to avoid weakening the *spring*, cartridges should only be kept in it when necessary.   A failure of the *spring* to raise the *platform* can usually be overcome by tapping the bottom of the *magazine* smartly with the palm of the hand. If the failure recurs, the rifle should be taken to the armourer for examination and repair.

(*d*) The *bolts* of rifles are not to be exchanged. Each *bolt* is carefully fitted to its own rifle, so that the parts which take the shock of the explosion have an even bearing, and the use of a wrong *bolt* may affect the accuracy of the rifle. The number stamped on the back of the *bolt lever* should agree with that stamped on the right front of the *body*.

(*e*) No N.C.O. or soldier is permitted to take to pieces any portion of the *action*, except as prescribed for cleaning, nor is he to loosen or tighten any of the screws.

39. *Protection of weapons and equipment from gas.*

1. If weapons or equipment have been splashed with mustard gas, chloride of lime may be used to disinfect them. Any dirt should first be removed as far as possible, and the surface to be cleaned will be sprinkled with a thin layer of chloride of lime. This should be washed off after 15 to 20 minutes and the object rinsed thoroughly with water. Parts which cannot be treated with the dry powder should be covered with a paste of chloride of lime, which should afterwards be washed off as described above. Any delicate parts of the mechanism (*sights, breech,* &c.) which would be injured by chloride of lime should be cleaned by polishing with dry rags. The rags must be buried after the operation. They should not be burnt. All cleaned parts should be dried and re-oiled. Men detailed to clean weapons and equipment

suspected of contamination with mustard gas must be provided with anti-gas gloves.

2. Certain gases have a corrosive action on metals. This action is greatly assisted by moisture, which dissolves and retains the gas, so that corrosion continues until the surface is cleaned. Metal surfaces which are covered with mineral oil are not affected, provided they are cleaned and re-oiled after exposure. The following precautions should be taken :—

    (a) Weapons should be kept oiled, and, after exposure to gas, should be cleaned and re-oiled. If exposed to high concentrations of a corrosive gas, they should in addition be stripped at the earliest opportunity and the parts washed in boiling water containing a little soda.

    (b) S.A.A. may be seriously affected by gas. Ammunition boxes should be kept closed.

        In position warfare, ammunition should be stored in shelters or recesses in the parapet, protected by a moistened curtain.

3. *Action during an enemy gas attack.*—The troops armed with the rifle will maintain a slow rate of fire, and occasional short bursts will be fired from machine guns to ensure that all weapons are in working order.

Troops in positions where it is not possible or advisable to fire, *e.g.*, supports and reserves, if in the area affected by gas, should close the *cut-off* and occasionally work the *bolt* backwards and forwards.

4. *Action after a gas attack.*—(a) Rifles and machine guns must be cleaned after a gas attack. Oil cleaning will prevent corrosion for 12 hours, but the first opportunity must be

taken to clean all parts in boiling water containing a little soda.

(*b*) S.A.A. must be carefully examined. All rounds affected by the gas must be replaced by new cartridges immediately. They will be cleaned and re-issued immediately so that they can be fired at the first suitable opportunity.

40. *Examination of arms.*

1. It is necessary for all company officers and N.C.Os. to possess a competent knowledge of the inspection and care of small arms.

2. Commanding officers will therefore arrange that they shall be instructed annually by the regimental armourer in repairing simple faults likely to occur in the field with such tools as would be available, and in the examination of the various components as directed in the following paras. :—

Rifles.

   i. The interior of the *barrel* for rust, cuts, bulges and fouling.

   ii. The *foresight* ; that the *blade* is not deformed and that the *nose-cap* is not loose.

   iii. The *backsight leaf*, for firmness of the joint ; that it is not bent ; that the *slide* moves smoothly ; that the *thumb-piece* and *fine adjustment worm* work freely and engage in the *rack* on the side of the *leaf* ; and that the U is not deformed.

   iv. The *magazine* ; that it is not dented, and that the *platform* works freely.

v. The *bolt*; that it bears the same number as the *body*; that the *striker* is not screwed too far into the *cocking-piece*; also that the *striker keeper screw* is not broken, is in its proper position, and that the *bolt* works smoothly.

vi. The *striker point*; that it is the correct shape and projects sufficiently through the face of the *bolt-head*.

vii. The *sear*; for height of the *nose*, which should just clear the bottom of the *resisting lug* on the *bolt*.

viii. The *cocking-piece*; for firmness on the *striker*, that the *bents* are in good condition, and that the *sear nose* bears properly.

ix. The *safety catch* and *locking bolt*; that the *safety catch* engages in the *camway* of the *bolt* and locks it; that it does not move too easily; and that the *cocking-piece* is withdrawn slightly to the rear when the *locking bolt* is applied, whether it is at " full cock " or the " fired " position.

x. The *cocking-piece* and *striker*; that they fly forward freely on pressing the *trigger*.

3. The action to be taken in the event of any rifle or ammunition being found defective is laid down in Sec. 42.

41. *Fitting the butt to the individual.*

1. Non-commissioned officers and men are to be fitted with rifles having long, normal, or short *butts*, according to their build.

2. This fitting is of the utmost importance and must receive the personal attention of the company or platoon commander.

3. The choice should be made after tests carried out in the standing and lying positions, and should be based on the readiness with which the firer brings his rifle up to the firing position and aligns his *sights* without letting his nose and mouth come into close proximity to the thumb and fingers of his right hand.

4. The *butt* selected should be that which can be used most comfortably whether firing in the correct standing or lying positions.

42. *Care of ammunition.*

1. Commanding officers will report in the regimental annual return any defects in the rifles or ammunition on their charge which have not been satisfactorily remedied.

2. **Miss-fires.**—A miss-fire arises from :—

    i. A defective cartridge.
    ii. A defective rifle.

In case i, the cartridge will be tried in another rifle and, if it still fails to fire, a report will be made in accordance with the instructions contained in the King's Regulations.

In case ii, the rifle will be taken to the armourer for examination.

3. **Storage of ammunition.**—Ammunition should be kept perfectly dry and clean, and should not be exposed to extremes of temperature.

4. No cartridges, whether ball, blank, miniature or dummy, other than those supplied by Government, may be used in service rifles.

5. In making reports on defective small arm ammunition, in accordance with the King's Regulations, the following definitions will be used :—

    i. Burst cases.
    ii. Separations.
    iii. Split cases.
    iv. Fluted cases.
    v. Blowbacks.
    vi. Missfires.

6. Burst cases, as distinguished from separations, may be of two kinds, viz., circumferential or longitudinal, and in reporting them, their position, whether in or above the base, should be clearly stated.

7. Separations are failures which are due to the case being stretched on firing, owing to excessive backward play of the *bolthead* in the rifle. Separations may be partial or complete, and may take place in any part of the case. They are distinguished from bursts by the fact that the torn edges of the metal are not fused. In case of doubt as to whether the casualty is a " burst " or a " separation," the rifle should be overhauled.

8. Split cases are those which burst at the *neck* or *shoulder*.

9. Fluted cases are those in which the powder gas has penetrated between the neck of the *case* and the walls of the *chamber* and has forced the metal inwards.

10. A blowback is an escape of gas between the cap and the sides of the *cap chamber*. This term is not to be used to denote an escape of gas due to bursts or other causes.

11. The instructions in this section apply to all small arm ammunition.

43. Mechanism.

1. *Recruit's mechanism.*—To ensure that the recruit has a knowledge of this subject, he will receive instruction in it as soon as he has been issued with his rifle (*see* Recruit's Initial Lesson). This ensures that the recruit will know how to remove and replace certain parts of his rifle without damaging them in any way. It is unnecessary to mention the weights or measurements of rifles or bayonets.

2. Instruction will be given in the following :—

(*a*) How to remove the *bolt* and *magazine.*
(*b*) How to remove the *magazine platform.*
(*c*) How to replace the *magazine platform.*
(*d*) How to replace the *bolt* and *magazine.*   (*See Note.*)
(*e*) Always to see that the *bolt lever* is in the lowest position before applying the *safety catch.*
(*f*) Half cock and how to re-cock.

Note.—When teaching recruits how to replace their *bolts* the following points will be brought out :—

He should always see that :—

i. He has got his own *bolt.*
ii. *Bolt-head* is screwed fully home.
iii. *Cocking-piece* and *resisting lug* are in one straight line.
iv. *Safety catch* is forward.
v. When applying the *safety catch* with the forefinger, always ensure by the aid of the remaining fingers that the *bolt lever* is as far down as it will go.

3. *Trained men's mechanism.*—To ensure that trained men have retained their knowledge of mechanism, instructors

will question them on the subject, *e.g.*, " Explain how to replace your *bolt*." If the man does not know he must have further instruction ; should he make only a slight mistake, the instructor will point this out at once.

4. The instructor should only question the men on what has been taught to them as recruits ; he should not be satisfied with a verbal answer ; he should make the men actually perform whatever he requires them to do.

5. *Instructors' mechanism.*—Officers, W.Os. and N.C.Os. must have a thorough knowledge of the *breech mechanism* of their rifles. It is necessary that they should know the different parts of the *bolt, striker*, &c., that move when the *bolt lever* is raised, drawn back, and so on. In teaching this subject, instructors will find the *skeleton action* most useful, and dummy cartridges should be used. By this means the young officer or N.C.O. will be able to see exactly what takes place on each movement.

6. *Action of the mechanism.*—On raising the *bolt lever*, the *bolt* is rotated to the left, thereby forcing the *stud* on the *cocking-piece* to move backward from the *long* to the *short groove* in the rear end of the *bolt* ; this action withdraws the *striker* about one-eighth of an inch. At the same time, a *steel lug* on the under side of the *bolt* works down an *inclined slot* on the left side of the *body*, withdrawing the *bolt* about one-eighth of an inch and effecting primary extraction.

7. The *charger* containing 5 cartridges is placed between the *guides*, and the cartridges are forced into the *magazine* by the thumb.

8. On pushing the *bolt* forward, the *charger* is thrown out and the *full bent* of the *cocking-piece* is brought against the *nose of the sear*. The *cocking-piece* and *striker* are thus held

stationary whilst the *bolt* travels forward, the *mainspring* being compressed between the *collar* of the *striker* and the rear end of the *mainspring chamber* in the *bolt*.

9. During the forward movement, the lower part of the *bolt-head* engages behind the upper part of the base of the top cartridge in the *magazine* and pushes the cartridge into the *chamber*.

10. On turning the *bolt* to the right, the *breech* is finally closed by the *rib* on the *bolt* working over the *resisting shoulder* on the right side of the *body* ; at the same time the *lug on the bolt* works into the *recess* cut on the left side of the *body*.

11. On pressing the *trigger* the two *ribs* on the *trigger* bear in succession on the *lower arm* of the *sear* and produce a double-pull off ; the first pressure bringing the *nose of the sear* to the bottom of the *bent of the cocking-piece*, and the second pressure finally releasing the *cocking-piece* ; the *mainspring* then carries the *striker* forward, exploding the *charge*.

12. The shock of discharge is taken equally on either side of the *body* ; on the right, by the *bolt rib* bearing against the *resisting shoulder*, and on the left by the *bolt lug* bearing against the *rear wall* of the *recess in the body*.

13. If the *bolt* has not been properly turned over when the *trigger* is pressed, one of two results will occur :—

    i. Either the *stud on the cocking-piece* causes the *breech* to close automatically by striking against the rounded corner of the division between the *two grooves* of the *bolt*, causing the *bolt* to turn down and the *breech* to close ;

    ii. Or the *stud on the cocking-piece* strikes full against the division between the two *grooves*, and prevents the *striker* flying forward

If the *bolt* is then closed by hand, the whole *action* becomes locke'd as the *sear nose* is engaged by the *half bent*, which is under-cut, whilst the *cocking-piece stud* travels half-way down the *longer groove*. The result is that the *trigger* cannot be pressed, nor can the *bolt* be rotated, until the *action* is placed at full-cock by drawing back the *cocking-piece.*

14. On opening and drawing back the *bolt*, the cartridge case is drawn out of the *chamber* by the *extractor* and is ejected. To ensure perfect ejection, an *ejector screw* is fitted on the left inside the *bolt way*.

15. The *safety-catch* may be used when the *cocking-piece* is either at full-cock or in the fired position. When the *safety catch* is applied the *cocking-piece* cannot be moved backward or forward, nor the *bolt* be rotated. Care should be taken to see that the *bolt lever* is as far down as it will go before applying the *safety catch*.

16. Instruction will also be given in the means of safety on the rifle :—

    (a) *Gas escapes.*

    (b) Two *studs* (on *bolt* and *cocking-piece*).

    (c) Half cock.

RECAPITULATION OF CARE AND MECHANISM OF THE RIFLE IN THE FORM OF NOTES FOR THE INSTRUCTOR.

Recruit's Initial lesson.

Object.—So that recruit will not develop bad habits before commencing rifle training parades.

Subjects.—(To be taught immediately recruits receive their rifles) :—

(*a*) Teach the man how to recognise his own rifle.

(*b*) (i) Loading.

(ii) Unloading

(iii) Charging magazines

(iv) Trigger pressing (*See* Sec. **55**).

(v) Recruits' mechanism (*See* Sec. **43**).

(*c*) Daily cleaning. Instructor demonstrates the following points. The section imitates him :—

   i. How to remove oil bottle and pull-through from the *butt trap*.

   ii. How to remove the *bolt* and *magazine* (put in a clean place).

   iii. See that the *weight* of the *pull-through* is not bent, run cord through fingers to see that it is not worn, to straighten it out and to remove any grit.

   iv. Work oil into flannelette with forefinger and thumb.

   v. Oil the *barrel* by pulling through from *breech* to *muzzle* ; a straight pull without pause.

   vi. Clean outside of rifle with an oily rag, instructor mentioning main parts of rifle.

   vii. How to replace the *bolt* and *magazine*.

   viii. How to replace the oil bottle and pull-through in the *butt trap*.

Note.—This method of cleaning is to be carried out daily by every man from the time he is issued with his rifle.

Lesson 2.—Materials and wear.

Explain importance.—Unless the rifle is kept perfectly clean the best results will not be obtained either on the range or on active service.

Subjects—

I.—Materials.

(*a*) Oil bottle containing service oil.

(*b*) Flannelette 4-in. by 2-in. for cleaning the barrel ; 4-in. by 1½-in. for oiling purposes.

(*c*) Pull-through.

(*d*) Gauze.

(*e*) Stick cleaning chamber

II.—Materials. How used.

(*a*) **Pull-through and its uses.**

  i. Explain the three loops—weight.

  ii. Always insert from the *breech* end.

  iii. Pull through straight from *breech* to *muzzle* and do not pause.

  iv. Flannelette in middle loop must surround the cord

(*b*) **Gauze. When used.**

  i. On active service it is issued on the pull-through.

  ii. At other times, when necessary to remove hard fouling after obtaining permission of an officer.

(c) **Gauze.   How to use.**

  i. Explain how it is put on the pull-through; the
    gauze must be in the shape of the letter " S."
  ii. Must fit the *bore* tightly—its object, for removing
    rust and hard fouling.
  iii. Oiled, and jagged ends turned in, before using in
    order not to scratch the *bore*.
  iv. Must only be packed with soft material, *i.e.*, flannel-
    ette.

(d) **Stick cleaning chamber.**—*See* Sec. **38, 4** (*d*).

III.—**How to Examine the Bore.**

Hold the eye close to the *muzzle* and look into the *bore*
but not through it; gradually draw the eye back, looking
for rust, cuts and metallic fouling.   Look from *breech* end to
examine the *chamber*.

IV.—**Causes of wear :—**

  (*a*) Friction of the bullet.
  (*b*) Heat due to explosion.
  (*c*) Friction due to the pull-through gauze.

V.—**Fouling (three kinds) :—**

  i. *Superficial.*—Always arises after firing, especially
    after blank.
  ii. *Internal.*—Caused by gas being forced into the pores
    of metal.
  iii. *Metallic.*—Caused by a portion of the nickel envelope
    remaining in the *bore*; only to be removed by
    an armourer.

Lesson 3.—Cleaning before and after Firing.

Subjects—

I.—Before firing.

   i. Remove the *bolt* and *magazine*.
  ii. Thoroughly dry the *bore* and *chamber*.
 iii. Clean the exterior of rifle as for daily cleaning.
  iv. *Bolt* to be slightly oiled.
   v. *Gas escapes* to be clear, face of *bolt* free from oil. See that *magazine spring* is in good order.

Note.—In sandy or dusty countries the *bolt* should be dry.

II.—After firing.

   i. Remove the *bolt* and *magazine*.
  ii. Pull through the *bore* to remove superficial fouling.
 iii. Pour boiling water through the *bore* (about 6 pints, special funnel to be used).
  iv. Thoroughly dry the *bore*.
   v. Clean the exterior as for daily cleaning, meanwhile allowing the *bore* to cool. Special attention to be paid to the face of the *bolt* and the *bayonet boss*.
  vi. Oil the *bore*.

Note.—(*a*) Special attention should be paid to the *bore* for at least three days after firing has taken place.

     (*b*) When blank ammunition has been used the rifle should be cleaned as above, but special attention to the *bore* is only required for one day.

(c) When blank firing precedes practice with ball, the rifle (*bore, magazine* and face of *bolt*), should be cleaned before firing with ball ammunition.

(d) If rifle cannot be cleaned at once the *bore* should be oiled and the rifle cleaned at the first opportunity.

III.—Care of rifle (general points).

i. *Leaf* of the *backsight* lowered when not in use.

ii. *Mainspring* of the *bolt* not compressed unnecessarily.

iii. Dummies not to be left in the *magazine* after parades.

iv. *Bolt* will never be exchanged.

v. No unnecessary rubbing of browned portions.

vi. Screws on rifle not to be touched.

vii. No material other than that issued from store to be used in cleaning the rifle.

Lesson 4.—Cleaning in the Field, and Jams.

Subjects—

I.—Cleaning in the Field.

(a) Rifle (*see* Sec. 38).

(b) Ammunition (*see* Sec. 42).

(c) Precautions against gas (*see* Sec. 39).

II.—Jams.

Causes :

i. Faulty manipulation of the *bolt*.

ii. Dirt or oil in the *magazine*.

iii. Dirty, damaged or defective ammunition.

iv. Some mechanical defect (worn or damaged parts).

Types and remedies.

(a) No round enters the *chamber*.
  To remedy :
    i. Draw back the *bolt*.
    ii. Press rounds well into the *magazine*, releasing
        them suddenly.
    iii. Tap the bottom of *magazine* sharply.

(b) Bullet enters the *chamber* obliquely.
  To remedy :
    i. Draw back the *bolt*.
    ii. Pull back the round with the forefinger, and
        push the round back into the *magazine*.

(c) Two rounds side by side in the *magazine*.
  To remedy :
    i. Push one round down sharply with the forefinger.

(d) Damaged *lips* of *magazine*.
  To remedy :
    i. Take the *magazine* to the armourer.
  To remedy on active service :
    i. Remove the *magazine*, and with a round of S.A.A.,
       lever up the *lips*.

e) Badly filled *charger*.
  To remedy :
    i. Remove the rounds from the *charger* and refill.
    ii. On active service reload with a complete new
        charger.

(f) Rifle half cocked.
  To remedy :
    i. Pull back the *cocking piece.*

(*g*) Empty case remaining in the *bolt way*.
   To remedy:
      i. Remove by turning the rifle over to the right.

(*h*) Missfire.
   To remedy:
      Reload.   If missfire recurs, examine *striker*.

Kit required.—Rifle and dummy cartridges.

Lesson 5.—Mechanism and Examination of Arms.

   Subjects—

I. Mechanism.

   (*a*) Trained men (*see* Sec. **43, 3**).

   (*b*) Instructors (*see* Sec. **43, 5**).

II. Examination of Arms.

   Officers, W.Os. and N.C.Os. only (*see* Sec. **40**).

AIMING INSTRUCTION.

44. *General.*

1. The purpose of aiming instruction is to teach men to aim correctly at any object, however difficult to see.

2. *Sights* are placed on the rifle in order to give both **direction and elevation.**

By **elevation** is meant the tilting of the *muzzle* as much above the point to be hit, as the bullet would fall below it if the *barrel* was pointed straight at it.

45. *Accuracy.*

1. Especial care will be taken that the *sights* of any rifle used in aiming instruction are in perfect order.

2. The aiming mark **in the earlier stages** will be a *grouping target* placed at a distance not exceeding 100 yards. When the habit of accuracy has been acquired, service targets will be used. Increased experience should compensate for the shape and comparative invisibility of these targets, so that the degree of accuracy ought to be maintained.

3. The instructor must inspect the *sights* frequently to ensure that they are correctly adjusted in accordance with his orders.
He will explain the following rules, and demonstrate the results to be anticipated from common errors in aiming :—

    i. The *backsight* must be kept upright.

    ii. The left eye (if as is normal the man shoots from the right shoulder) must be closed. In the opposite case the right eye must be shut.

    iii. Aim will be taken by aligning the *sights* on the centre of the lowest part of the mark, the top of the *foresight* being in the centre of, and in line with, the shoulders of the U of the *backsight*.

4. When these principles have been mastered, the instructor will loosen the *sling*, adjust the *sights* for any given range and

aim from a rest at the target, taking care that his eye is
immediately above the *butt-plate*. It will be convenient to
use a sandbag on a tripod to steady the head during the
aiming. Having aimed, he will call on each individual to
observe the correct method of aligning the *sights* on a mark.
Each recruit will then act similarly, when the instructor will
examine the aim, point out errors, and explain how they
would have affected the accuracy of the shot, and how they
are to be avoided. He should occasionally call on a man
to point out any errors which may have been made by his
comrades.

5. Extreme accuracy of aim must be insisted on even during
the first lesson.

46. *Common faults in aiming.*

1. The most common faults in aiming are :—

  i. Taking too much, or too little, *foresight* into the U of
     the *backsight*, causing the bullet to strike high
     or low respectively.

  ii. Inaccurate centring, *i.e.*, failure to get the blade of
      the *foresight* in the exact centre of the U of the
      backsight.

The recruit should understand that this inaccuracy will
deflect the *muzzle* of the rifle to the side on which the line of
aim is taken, *e.g.*, if aim be taken over the right edge of the
U, the direction of the line of fire will be to the right of the
line of sight.

  iii. Fixing the eye on the *foresight* and not on the object.
       If the eye is focussed on the *foresight* only, the
       firer will retain only a blurred image of the target.

iv. Inclining the *backsight* to one side. In this case the bullet will strike low, and to the side to which the *sights* are inclined.

47. *Adjustment of sights.*

1. **To adjust the backsight.**—Hold the rifle in the loading position so that the lines on the *backsight* can be clearly seen. Press in the *stud* on the side of the *slide* with the left thumb ; move the *slide* until the line is even with the graduation on the *leaf*, giving the elevation for the distance named. Be careful that it is firmly fixed.

2. **To adjust the slide.**—If when the *sights* are set at 200 yards, it is found that the line on the *slide* does not exactly coincide with the graduation on the *leaf*, then adjust it as follows :—

> Press the *stud* on the *slide* with the thumb of the left hand until the *worm wheel* can be easily revolved ; turn the *worm wheel* with the thumb nail of the right hand, until the lines coincide. The *stud* must not be pressed to such an extent that the *worm wheel* is entirely disengaged from *the rack.*

AIMING INSTRUCTION.

INSTRUCTOR'S NOTES.

Lesson 1.—Accuracy of aim.

Preliminary.

1. **Sights.**—The *sights* of all rifles must be in perfect order. They will always be adjusted to the actual distance during this instruction.

2. Each lesson will be repeated as often as necessary until the recruit is proficient, before proceeding to a more advanced one.

3. **System of instruction.**—To illustrate principles or check faults a free use will be made of large diagrams on paper, blackboard or ground; by practical illustration with the rifle, and by the use of suitable appliances, *e.g.*, accuracy of aim—paper in front of *muzzle* (*see* Special Note 1 below).

Subjects—

I.—**Elementary aiming.   Grouping Target.**

   i. Test *sights*.

   ii. Explain *sights* and show a correct aim by a diagram.

   iii. Explain the three rules of aiming; the third rule by diagram.

   iv. Teach how to lay an aim and explain the following :—

      (*a*) Elbow and head rested.

      (*b*) Eye over the heel of the *butt*.

      (*c*) Look at mark.

   v. Let each recruit view aim.

   vi. Illustrate elevation (using two rifles) by removing *bolts* and laying aims—*sights* being adjusted to 200 and 1,000 yards respectively.

   vii. Let each recruit view aims and look through the *bores*, instructor bringing out the following :—

      (*a*) *Sights* 200.—*Sights* and *bore* are pointing at mark.

      (*b*) *Sights* 1,000.—*Sights* on mark, *barrel* elevated to allow for fall of bullet.

    viii. Recruits lay aims ; instructor checks, only dealing with faults as they occur.

    ix. Teach and give the section practice in adjustment of *sights*.

II.—Aiming at " Small," and " Large " and Silhouette figure targets 200 to 600 yards.

    i. When the recruits can lay an aim at the grouping target, proceed with " Small " and then " Large " targets ; afterwards with " silhouette figure " targets.

    ii. Instructor shows a correct aim at each target before the recruits aim.

    iii. Check faults as for grouping target.

Special Notes.

1. When checking, for inaccurate centring or elevation, the aim laid by a recruit, the instructor must always get his eye in the correct position and his head rested. If the aim is found to be incorrect, make the recruit look at it again ; if he sees it is wrong, let him lay another, but if he still thinks it is correct, call another recruit to look at the aim. Should this recruit see that the aim is wrong, and fail to convince the recruit who laid the aim, the instructor must convince him by holding a piece of white paper in front of the *muzzle*. Let the recruit who laid the incorrect aim get behind the rifle and (making sure he has a correct position) the instructor tells him to get the tip of the *foresight* in line with the shoulders and in the centre of the U of the *backsight*. Then remove the

paper quickly, replacing it after a short pause and ask the recruit where his aim was. This will usually convince the man that his aim was incorrect.

2. Common faults.

i. Inclined *sights*. Illustrate.

ii. Inaccurate centring of *foresight*.

iii. Varying amount of *foresight*. Illustrate (ii) and (iii) with paper method if necessary.

iv. Focussing the *sights* instead of the mark.

3. Reasons for aiming at the centre of the lowest part of the mark.

i. Whole mark is kept in view.

ii. Better chance of hitting a vanishing target.

iii. Counteracts tendency to shoot high.

iv. Assists close grouping in collective fire.

4. Reasons for full sight.

i. Less chance of varying amount of *foresight*.

ii. Facilitates a rapid aim.

Kit required.—Grouping target. Small, large, and silhouette figure targets, 200 yards to 600 yards. Aiming rest. Tripod. Sandbag. Paper and pencil.

48. *Aiming off for wind.*

1. The recruit should be taught to discriminate between mild, fresh, and strong winds, by means of the effect which they exercise on natural objects, *e.g.*, trees, grass. He should

be taught to note the direction of the wind as *front, rear, right angle,* or *oblique.*

2. The approximate allowances in deflection for these winds will be taught.

Practice will be afforded in aiming off " small " and " large " and Silhouette figure targets according to the range, and the strength and direction of the wind.

In aiming off in feet, all distances are taken from the centre of the lowest part of the mark ; when using the " target breadth " method the target's breadth will be measured from the edge of the target.

3. Practices should be limited to 600 yards, but in addition there must be practice in aiming off at all ranges according to orders, the allowance being indicated if possible by reference to the breadth of the target, by the selection of an auxiliary aiming point, or by aiming off in degrees—using the *foresight.*

WIND TABLE.

Range.	Mild.	Fresh.	Strong.	
	10 m.p.h.	20 m.p.h.	30 m.p.h.	
200 yds.	6 in.	1 ft.	1½ ft.	
300 yds.	1 ft.	2 ft.	3 ft.	Halve allowance for
400 yds.	1½ ft.	3 ft.	4½ ft.	oblique winds.
500 yds.	2 ft.	4 ft.	6 ft.	

4. It is necessary to employ a man at the target to indicate the correct point of aim with a marking disc after each aim taken by the recruit. The amount of allowance made will be checked by the instructor.

AIMING INSTRUCTION.

INSTRUCTOR'S NOTES.

Lesson 2.—Aiming off for wind.

Subjects—

I.—Small Aiming mark at 10 yards.

Object—Keeping elevation only.

i. Prove necessity.

ii. Pin up an *auxiliary aiming mark*—section take aim— check if faults occur.

iii. Explain ; elevation is kept by tip of *foresight* being in line with shoulders of U of *backsight* and the mark resting on the shoulders. Show diagram. Remove *auxiliary aiming mark*, and let the section view the relation of the *sights* to the *stationary aiming mark*.

iv. Section practice—aims being taken at visible vertical lines drawn on either side of the mark—not less than 1 inch, and not more than 2 inches away.

NOTE.—In order that the instructor can ascertain that any aim to a flank is correctly maintained as regards elevation, he will draw an invisible horizontal line through tne lowest visible part of the aiming mark.

v. Pin up *auxiliary aiming mark*, to check aim, looking chiefly for elevation. Give plenty of practice.

vi. Explain table and various kinds of winds and how to determine strength.

II.— Small and large targets, 200-600 yards (in feet).

Teach dimensions.

		Bull.	Inner.	Magpie.	Target.
Small target	...	12 in.	24 in.	36 in.	4 ft. × 4 ft.
Large target	...	24 in.	36 in.	48 in.	6 ft. × 6 ft.

Measurements are in feet from the centre of the lowest part of mark.

ii. Man at target places the *auxiliary aiming mark*, 1 foot left or right.

iii. Section take aim—check—faults rectified.

iv. *Auxiliary* removed and the recruit views, to see how one foot aimed off appears.

v. Practice.

(*a*) Aiming off for definite number of feet.

(*b*) Problems for different winds.

vi. Check aim by *auxiliary aiming mark.*

III.—Silhouette figures — Average width 18 in. 200-600 yards.

Measurements are in *target breadths* from the edge of the target.

i. Man places *auxiliary figure* one breadth right or left, marking extreme edge with a stick ; *auxiliary* is then removed.

ii. Section aim at stick—check—faults rectified.

iii. Practice as in "II" but in *target's breadths*. Six inches of error will be allowed on either side of correct point of aim.

Kit   required.—Aiming   rests.   Tripods   and   sandbags. Silhouette figure targets.

49. *Use of degrees in aiming off (wind, &c., in collective fire).*

1. It is necessary for officers and N.C.Os. to know the effect of wind over 600 yards.

2. The point of aim is indicated :—

    i. By use of an *auxiliary aiming mark.*

    ii. With reference to the breadth of target.

    iii. By aiming off in degrees, using the *foresight.*

{ As explained in Lesson 2.

TABLE.

(Collective Fire.)

Range.	Mild.	Fresh.	Strong.
0— 700 800—1200	0° $\frac{1}{4}$	$\frac{1}{4}^{\circ}$ $\frac{1}{2}$	$\frac{1}{2}^{\circ}$ $1\frac{1}{4}$

N.B.—The use of degrees does away entirely with all estimating in feet or yards. The fire unit leader has only to estimate (*a*) the range and (*b*) the strength of the wind, and then apply this Table.

INSTRUCTOR'S NOTES.

Lesson 3.—Aiming off—collective.

Subject—

    I.—This exercise should be carried out collectively at the longer ranges. It should be demonstrated that the use of *target breadths, auxiliary aiming marks or degrees* is better than the use of feet and yards. Use any suitable targets either natural or artificial. Aiming off in feet is mainly useful for target practice only, and not for field work.

    Kit required.—Rifle rests. Man with flag.

50. *Aiming up or down.*

    1. For alteration of sights or point of aim in range and battle practices the recruit requires instruction in the elevation table.

ELEVATION TABLE.

Range.	Eleva-tion.	Vertical Rise.		Eleva-tion.	Vertical Rise.	
		Ins.	How obtained.		Ins.	How obtained.
200	300	6	2 × 3 = 6	400	12	Double amount obtained for 300.
300	400	12	3 × 4 = 12	500	24	Double amount obtained for 400.
400	500	20	4 × 5 = 20	600	40	Double amount obtained for 500.
400	...	...	...	550	30	4 × 5, and add ½ amount again, i.e., 4 × 5 plus ½ amount = 20 plus 10 = 30.
		Vertical Drop.			Vertical Drop.	
		Ins.	How obtained.		Ins.	How obtained.
500	400	20	5 × 4 = 20	300	40	Double amount obtained for 400.
400	300	12	4 × 3 = 12	200	24	Double amount obtained for 300.
400	...	...	...	250	18	4 × 3, and add ½ amount again, i.e., 4 × 3 plus ½ amount = 12 plus 6 = 18.

NOTE.—Units—*i.e.*, 2, 3, &c.—refer to the initial figures of hundreds of yards.

2. On the battlefield, better results will be obtained by correcting errors by alteration of sights than by aiming up or down—which is explained below, and which should only be used when time is the essential factor. (This will be rare since the alteration of sights only takes 3 seconds.)

3. If it is necessary to aim up or down the aim should be directed at a point not more than 3 ft. above or below the 6 o'clock line.

INSTRUCTOR'S NOTES.

Lesson 4.—Elevation table and aiming up or down.

Subjects—

I. Elevation.

> The use of the table should be taught with Small and Large targets at actual distances, with the marking disc to show the supposed strike of the bullets.

II. Aiming up or down.

Object.—To avoid making minor alterations of *sights* when time does not permit.

Limits.—Three feet up or down.

Practice.—At Small and Large targets.

Example :—Firer observes the strike of bullet to be low or high, during a rapid or snapshooting practice. As time does not permit him to alter his sights he must aim up or down.

Kit required.—Rifle and rests. Tripods. Sandbags. Small and Large targets. Auxiliary aiming mark. 1 man per target (to work marking disc). 1 signalling flag.

III. Later, practice should be given in the elevation table
(section 50) and the wind table (*see* Sec. 48)
combined.

51. *Rapidity of aim.*

1. Rapidity of aim is essential for rapid fire and snapshooting. The object is to quicken the aim while retaining
absolute accuracy and proper trigger release.

INSTRUCTORS' NOTES.

Lesson 5.—Rapidity of aim.

Preliminary—

1. Examine rifles and dummies—extend section—point out
any suitable targets—ground arms.

2. Instructor calls the section to his right side. Explain
that rapidity of aim is essential for rapid fire and snapshooting.

Subjects.

I.—Snapshooting.

> i. Demonstrate snapshooting and explain how time is
> saved.
> Correct position must be adopted.
> Rifle brought quickly to aim.
> *Sights* quickly aligned and no dwelling on the aim.
> ii. Send the section back and give the commands " Take
> up Arms," " Load," and a sight adjustment.
> iii. Give the command " Watch your Front." (Section
> push forward their *safety catches.*)
> iv. Section fire one round on command " Fire " (no time
> limit at first).

v. Instructor, taking each individual in turn, checks
with eye disc. The men work on the command
" Fire."

vi. Section is opened in two ranks, facing each other at
6 paces. Men of one rank check the aim of men
opposite, using eye discs if available ; instructor
occasionally checks with eye disc.

II.—**Later lessons.**—Men in front with silhouette figure
targets representing enemy.

i. 1st Practice. Fixed bayonets.
Target about 100 yards away.
Long exposures (5 seconds).
Target appears at same place each time.

ii. 2nd Practice. Fixed bayonets.
Targets longer distance up to 300 yards.
Shorter exposures.
Targets appear in different places.

Kit required.—Aim correctors. Silhouette targets for later
lessons and 1 man per target. 1 signal flag.

52. *Aiming off for movement.*

1. The following instructions for aiming at moving targets
will be given during the latter part of preliminary training.
When practice in this form of shooting is carried out on
30 yards or miniature ranges, the pace of movement should be
regulated in strict accordance with that of service targets.

2. When firing at targets crossing the front, the aim will
first be taken on the object. Then, following the object
sideways, the aim will be carried in advance and kept in
front of the object until the rifle has been fired. The distance

to which the aim should be carried in advance of the target
will vary according to the range, rate of movement, and
direction of movement.

3. Up to 500 yards range, aim should be taken at the
following distances in advance of the object :—

TABLE OF ALLOWANCES.

Man walking	...	...	1 ft.	
Man doubling	...	...	2 ft.	For each
Horseman trotting	...	...	3 ft.	100 yards.
Horseman galloping	...	...	4 ft.	

For oblique movement, halve the allowance.

4. Fire will rarely be effective at a single man moving
across the front at more than 300 yards range, or at a single
horseman above 500 yards. At ranges beyond 500 yards
aim should be taken at the head of a body of troops moving
to a flank.

INSTRUCTORS' NOTES.

Lesson 6.—Aiming off for movement.

Preliminary.

1. Examine rifle and dummies—extend section—point out
suitable target. Ground arms.

2. Instructor calls the section round him and explains the
necessity for aiming off.

Subjects :—

I.—Demonstrate the following :—

    i. *Sights* are first brought on mark.

    ii. Aim the required amount in front of the object.

    iii. Automatic swing of rifle.

iv. *Trigger* pressed while rifle is on the swing, continue swing after pressing the *trigger*.

Squad stand **behind** the instructor in order to be able to watch the movements of his rifle.

II.—**Teach the movement table,** and the limits for fire by individuals.

III.—i. Section practise automatic swing of rifle, only taking first pressure.

  ii. Instructor takes one man at a time, who views how to aim off by looking into the aim corrector.

  iii. Having looked into the *aim corrector* the **man returns** to the section and continues to practice, completing second pressure.

  iv. Instructor checks each man's progress in turn by means of an aim corrector.

IV. **Later lessons.**—Practice at actual distances up to 300 yards. A man is employed to move about in front of the section ; he should move obliquely as well as directly across the front.

Kit required.—Aim corrector. Man to act as moving target.

53. *Aiming at ground and marking down an enemy.*

1. The eyesight must be gradually trained in aiming at figures or other service targets and at ground which might conceal an enemy. For this latter purpose a man will be directed to show himself for a few seconds at different ranges. The squad will then aim, from rests, at the ground which they believe to be occupied. After a short interval the man will stand up, whereupon errors will be corrected and criticized.

Firing Instruction.

54. *Object of firing instruction.*

1. The object of all Firing Instruction is to teach men to handle their rifles correctly both in the open and behind cover.

55. *Trigger pressing.*

Note.—Taught in Care of Rifle (Recruit's Initial Lesson.)

1. Before he is permitted to practice *trigger* pressing by himself, the recruit will be given several lessons in the correct way of pressing the *trigger*. The rifle will be rested and the recruit will be seated with his elbows rested. The instructor will, as a preliminary step, ensure that the recruit can move his trigger finger freely.

2. The instructor will explain.

    i. That as the *trigger* has a double pressure, two distinct pressures are necessary to fire the rifle. (The strength of the first is 3 to 4 lbs.; that of the second, about 2 lbs., making a total of 5 to 6 lbs.) The first should be taken when the rifle has been brought into the position for aiming; the second, when the sights are aligned on the mark.

    ii. That the direction of the pressure is diagonally across the *small of the butt.*

    iii. That the first joint of the forefinger should be placed round the *lower* part of the *trigger.*

iv. That, in order not to disturb the aim, the breathing
must be restrained when pressing the *trigger*.

3. In order that he may learn by experience the pressure
required to release the *cocking-piece*, the soldier will also :—

i. Be directed to place his forefinger under that of the
instructor, but without exerting pressure, whilst
the instructor carries out the motion.

ii Then, to enable the instructor to ascertain whether
the method is understood, the soldier will place
his hand over that of the instructor, and exert
the pressure.

iii. Finally, the soldier himself will aim and press the
trigger, while the instructor uses the *aim corrector*.
The main object is to release the *cocking-piece*
without disturbing the aim.

4. The recruit will always say after the *spring* is released
whether the true aim was maintained. If not, he must state
definitely the direction in which the rifle was pointing at the
moment of discharge.

5. From time to time the instructor will test the aim and
trigger release of each recruit with an *aim corrector*, and, if
necessary, further lessons in trigger pressing will be given.
Practice with miniature ammunition should be given, to
develop steadiness before practice is begun with ·303″
ammunition.

6. Trigger pressing requires most careful individual instruction, during which the necessity for determination and strong
personal effort will be impressed on the mind of every recruit.

7. The use of the *sling* for steadying the rifle during firing
is not to be taught.

Instructors' Notes.

Lesson 1.—Trigger Pressing.

Preliminary.

Explain its importance. Unless the *trigger* is properly pressed results in shooting will not be good.

Subjects—

I.—*Instructor demonstrates* each phase. The recruits practice.

    i. Test each recruit's trigger finger.

    ii. Teach how to cock the *action*.

    iii. Show correct grip with the right hand.

    iv. How to apply forefinger to the *trigger*, first joint on the lowest part of the *trigger*.

    v. Teach how first pressure is taken.

    vi. Explain and illustrate how second pressure is taken; right hand kept still and breathing restrained.

II.—*Section practice.*—Each recruit in turn places his hand over that of the instructor.

Special Notes.

1. Rifle and elbows should be rested.

2. In the case of a backward recruit the instructor would place his hand over the recruit's to show the correct method of pressing the trigger.

3. Recruits should not use the left hand for this purpose.

Kit required.—Any suitable rest.

56. *Loading, unloading, and charging magazines.*

Note.—Taught in Care of Arms (Recruit's Initial Lesson).

1. Load—

   i. Turn the *safety catch* completely over to the front with the thumb of the right hand.

   ii. Pull out the *cut-off*, first pressing it downwards with the thumb.

   iii. Seize the *knob* of the *bolt* with the forefinger and thumb of the right hand, turn it sharply upwards, and draw back the *bolt* to its full extent.

   iv. Take a *charger* between the thumb and first two fingers of the right hand, and place it vertically in the *guides*.

   v. Then, placing the ball of the thumb immediately in front of the *charger*, and hooking the forefinger under the *cut-off*, force the cartridges down with a firm and continuous pressure until the top cartridge has engaged in the *magazine*. *N.B.*—If there is no *cut-off*, hook the finger under the woodwork.

   vi. Force the *bolt* sharply home with the thumb and forefinger, turning the *knob* well down, and, with the forefinger of the right hand, turn the *safety catch* completely over to the rear, ensuring at the same time, by means of the remaining fingers, that the *bolt-lever* is fully down.

2. To Unload—

(*a*)—i. As when loading, but after drawing back the *bolt* work the *bolt* rapidly backwards and forwards (without turning the knob down) until the cartridges are removed from the *magazine* and *chamber.*

ii. Close the *breech*, press the *trigger*, close the *cut-off* by placing the right hand over the *bolt*, and apply the *safety catch.*

(b) **Another Method.**—Remove the *magazine* and take out the cartridges.

3. **Charging Magazines.**—The *magazine* will hold two chargers of five cartridges each, but should, in ordinary circumstances, be loaded with one only. If it is desired to charge the *magazine* without loading the rifle, the top cartridge may be pressed downwards with the thumb and the *cut-off* closed.

N.B.—When using a rifle which is not fitted with a *cut-off*, and it is required to " Charge Magazines," keep the pressure on the top cartridge with the thumb of the right hand and draw the *bolt head* over it with the little finger, close the *breech*, press the *trigger*, and apply the *safety-catch.*

57. *The standing position.*

1. The standing position will, as a rule, be used to fire over high cover or to take a snap shot, during an advance, so that the pace is not materially checked. The shot will not be fired while actually on the move, but the firer will halt for a moment. shoot, and then continue the advance.

It is a convenient position for elementary instruction, but when recruits have acquired facility in handling the rifle, they will be practised normally in the lying and kneeling positions.

**2. To Load—*

i. Turn half right.

ii. Carry the left foot to the left and slightly forward, so that the body is equally balanced on both feet.

iii. Bring the rifle to the right side with the *muzzle* pointing upwards, *small of the butt* just in front of the hip, grasping the *stock* with the left hand immediately in front of the *magazine*.

iv. Then load the rifle as already taught.

3. To adjust sights.—This will be done as already taught in lesson 1 Aiming Instruction, and without any unnecessary movement.

4. To aim and fire—

i. Direct the eyes on the mark.

ii. Then bring the rifle into the hollow of the right shoulder, press it in with the left hand, grasp the *small* firmly with the thumb and three fingers of the right hand, place the forefinger round the lower part of the *trigger*, and take the first pressure ; the *backsight* to be upright, left elbow well under the rifle, right elbow a little lower than, and well to the front of, the right shoulder.

iii. As the rifle touches the shoulder bring the cheek down on the *butt*, keeping the face well back from the right hand and *cocking-piece*. Close the left eye, align the *sights* on the mark, restrain the breathing,

---

* The command " Load " is only required for drill purposes.
After a rifle is once loaded the soldier is responsible that his *magazine* is kept filled until the command " UNLOAD " is given.

take the second pressure (and declare the point of aim).

    iv. After a pause bring the rifle to the loading position, and reload.

Great care must be exercised to ensure that the forefinger is not placed on the *trigger* before the rifle is in contact with the shoulder, and that a firm grip is maintained with both hands while firing.

    5. *To unload.*—As already taught.   Lower the *sights* and order arms.

INSTRUCTORS' NOTES.

Lesson 2.—Standing Position.

Preliminary.

    1. For practising the firing positions the section will be formed in a straight line, and sufficient targets must be provided.

    2. The essential points of the firing positions are to be insisted upon from the beginning as the foundation of fire discipline. The instructor's attention is called to the main points (*a*) to (*g*) in the first stage of fire discipline training.

    3. The **trigger release** of all rifles should always be in perfect order.

    4. Rifles must fit the firers.

    5. Individual instruction is necessary ; squads to be small **:** the normal positions suit nearly all men.

    6. Any tendency to shoot from the left shoulder will be discouraged. A recruit with normal vision learning to use a rifle for the first time can be taught to fire from the right shoulder, for which the rifle is constructed, as easily as from the left.

PLATE 21.

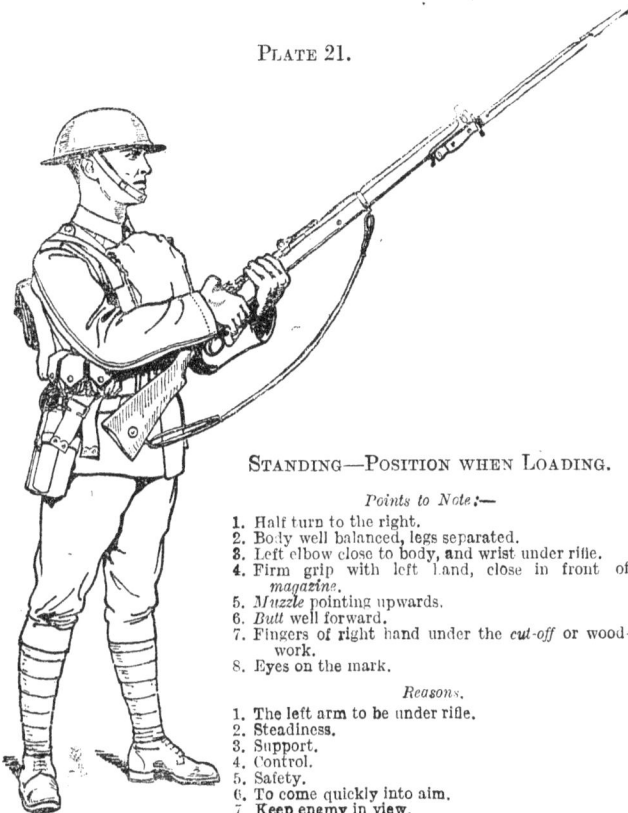

STANDING—POSITION WHEN LOADING.

Points to Note :—

1. Half turn to the right.
2. Body well balanced, legs separated.
3. Left elbow close to body, and wrist under rifle.
4. Firm grip with left hand, close in front of *magazine.*
5. *Muzzle* pointing upwards.
6. *Butt* well forward.
7. Fingers of right hand under the *cut-off* or woodwork.
8. Eyes on the mark.

Reasons.

1. The left arm to be under rifle.
2. Steadiness.
3. Support.
4. Control.
5. Safety.
6. To come quickly into aim.
7. Keep enemy in view.

Subjects.

I.—Standing position—

i. Examine rifle and dummies—extend section—instructor names his own target—point out suitable targets for section.

ii. Explain that you are about to teach how to fire the rifle.

iii. Demonstrate the whole position, naming each phase whilst doing so :—

(*a*) Loading.

(*b*) *Sight* setting—give range.

(*c*) Aiming and firing.

(*d*) Unloading.

iv. Explain when the position is used—to prevent delaying the advance and for firing over high cover. Give example.

II.—Loading position—

i. Section imitates the instructor in coming to the loading position, and returning to the order—faults only to be checked as they occur.

ii. The section practice—instructor inspects each recruit separately. He should never touch a man, but should correct him by force of example.

iii. Call section round you, and explain a few reasons while the section rests.

iv. Send section back and give them further practice—check faults and question.

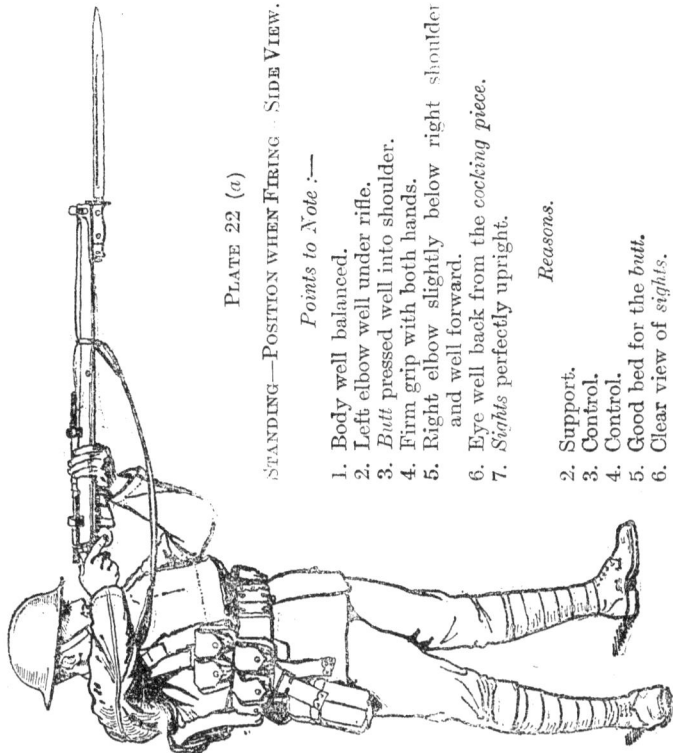

Plate 22 (a)

Standing—Position when Firing : Side View.

Points to Note :—

1. Body well balanced.
2. Left elbow well under rifle.
3. *Butt* pressed well into shoulder.
4. Firm grip with both hands.
5. Right elbow slightly below right shoulder and well forward.
6. Eye well back from the *cocking piece.*
7. *Sights* perfectly upright.

Reasons.

2. Support.
3. Control.
4. Control.
5. Good bed for the *butt.*
6. Clear view of *sights.*

PLATE 22 (*b*).

STANDING—POSITION WHEN FIRING—FRONT VIEW.

Points to Note :—

1. Body well balanced.
2. Left elbow well under rifle.
3. Good bed for the *butt.*
4. Firm grip with both hands.

5. Eye well back from the *cocking-piece.*
6. *Sights* perfectly upright.

III.—**Loading, sight-setting, unloading**—

    i. Make the section adopt the loading position.

    ii. Briefly explain how to load, adjust sights, and unload. The section imitates the instructor in all these movements.

    iii. Give the section practice in loading and sight-setting; check any faults, examine *sights*, call out fresh adjustments (for practice), while moving along the section.

    iv. Make the section unload and return to the order; check to see if *sights* are lowered and *safety-catch* is turned to the rear.

IV.—**Aiming and firing**—

    i. Give command " **Standing, Load,**" and a sighting elevation. (Rest.)

    ii. Teach how to come to the aiming position, giving the essential points. Section imitate the instructor—practice.

    iii. Give reasons—further practice—check faults.

    iv. Teach how to fire the rifle, explaining :—

        (a) *Trigger* only released when *sights* are correctly aligned.

        (b) After slight pause return smartly to the loading position, and reload quickly.

        (c) Declare point of aim, *i.e.*, " Correct," " High," " Low," &c.

        (d) Re-charge *magazine* after firing five rounds.

    v. Section practice—check faults.

    vi. Practice finished, give command " **Unload.**"

V.—How to get the eye back from the cocking-piece (essential for a clear view of the sights)—

- i. Raise the head a little and draw it back.

   ii. Raise the *butt* a little higher in the shoulder

   iii. Turn the body squarer to the target.

   iv. If these methods fail, obtain a longer *butt*.

Kit required.—Any suitable targets or aiming marks.

58. *The lying position.*

1. The lying position will generally be adopted by troops on open ground, or when firing from continuous low cover, or from behind small rocks, trees, ant-heaps and similar cover.

2.—i. To lie down. Turn half right and bring the rifle to the right side as when standing grasping the rifle in the left hand at the point of balance. Place the right hand on the ground, and lie down. The firer will thus be lying obliquely to the line of fire. The legs should be separated, the left shoulder well forward, the left arm extended to the front, and the rifle resting on the ground in a convenient position, with its *muzzle* pointing to the target.

   ii. To load. As when standing.

   iii. To unload. As when standing.

   iv. To adjust *sights*. Quit the rifle with the right hand, draw the rifle back with the left hand (without any unnecessary movement of the body) until the lines on the *backsight* can be clearly seen. Then adjust the *sights*, as when standing, and resume the loading position.

   v. To aim and fire—proceed as when standing (without moving the elbows or body).

PLATE 23.

LYING—POSITION WHEN LOADING.

Points to Note :—

1. Body oblique to line of fire.
2. Legs separated.
3. Heels on the ground.
4. Elbows closed slightly inwards.
5. Rifle at full extent of left arm.
6. *Butt* well forward.
7. Rifle resting on the ground.
8. *Muzzle* pointing to the front.

Reasons.

1. To get left forearm under rifle.
2. Steadiness.
3. Steadiness and safety.
4. Prevent elbows moving when coming into aim.
5. Coming quickly and cleanly to aim.
6. Coming quickly and cleanly to aim.
7. Steady for loading.
8. Safety.

PLATE 24.

ADJUSTMENT OF SIGHTS.

Fig. A.

Points to Note :—

1. Firer's body is not raised.
2. Right hand is clear of rifle.
3. *Slide* adjusted with left thumb.

Fig. B.

PLATE 25 (*a*).

LYING—POSITION WHEN FIRING—SIDE VIEW.

Points to Note :—

1. Both elbows on the ground.
2. Good bed for the *butt.*
3. Firm grip with both hands.
4. Eye well back from the *cocking piece.*

PLATE 25 (*b*).

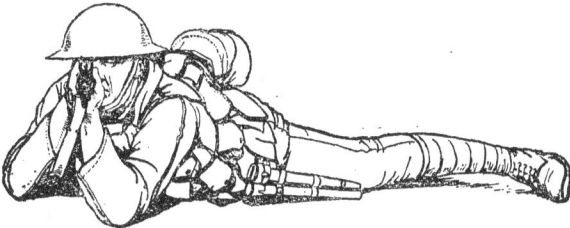

LYING—POSITION WHEN FIRING—FRONT VIEW.

Points to Note :—

1. Body oblique to line of fire.
2. Left elbow well under rifle.
3. *Sight* perfectly upright.
4. Elbows closed slightly inwards.

INSTRUCTORS' NOTES.

Lesson 3.—Lying position.

Preliminary.

1. Recruits will be trained to adopt the lying position rapidly, and to perform the loading and aiming motions with as little movement as possible. The oblique angle of the body is not to be exaggerated.

2. To avoid tiring the men, the instructor, for purposes of brief explanation or demonstration, may give the order " REST," whereupon *safety catches* will be applied and the men will rest in an easy posture ; the men will return to the loading position on the order " POSITION."

Subjects—

I.—**Sequence of instruction** will be the same as for the standing position.

II.—When in the aiming position the rifle may be raised or lowered on to the target by moving the body either backwards or forwards, pivoted on the elbows.

(To be taught before the men actually fire in this position.)

Kit required.—Any suitable targets or aiming marks, and ground sheets.

59. *The kneeling position.*

1. Kneeling is used mainly when firing from continuous cover, such as a low wall, bank, or in long grass, crops, &c., which would obstruct the line of sight if the lying position was adopted.

2. **To kneel.**—*Loading position.*—Take a walking pace forward to the right front with the left foot, at the same

PLATE 26.

KNEELING—POSITION WHEN
LOADING.

Points to Note :—

1. Body well balanced, left foot
carried well to right front.
2. Body supported on right heel.
3. Left forearm resting behind
left knee.
4. *Butt* resting on inside of right
thigh, and well forward.
5. Left heel slightly behind left
knee.

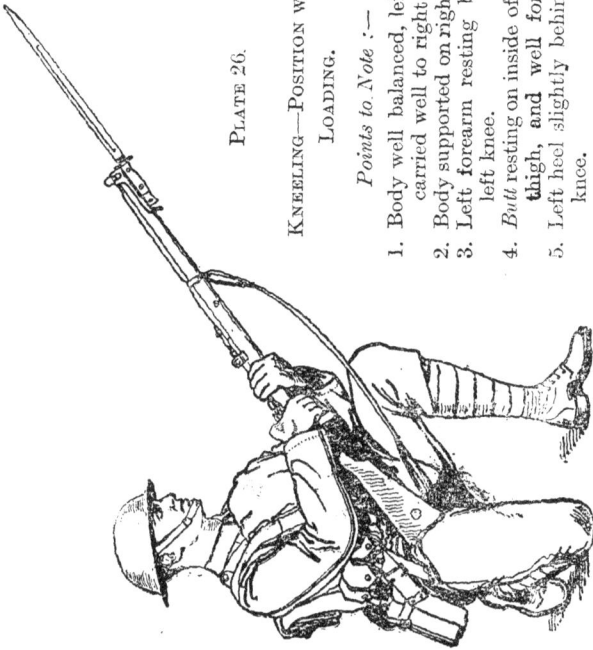

time grasping the rifle in the left hand as when standing, kneel down on the right knee : if possible sink the body on to the right heel, left forearm to rest behind the left knee, *butt* of the rifle resting on the right thigh.

3. *Firing position.*—The left knee will be in advance of the left heel, and the left elbow rested on or over the left knee ; the left leg, hand and arm, and the right shoulder, should be in the same vertical plane as seen from the front.

4. **To load.**—Adjust the *sights*, aim, fire, and unload as when standing.

INSTRUCTORS' NOTES.

Lesson 4.—Kneeling position.

Subjects :—

I.—*Sequence* as for the standing position.

II.—When in the aiming position, the rifle may be raised or lowered on to the target by moving the knee, elbow, or body—all methods are permitted.

(Taught before the men fire the rifle in this position.)

SPECIAL NOTE.

Loading, sight-setting and unloading need not be taught in detail in this lesson. Words of command only are necessary.

Kit required.—As for the lying position.

60. *The sitting position.*

1. The sitting position is suitable when on a steep slope. The right shoulder should be kept well back, and the left forearm supported by the thigh ; the right elbow may rest against the right knee, or be unsupported.

PLATE 27 (a).

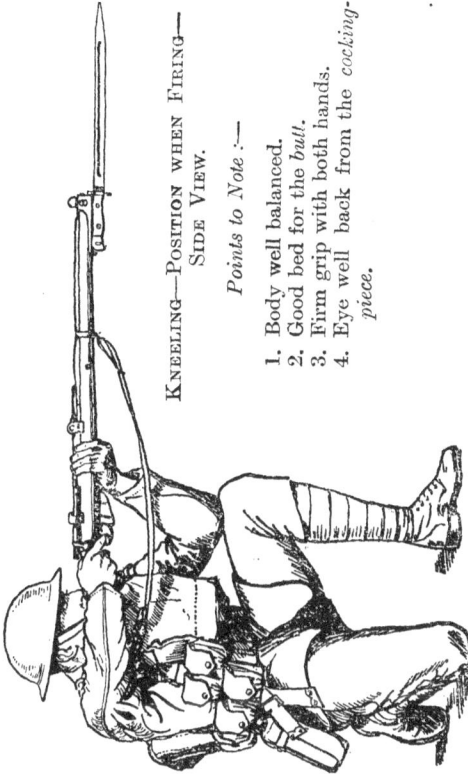

KNEELING—POSITION WHEN FIRING—
SIDE VIEW.

Points to Note :—

1. Body well balanced.
2. Good bed for the *butt*.
3. Firm grip with both hands.
4. Eye well back from the *cocking-piece*.

PLATE **27** (*b*).

KNEELING—POSITION WHEN FIRING—FRONT VIEW.

Points to Note :—

1. Body well balanced.
2. *Sights* perfectly upright.
3. Left leg, forearm, rifle and right shoulder in one vertical plane.
4. Left elbow resting in rear or over the knee cap.

PLATE 28.

SITTING—POSITION WHEN LOADING.

Points to Note—

1. Body upright and oblique to line of fire.
2. Left elbow resting on thigh.
3. *Butt* resting inside right thigh.
4. Both feet in most convenient position, according to the slope of the ground.

PLATE 29.

Sitting—Position when Firing—Across a Valley:

Points to Note :—

1. Good bed for the *butt*.
2. Both elbows rested when possible.

PLATE 30.

SITTING—POSITION WHEN FIRING—DOWN A STEEP SLOPE.

Points to Note :—

1. *Sights* perfectly upright.   3. Left forearm resting along left thigh.
2. Good bed for the *butt*.   4. Right elbow raised according to slope.

INSTRUCTORS' NOTES.

Lesson 5. Sitting Position.

None are necessary, as the plates explain themselves. The exercise must, however, be carried out on ground suitable for this position.

Kit required.—As for the lying position.

61. *Handling the rifle behind cover.*

1. Besides teaching the firing positions already described, the instructor will explain to his section the best means of using various forms of cover for fire effect and protection, practising the men in adapting themselves to various forms of cover in all positions. (*See* Infantry Training, Vol. II., (1921) Sec. 9, 5.)

2. The value of cover from view and the means of concealment afforded by small folds in the ground or even a few tufts of grass will be demonstrated. The tendency to attract attention by exaggerated movements of the head, arms or rifle, in loading and aiming, will be pointed out and checked.

3. Plates 31 to 39 show the main points to fulfil in using cover of various kinds.

Note.—The normal positions for loading are as in the plates. In the event, however, of more than 5 rounds being named in a fire order, the *magazine* will be recharged with the rifle still maintained on top of the cover.

PLATE 31.

STANDING IN A TRENCH—POSITION WHEN LOADING.

Points to Note :—

1. Firer, rifle and bayonet under cover.
2. Left foot on fire-step when possible.
3. Rifle rested on the ground.
4. *Muzzle* clear of cover.

PLATE 32.

STANDING IN A TRENCH—POSITION OF OBSERVATION.

Points to Note :—

1. No undue exposure.
2. Rifle rested on the ground.
3. *Sling* to the right.

P<small>LATE</small> 33.

STANDING IN A TRENCH—POSITION OF READINESS.

Points to Note :—

1. No undue exposure.
2. Left hand near *nose cap.*
3. Right hand grasping *small* of *butt.*

PLATE 34 (a).

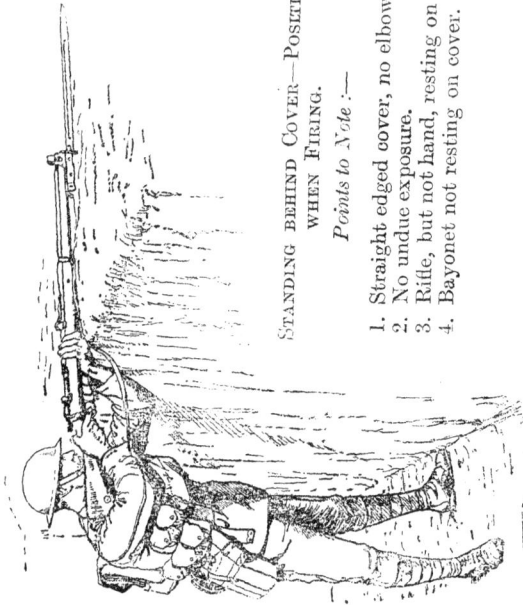

STANDING BEHIND COVER—POSITION WHEN FIRING.

Points to Note :—

1. Straight edged cover, no elbow rest.
2. No undue exposure.
3. Rifle, but not hand, resting on cover.
4. Bayonet not resting on cover.

PLATE 34 (*b*).

STANDING BEHIND COVER—POSITION WHEN FIRING—
FRONT VIEW.

Points to Note :—

1. No undue exposure.
2. *Sights* perfectly upright.
3. Bayonet not resting on cover.

PLATE 35.

KNEELING BEHIND COVER—POSITION WHEN LOADING.

Points to Note :—

1. Firer, rifle and bayonet under cover.
2. Rifle resting on the ground.
3. *Muzzle* clear of cover.
4. Left hand near *nose-cap.*
5. *Sights* to be adjusted with right hand.

PLATE 36.

KNEELING BEHIND COVER—POSITION OF READINESS.

Points to Note :—

No undue exposure.

Rifle and bayonet under cover.

Rifle resting on the ground.

Muzzle clear of cover.

5. Left hand near *nose-cap.*

6. Right hand grasping *small* of *butt.*

7. *Sling* to the right.

PLATE 37.

KNEELING BEHIND COVER.—POSITION WHEN FIRING.

Points to Note :—

1. No undue exposure.
2. Rifle, but not hand, resting on cover.
3. Left elbow resting on left thigh when possible.
4. Bayonet not resting on cover.

PLATE 38 (*a*).

LYING—FIRING ROUND COVER—POSITION WHEN FIRING—
SIDE VIEW.

Points to Note :—

1. No undue exposure.   2. *Backsight* clear of cover.

PLATE 38 (*b*).

LYING—FIRING ROUND COVER—POSITION WHEN FIRING—
FRONT VIEW.

Points to Note :—

1. No undue exposure.
2. Side of rifle only resting against cover.
3. *Sights* perfectly upright.

PLATE 39 (a).

LYING BEHIND COVER—SMALL FOLD IN GROUND—SIDE VIEW.

Points to Note :—

1. No undue exposure.   2. *Muzzle* of rifle clears cover in front.

PLATE 39 (*b*).

LYING BEHIND COVER—SMALL FOLD IN GROUND—FRONT VIEW.

Points to Note :—

1. No undue exposure.
2. *Muzzle* of rifle clear of cover.

INSTRUCTORS' NOTES.

Lesson 6.—Positions behind cover.

Preliminary.

1. When engaged with the enemy, every man will be in a position of readiness : if not engaged, a look-out or sentry will keep watch.

2. Eyes must be kept on the target between shots, but it is permissible to glance down to insert a fresh *charger*.

3. All positions must be taught ; correct uses of cover explained ; each kind of cover which is used will be discussed —walls, trenches, shell holes, isolated cover, folds in the ground ; cover from view will be demonstrated.

4. When handling the rifle behind cover, the position to be adopted will not be named. The man adapts his position and action to the type of cover behind which he is sheltering.

5. Men must adapt themselves to cover according to their build. Any two men will rarely take up exactly the same position.

6. Points to bring out :—

   (*a*) Modification of position to suit the cover, **without sacrificing fire effect.**

   (*b*) Rifle properly rested.

   (*c*) No undue movement or over-exposure.

7. Good cover should :—

   (*a*) Have a good field of fire.

   (*b*) Permit free use of the rifle.

   (*c*) Be bullet-proof ; " Cover from view only " excepted.

   (*d*) Be inconspicuous.

   (*e*) Be easy to advance from.

Subjects—

I.—i. Examine rifles and dummies. Bayonets to be fixed.

    ii. Instructor demonstrates correct methods for slow, snapshooting, and rapid fire. Section watch from the right flank. Instructor then teaches methods in detail.

II.—Teach the method of loading and adjustment of sights (no standardized position).

    i. Men and bayonet below cover.

    ii. As close to cover as possible.

III.—Show position of readiness.

    i. *Safety catch* forward.

    ii. Take up a position which enables the rifle to be brought quickly to the aim, *magazine* to the right (*see* Plate 36).

    iii. Give the section practice, and check faults.

IV.—Teach how to aim and fire.

    i. The rifle, but not the hand, rested near the point of balance on or against the cover.

    ii. No undue exposure.

    iii. No unnecessary movements.

    iv. Give practice, check faults.

V.—Teach Snapshooting—Demonstrate from the position of readiness, explaining the following points :—

    i. Keep the head still.

    ii. Reload with *butt* in the shoulder.

    iii. If no more enemy appear, return to the position of readiness.

iv. After firing five rounds return under cover and recharge *magazine*; then adopt the position of
   readiness.
v. Give practice, check faults.

VI.—**Teach rapid fire**—Demonstrate from the position of
   readiness :—
   i. Right elbow kept down when working the *bolt*.
   ii. Give practice, check faults.

SPECIAL NOTES.

1. **Kneeling behind cover.**—Sequence as for standing.

   (*a*) Kneel on either or both knees.
   (*b*) *Magazine* turned to right in loading position.
   (*c*) Knee close to cover in aiming position.
   (*d*) Give practice, and check faults.

2. **Firing round cover.**

   (*a*) Side of rifle rested. *Backsight* clear of rear edge of
         cover.
   (*b*) Fire round right side.
   (*c*) No unnecessary exposure.
   (*d*) Give practice, and check faults.

3. **Isolated cover.**—Dangerous to use if conspicuous.

   (*a*) Demonstrate correct position.
   (*b*) Instructor calls section round him and explains
         correct position, *i.e.*, lie straight behind cover,
         with legs closed.
   (*c*) No unnecessary movement when loading and adjust-
         ing *sights*.

(d) Side of rifle rested, *backsight* not touching the rear edge of the cover.

Note.—At the end of this lesson the section view the complete demonstration from the front.

Kit Required.—Rifles, dummy cartridges and suitable cover—artificial or natural.

62. *Automatic alignment.*

1. Automatic alignment is the natural action of a man trained in the use of the rifle whereby he automatically brings his weapon into an approximate alignment on to the target. Constant practice is essential for this to be done correctly. Muscle exercise No. 1 will be found useful in this respect.

2. Snapshooting trains the combination between hand and eye ; training in automatic alignment trains the hand to work in combination with the eye and the ear.

3. **Night firing.**—Men should be exercised in the following automatic method of aligning their rifles for night firing :—

　　　i. Aiming marks should be selected within 100 yards of the section.

　　　ii. The men should be ordered to bring their rifles into the firing position with both eyes shut.

　　　iii. The right eye should then be opened, and the approximate alignment of the rifle verified.

After some practice each man will be able to ascertain his individual error, whether vertical or lateral. He should correct this by practice until he is able, with his eyes shut, to align the rifle with approximate accuracy.

4. Practice should also be given in aligning the rifle at sounds, such as the opening and closing of a rifle bolt by a

man hidden behind a bush, the rattling of tins on a wire, and so on.

This exercise should first be practised in the daytime. When proficiency is attained, men should be exercised in firing a few rounds after dark (or in daylight using smoked glasses) at large screens at a range not exceeding 300 yards, in order to demonstrate the value of the instruction received. The position of the screen should be indicated by some rough expedient to represent the flash of a rifle, or by a noise being made close to the target by a man in a pit.

5. Much material effect cannot be expected, save possibly against an enemy in movement, but the moral effect should be considerable.

Troops in a position commanding open ground or an approach which may be used by the enemy, may arrange to sweep it with fire by various means. These comprise— Laying rifles and light automatics in rests constructed by daylight ; preparing illuminated aiming marks giving a horizontal line of sight ; or by firing at the flashes of the enemy's rifles.

INSTRUCTORS' NOTES.

Lesson 7.—Automatic Alignment.

Subjects—

I. 1st stage.—At the halt at targets within 50 yards :—

(a) By looking at the target, then closing the eyes and trying to align the rifle on the target.

(b) By endeavouring to locate a hidden target by sound and then trying to align the rifle on the target.

II. 2nd *stage.*—At hidden targets in various places, the section being on the move.

III. 3rd *stage.*—With ball ammunition at night on targets up to 300 yards (at the halt).

(Smoked glasses will enable the 3rd stage to be carried out in daylight.)

63. *Muscle exercises.*

1. To accustom the muscles to the strain of prolonged firing, the following exercises will be carried out frequently during the elementary training of recruits and also by trained soldiers. Care must be taken that men are not unduly fatigued.

2. In each practice a conspicuous object, representing the target, will be indicated, and the rifle will invariably be thrown into approximate alignment with it. In the first, third and fourth exercises the correct aiming position will be adopted (including taking the first pressure, bringing the cheek to the *butt*, and closing the left eye), but without actually aligning the *sights.* In the second exercise the first pressure will be taken when the right hand grasps the rifle, but the head will not be lowered, the left eye will not be closed, nor will the *sights* be aligned.

3. These exercises are designed to strengthen the muscles of the forearm and the biceps and to work men up to a high standard of efficiency during prolonged or rapid fire without undue fatigue.

4. Dummy cartridges will not be used.

5. Bayonets will be fixed, except in 2nd Practice.

1st Practice.

Caution : *Muscle exercise.   1st Practice.*

" Load "—(any position).

" One."—Bring the rifle to the position for aiming, return after a short pause to the position for loading, and continue the practice.

" Unload."

2nd Practice.

Caution : *Muscle exercise.   2nd Practice.*

" Load " (any position).

" One."—Bring the rifle to the position for aiming.

" Two."—Quit the rifle with the right hand.

" Three."—Seize the rifle with the right hand, and at the same time quit it with the left hand.

Note.—The words " Two " and " Three " will be given at intervals of about 10 seconds.

" Unload."

3rd Practice.

Caution : *Muscle exercise.   3rd Practice.*

" Load " (any position).

" One."—Bring the rifle to the position for aiming.

Note.—The men will be trained progressively to hold the rifle in this position until they can do so without fatigue for two minutes.

" Unload."

4th Practice.

Caution : *Muscle exercise.   4th Practice.*

" Standing—Load."

" On guard."—Come " on guard," with either foot forward.
Safety catch back.

" Aim."—Advance the rear foot, push forward the *safety catch*, align the *sights* and take the first pressure.

Note.--The words " On guard " and " Aim " will be repeated at intervals of four seconds.

" Unload."

64. *Quickening exercises.*

1. The following are examples of quickening exercises :—
> A. With ammunition.
> B. Without ammunition.

2. These exercises are useful for smartening recruits when they have reached a fair standard of knowledge, and, secondly, for quickening the trained soldier. Many other exercises of a similar nature can be devised by instructors.

A. WITH AMMUNITION.

(To be carried out with ammunition on 30 yards or miniature ranges, in all positions, with or without using cover.

3. *Speed and accuracy—*
> *Competition* between 2 firers or between 2 pairs of firers.
> *Targets.*—Any small targets (*e.g.*, tiles, old tins, &c.) that will fall or break when struck.
> *Method of conducting.*—Firers standing at ease, rifles unloaded ; on the word " Go " they load, adjust *sights* and fire.

The first firer, or pair of firers, who knock down all their targets win.

4. *Fire and movement—*
> *Competition* between any number of firers, who for safety will fire singly.
> *Targets* as in No. 1, number as required.

Method of conducting.—Firer standing at ease, rifle unloaded ; on the word " Go " he lies down, loads,
adjusts *sights* and fires 2 rounds ; he jumps into
a trench and fires 2 rounds ; and then over the
top and fires 2 rounds kneeling in the open.

Time limit. —One minute, or less, according to proficiency.
The winner is the man who gets most targets down.

B.—WITHOUT AMMUNITION.

(If ranges and ammunition are not available the following
exercises are suitable.)

6. *Quick handling and firing.*—Section in two ranks 6 paces
distant ; front rank with aiming discs (lying, kneeling or
standing as required) ; rear rank turned about, their rifles
on the ground with *bolts* and *magazines* out. *Magazine plat-
forms* removed ; *safety catches* applied ; *sights* set at 1,000 ;
cocking piece in wrong groove ; bayonets off ; 5 dummy
cartridges loose, and empty *charger,* lying near rifle.

On the words " 400—Go," each firer reassembles all
parts of the rifle, fixes bayonet, loads with dummy cartridges, adjusts his *sights,* and (in a position similar to that
adopted by his front rank man) fires 5 rounds at the eye disc.

The winner is the firer who gets the most accurate shots in
the shortest time, including recharging his *magazine.*

Front and rear ranks will then change over.

Note.—The instructor must watch the firers very closly.

7. *Rapid loading competition.*—Dummy cartridges placed
on the ground in *chargers* (number unlimited) 50 yards in
front of the men.

On the word " Go " they double to their ammunition, and carry out loading and unloading as rapidly as possible in the lying position.   The rifle must be held in the correct loading position.

Time limit.—One minute.

One half section to check the action of the other half ; then change over.

The best man in each section can similarly compete to decide who is the best in the platoon or party.

8. *Loader versus filler.*—The section will be divided into pairs.   One man of each pair takes up a loading position and is given 5 *chargers* of dummy cartridges.   As fast as he loads and unloads his rifle the filler picks up the cartridges, replaces them in *chargers* and supplies the loader with ammunition.

If the loader can call, " I am waiting," before he has loaded and unloaded 12 *chargers,* he wins.

If, however, the filler can keep the loader supplied until the latter has loaded and unloaded 12 *chargers,* the filler wins.

The men of each pair then change over.

65. *Rapid fire training.*

To be carried out in all positions with bayonets fixed, either as a separate exercise or, when men are sufficiently advanced, during firing instruction.

Each practice will be demonstrated by the instructor.

Practice I—Clean and Quick loading.

Command.	Points to note and criticise.
" Load " or " Standing") (" Kneeling ") " Load."	All movements carried out correctly and smartly. *Magazine* charged in one clean motion. *Pouch* rebuttoned. *Safety catch* applied. Firm grip with both hands. Eyes on target (but it is permissible to glance down to insert *charger*).
(Safety catches forward.)	
" Re-load " ... ... Repeat 4 times at intervals of one second. " Load " with another *charger* and repeat.	Instant opening and closing of *breech* in one movement. *Bolt* withdrawn to full extent each time. Correct grip with right hand as soon as *breech* is closed.
" Rest " or " Order Arms."	*Safety catches* applied.

Practice II—Reloading at shoulder and first pressure.

" Load "	As in Practice I.
" Aim "	*Safety catches* forward. First pressure taken.
" Re-load " ... As in Practice I, but given at intervals of 2 secs.	Rifle kept in shoulder. First pressure only taken. Firm grip. Correct position of *butt* in shoulder. Cheek on *butt*, and head kept as still as possible.

Command.   Points to note and criticise.

" Rest " or **" Order**   *Safety catches* applied.
Arms. '

Aids to rapid fire—

(*a*) *Action* to be " bright clean " and slightly oiled.

(*b*) Vice-like grip with the left hand.

(*c*) Correct grip with the right hand.

(*d*) Tilt the rifle slightly to right when reloading.

(*e*) Keep the head still.

(*f*) Count the number of rounds

Practice III—(Rapid fire).

(Not to be practised until snapshooting has been taught.)

Section in two ranks, 6 paces apart, facing inwards and extended to 2 paces.

One rank fires, while the other, provided with aiming discs, checks.   The instructor will himself constantly check with the aiming disc.

" Load "   All points as in Practices I and II ;
(5 or 10 rounds.)   also—Accuracy and rapidity of
                          aim.

" Rapid fire."   Trigger pressure.
(Change over and   The man's rate of fire to be gradually
repeat.)   quickened.

Note.—If aiming discs are not available, the men fire at each other's eyes.

66. *Fire discipline training.*

General.

1. To ensure good results in fire discipline training the instructor must be quick to detect and remedy faults and be well grounded in his work.

2. The methods of carrying out fire discipline training laid down in this section should ensure that men obey orders rapidly and accurately, and, when left to themselves, use their rifles to the best tactical advantage.

3. Preliminary collective exercises consist of simple practices to teach accurate and quick obedience to fire orders, quick concentration of fire on various targets, while at the same time strict attention is paid to the individual action of the soldier in " Fire Discipline."

4. The normal firing position is *lying*; this will always be used unless other orders are given. The instructor will always make certain that the aiming mark he describes is visible to every member of his section.

5. Standing, kneeling and sitting positions will only be practised under conditions when they would be used; in wet weather, however, the standing positon may be used.

6. Rapid fire should never be ordered or allowed unless the target justifies its use.

7. A supposed position of the enemy will always be pointed out. The position of the instructor must be that of the fire unit leader in battle (except in the first stage " At the Halt ") until he has completed his fire orders; he will then move about to check faults.

8. Fire discipline training is carried out in two stages.

1st or elementary stage.

9. This stage is purely drill. As tactical situations, and hence the use of ground and cover, are not considered, it can be carried out in barracks; it is first carried out AT THE HALT and then on THE MOVE.

10. **At the halt** (with dummy cartridges). Easy service aiming marks will be used, and the ranges given must be

approximately correct. The section is halted at ease, extended to one or two paces.

    i. The instructor gives the order for loading.

    ii. He then gives the range, and the men adjust their *sights* (the instructor checks).

    iii. The fire order is then completed, and the men act on it.

    iv. They will continue to fire until the order to " Stop," is given, or until the named number of rounds have been fired.

11. The points which the instructor should note " At the Halt " are :—

    (*a*) Position adopted by the firer, dexterity in manipulation of *bolt*, loading, *safety catch*, and buttoning of pouch.

    (*b*) Correct adjustment of *sights*.

    (*c*) Recognition of target.

    (*d*) Difference between " Rapid " and " Slow " fire.

    (*e*) Difference between " Stop " and " Unload."

    (*f*) Alertness of the men in attending to fresh orders.

Every irregularity must be checked.

12. **On the move** (dummy cartridges will not be used). When the section is proficient at the halt, movement will be introduced.

Rifles will be loaded before the exercise begins ; the men are responsible for keeping their *magazines* charged.

    i. The section advances, extended.

    ii. On the command, or signal, " Halt," the section adopts the lying position (unless otherwise ordered).

iii. Fire orders are given (particular attention being paid to correct pauses so that each part of the order may be acted on before the next is begun).

The instructor will walk round his section, paying attention to the points previously mentioned.

2nd or more advanced stage (dummy cartridges will not be used).

13. This stage will be carried out in open country, on any suitable piece of ground having small undulations and minor irregular features, and is designed to teach and practise the men in the following :—

    i. The duties already practised in the 1st stage.
    ii. The use of ground and cover in relation to movement and how to obtain fire effect.
    iii Initiative and judgment.

14. The exercise is carried out as follows :—

    i. The section advances, extended.
    ii. A man appears (for about half a minute).
    iii. Instructor orders, " At the man—Fire."
    iv. The section halts, each man adopts the position he thinks suitable, according to the nature of the actual patch of ground over which he is moving; (he may find that he cannot see the target while he is lying down but that if he kneels he can do so, or by moving forward or back a yard or two he can get a better position), adjusts his *sights*, and fires.

15. The instructor will act as laid down in para. 7 above.

16. As proficiency increases, more difficult targets will be used, *e.g.*, men or carts passing on the road ; change of targets, aiming off, &c., will be used to vary this exercise.

17. Anticipatory fire orders may sometimes be given in this stage.

18. During this exercise the instructor should see that each man acts correctly in the following :—

(A) In both collective and individual fire.

    i. Recharges his *magazine* whenever necessary.
    ii. Makes proper use of the *safety catch*.
    iii. In the advance, gets up and down quickly.
    iv. Makes the best use of cover.
    v. Never presses the *trigger* unless his *sights* are aligned on the mark.
    vi. Observes the enemy.

(B) When a complete fire order has been given (in addition to A).

    vii. Adjusts the *sight* for the range ordered.
    viii. Recognises the aiming point described.
    ix. Counts the number of rounds fired.
    x. Limits his rate of fire to that ordered.

(C) When only a hasty and incomplete fire order has been received, or when the men are supposed to be acting individually (in addition to A).

    vii. Selects targets.
    viii. Judges distance.
    ix. Adjusts *sight*.
    x. Uses the rate of fire necessary,

TESTS OF ELEMENTARY TRAINING.

67. *General*.

1. These tests are most important, and if a platoon commander can satisfy himself that his men are able to pass all the tests, he can rest assured that so far as the groundwork of rifle training is concerned, he has an efficient platoon.

2. The platoon commander will keep a record of all the men in his platoon, showing the tests which they have passed, and the dates on which the tests were carried out.

3. This record will be inspected periodically by the company commander. Extracts from these records will furnish useful guides as to efficiency when men are transferred to other companies. Soldiers and recruits will themselves keep a record of their performances in their scoring books.

4. It is important that teaching should not be confused with testing. In the former a man is instructed by demonstration and explanation ; in the latter he is questioned, or ordered to carry out a certain exercise without any explanation or assistance, and either passes the qualifying standard or is relegated for further instruction.

5. Range practices and more advanced training will be a waste of ammunition and time, unless recruits have been thoroughly grounded, and trained men are kept efficient, in elementary training. The following system of tests has therefore been designed in order to :—

i. Provide a means of testing recruits in order to ensure that they have reached an efficient standard before they begin range practices.

ii. Ensure that trained soldiers have retained their efficiency.

iii. Prevent any detail of elementary training from being overlooked.

iv. Provide a standard to be attained by technical and other troops who are unable to devote as much time as is desirable to elementary training.

v. Enable non-commissioned officers and men, particularly those of the Militia and Territorial Army, to reach the required standard in their own time.

6. These tests are divided into :—

> A.—Oral
> B.—Inspection $\Big\}$ Tests.
> C.—Standard

Certain of the tests must be carried out individually, but in order to save time, as many as possible should be carried out collectively.

68. *Method of conducting the oral and inspection tests.*

A.—ORAL TESTS.

1. **Care of rifle and ammunition.**—A few questions should be put to each man.

2. **General knowledge.**—A few questions should be put to each man regarding the objects of, and reasons for, various details that have been taught him.

Qualifying standard.—Normally, three out of four to be answered correctly.

B.—INSPECTION TESTS.

3. Firing positions.—Men should be inspected in all firing positions, both in the open and behind cover, and those who make any serious faults will be failed.

4. Fire discipline.—The rapid execution of all orders, including the correct carrying out of all detail as laid down in " Fire Discipline Training," Second Stage A, B and C, Sec. **66**, 18.

An efficient standard must be reached in the above.

69. *Method of conducting the standard tests.*

1. Recognition of targets and aiming points.—The men being tested should each have an aiming rest. The commander will describe some difficult aiming point. The men lay their rifles on the point which they recognise from the description. Four points should be described for every man tested.

Standard : three out of four points described must be recognised.

2. Judging distance.—As for Quarterly Test, *see* Section 28.

3. Adjustment of sights.—Four distances will be named and sights examined. The position of the individual being tested will be varied, *i.e.*, standing, kneeling and lying.

Variations between distances ordered will not exceed 400 yards.

Standard : three correct adjustments out of four. Each within 3 seconds, time to be taken from the last sound of the range given to the moment when the *slide* is fixed.

4. Regulation aim.—Tested from aiming rests at a " small " target, 200 yards.

Standard : three out of four aims must be correct.

5. Trigger pressing.—Trigger pressing will be tested by means of the aim corrector.   (Accuracy of *aim* and correct *trigger* release are essential.)

Target.—Any distinct aiming mark.

Standard : three correct trigger releases out of four.

6. Aiming off for wind.—Tested with aiming rests.

(*a*) The men will be ordered to lay their rifles (up to two widths) right or left of a *Fig. 2 Silhouette target* at 300 yards. One foot (six inches either side) of lateral error only will be allowed, measured from the correct point of aim.   Vertical error should not exceed 1 foot.

Standard : three correct out of four.

(*b*) The men will also be tested in aiming off in degrees, using the foresight, etc.

Standard : three correct out of four.

7. Aiming off for movement.—Allowance in aiming off for movement will be tested with the aim corrector ; men failing to carry out the principles will be relegated to further practice.   The instructor will order a definite amount to be aimed off.

Standard : three correct aims out of four.

8. Rapidity of aim.—The time required to bring the rifle from the loading position to the shoulder, on the command

" fire " to align the *sights* on an aiming disc held to the eye, and press the *trigger,* will be measured with a stopwatch (or ordinary watch with a second hand). Position—lying.

The instructor will stop the watch when the *trigger* is pressed.

Standard : three out of four aims to be correct, each within four seconds.

9. **Rapidity of loading**.—The men to be tested will be equipped with a bandolier or pouches, and six *chargers* filled with dummy cartridges.

The *chargers* will be placed in the pouches or bandolier, which will be buttoned over them.

The time required to load, close the *bolt,* and eject the cartridges will be noted. The following conditions must be fulfilled :—

> The rifle held in the correct loading position ; one *charger* inserted at a time ; the pouch or bandolier, whether empty or not, buttoned up every time a *charger* is withdrawn.

Standard time : one minute.

10. **Rapidity of firing**.—This test will be a combination of 8 and 9. On the command " Rapid-Fire," each man will load with one *charger* at a time from the pouch or bandolier (the pouch being buttoned up each time a *charger* is withdrawn), and fire 10 rounds at an aiming disc held to the eye.

Standard time : one minute from the moment the command " Rapid-Fire " is given ; eight shots out of ten to be correct.

11. **Grouping with miniature cartridges.**—The grouping standards for miniature cartridge practice at 25 yards
will be :—

Marksman	...	...	...	...	1 inch ring.
First-class	...	...	...	...	2 inch ring.
Second-class	...	...	...	...	3 inch ring.

12. **Adjusting respirator, loading and sight setting.**—
The men to be tested will be in the lying position, respirators
in the " Alert " position. On the command " Gas—Four
Hundred " (or any other range not necessitating a movement
of the *slide* of more than 400 yards), the men will :—

(*a*) Put on their respirators.

(*b*) Load with five rounds from the pouch.

(*c*) Button up the pouch.

(*d*) Set their *sights* to the range ordered.

Standard time : 25 seconds.

N.B.—This test is to be carried out in fighting order.

EXERCISING THE TRAINED SOLDIER.

70. *System.*

1. When exercising the trained soldier, the method adopted
for recruit instruction will be modified and the system employed
will be that of—

" **Practising the soldier in the use of the weapons,
rather than teaching him, or testing him.**"

Only backward men should require teaching. Testing may be necessary in order to gauge the efficiency of the men of the Section or Class, and also to discover from time to time whether progress to efficiency is being made.

The aim of the instructor should be to ensure that all the men of his section are being practised according to their several individual requirements and efficiency, that interest is maintained and monotony avoided.

2. Detail should not be necessary except in the case of backward men.

3. When drawing up the programme of work, the instructor will so frame it that exercises which require muscular work and training in subjects at which men may sit or stand easy are alternated.

71. *Specimen programmes.*

1. The following programmes, each of one hour's duration, are inserted here with a view to assisting officers in carrying out the individual weapon training of their men. The programmes are divided into three categories :—

A.—Those suitable for indoor work, and for use in wet weather.

B.—Those suitable for use on the barrack square.

C.—Those suitable for work in open country.

A.—INDOOR.

No. 1. *Kit required.*—Eye Discs. Landscape Targets. Discharger. Dummy No. 36 Grenades.

Time.	Subject.	Detail
Mins.		
15	Rapid Fire Training, Practices 1, 2 and 3 ...	⎰ 1. Clean and quick handling. 2. Reloading at the shoulder and first pressure. 3. Rapid Fire.
10	Care of Arms	Cleaning the Rifle. Question and Answer.
5	Firing Instruction	Muscle Exercise No. 2.
10	Visual Training	Military Vocabulary.
10	Bombing	Changing Rifleman to Bomber.
10	Bombing	Description No. 36 Grenade.

No. 2. *Kit required.*—Dummy No. 36 Grenades. Respirators.

Time.	Subject.	Detail.
Mins.		
15	Firing Instruction	Loading and Firing ; *all* positions, in Respirators.
10	Care of Arms	Trained Men's mechanism.
15	Quickening Exercise	Loaders *v.* Fillers. Competitive. (With dummies.)
10	Bombing	Points before and after Throwing or Firing Live Grenades.
10	Quickening Exercise	Quick handling and firing. (With dummies.)

No. 3.   *Kit required.*—No. 37 W.P. Dummy Grenades.
Landscape Targets.

Time.	Subject.	Detail.
Mins. 10	Firing Instruction	Automatic Alignment. Elementary Stage (No. 1).
10	Aiming	Questions on Wind, Elevation and Movement Tables.
15	Quickening Exercise	Rapid Loading. Competitive. (With dummies.)
10	Bombing	Description and Handling No. 37 W.P. Grenades.
5	Firing Instruction	Muscle Exercise No. 3.
10	Visual Training	Recognition on Landscape Targets.

B.—BARRACK SQUARE.

No. 4.   *Kit required.*—Miniature " Small " and " Large "
Targets.   Aiming Rests.

Time.	Subject.	Detail.
Mins. 15	Firing Instruction	Lying Position. Bolt drill— Rifle.—(a) In loading position. (b) In aiming position.
10	Care of Rifle	Causes of Wear ⎫ Kinds of ⎬ Question Fouling ⎭ and Answer. Gas Escapes
15	Bayonet Training	Class Formation. High Port. Long Point. Controlled Charge.
15	Aiming Instruction	Accuracy of aim. Section lay aims— (a) Miniature Small Target.
5	Firing Instruction	(b) Miniature Large Target. Muscle Exercise No. 1.

No. 5.   *Kit required.*—" Small " and " Large " Miniature Targets. Discharger. Dummy No. 36 Grenades. Landscape Target. Training Sticks. Aiming Rests.

Time.	Subject.	Detail.
Mins.		
15	Fire Discipline Training	1st stage— (*a*) At halt. (*b*) On move.
10	Aiming Instruction	Lesson 2. Questions on Wind Table. Practice in aiming off and keeping elevation.
15	Bombing Instruction	Changing from Rifleman to Rifle Bomber.
10	Visual Training	Recognition on Landscape Target.
10	Bayonet Training	Lesson 3. Parries.

No. 6.   *Kit required.*—Eye disc. Training Sticks.

Time.	Subject.	Detail.
Mins.		
15	Firing Instruction	Rapid fire training. Practice I, II and III.
10	Section Battle Formations ...	Arrow head — line — file — single file. Extensions—at halt and on move.
10	Aiming Instruction	Questions on Wind, Elevation and movement tables.
10	Bayonet Instruction	Lesson 4. Practice long and short points at training stick.
10	Care of Arms	Questions on Cleaning.
5	Bombing Instruction	Loosening Exercises.

No. 7. *Kit required.*—Training Sticks. Discharger.

Time.	Subject.	Detail.
Mins. 15	Firing Instruction	Kneeling and Standing Positions. Advancing at the High Port, halting and coming to the aim, aligning the *sights* on some indicated point.
10	Care of Arms	Questions on jams and remedies, and on mechanism.
15	Bayonet Training	Fighting the ring (varied).
10	Bombing	Fixing Discharger and Range Setting.
10	Quickening Exercise	Rapid Loading Competition. (With dummies.)

C.—OPEN COUNTRY.

No. 8. *Kit required.*—Dummy Grenades. Aiming Rests.

Time.	Subject.	Detail.
Mins. 15	Bombing	Loosening Exercise and throwing practice.
10	Visual Training	Recognition.
15	Firing Instruction	Handling the rifle behind various forms of cover.
15	Judging Distance	At objects up to 800 yards, different methods to be practised.
5	Firing Instruction	Muscle Exercise No. 4.

No. 9. *Kit required.*—Silhouette Targets put out.   Discharger and Dummy Grenades.

Time.	Subject.	Detail.
Mins.		
15	Fire Discipline Training	Stage 2. In the open.
15	Visual Training	Stage 2. Silhouettes.
10	Quickening Exercise	Rapid Loading Competition.
20	Bombing	Changing from Rifleman to Rifle Bomber, and throwing dummy grenades from a fire position.

No. 10. *Kit required.*—Bayonet Sacks.   Silhouette Figs. 3, 4 and 5.   Dummy Grenades.

Time.	Subject.	Detail.
Mins.		
15	Bayonet Training	Lesson 4. Long point and short point at sacks.
10	Aiming Instruction	Snapshooting. Silhouettes, Nos. 3, 4 and 5. 100–300 yards. Exposures, 4 secs.
15	Bombing	Loosening Exercises. Throwing into cages.
10	Visual Training	Examination of ground. Description of Lines and Areas.
10	Quickening Exercise	Rapid Loading Competitions. (With dummies.)

Miniature and 30-Yards Ranges.

(See also Vol. III.)

---

72. General instructions for miniature ranges.

1. Practice on the miniature range should begin as soon as the recruit can adopt a good lying position, aim with accuracy, and press the *trigger ;* it should be spread over the period of elementary training which precedes range practices.

It is essential that the recruit should receive good instruction at the firing point, otherwise the ammunition is wasted and the recruit confirmed in his faults.

2. During this elementary training, frequent visits should be made to the miniature range, and the lessons of aiming, pressing the *trigger*, declaring the point of aim on discharge, &c., should be practically illustrated by means of miniature ammunition. Instruction on miniature ranges is in no sense a final training, but it is a useful and economical form of instruction.

3. The practices should conform to those to be fired later with ·303″ ammunition.

4. Target apparatus should be suitable for :—

    (a) Range practices.

    (b) Individual battle practices.

    (c) Section or platoon battle practices.

The elementary and other targets for use in miniature range instructional practices should be similar to those used on the classification range, and are supplied reduced to the correct scale.

5. The difficulties of service shooting can only be partly reproduced, *e.g.*, difficulty of estimating range, effect of

atmosphere on bullet, effect of atmosphere on eyesight, shock of discharge, will all be absent on the miniature range.

6. Cover of all kinds can be made with sandbags ; trenches should also be made where possible.

7. For Details of the **Empire Miniature Range Test,** see Table A, Appendix I, of Vol. II.

73. *Rifles and ammunition.*

1. **Rifles.**—The rifles used should be service pattern, ·22 inch R.F. The correct sighting for direct hits is about 300 yards, but each rifle on charge should be periodically tested by a good shot, and a board kept in the range showing the exact elevation and deflection required on each rifle for direct shooting on that particular range. (*See* Sec. 76, 3 and 7.) Before firing commences, the instructor will see that each rifle has its own correct sighting elevation and deflection.

2. The *windgauge* may be used to represent wind, and the firers taught to aim off so as to correct the deflection given, acting sometimes on their own judgment, sometimes according to orders for fire direction.

3. **Cleaning.**—Rifles should be cleaned after firing 60 rounds, and always before firing " rapid," and on conclusion of firing should be wiped out rag clean and left slightly oiled.

4. **Ammunition.**—Only ·22-inch miniature ammunition will be used on a miniature range.

74. *Safety precautions.*

1. **Range discipline.**—When rifles are being loaded, un-loaded, or inspected, they should be directed towards the target. When it is necessary to examine the targets, all men who are in position will unload, and lay down their rifles on

the firing point, with *bolts* open, and the red flag will be raised before anyone goes to the targets.

2. Firing will take place under the personal superintendence of a qualified instructor, who will ensure that all the conditions and safety precautions are strictly observed.

3. If miniature cartridge practice takes place on a classification range, the same orders for safety, &c., are to be observed as when service ammunition is used as miniature ammunition will carry as far as 1,400 yards.

75. *Practices.*

1. **Range practices.**—With or without a rest or cover, various positions :—

i. *Grouping.*—Rings 1, 2 and 3 inches. Recruits must reach a 3-inch standard.

ii. *Application.*—At " large " and " small " targets.

iii. *Snapshooting.*—At snapshooting targets.

iv. *Rapid fire.*—Can also be practised ; speed will be attained by quickening the aim and trigger release. A rate of at least 10 rounds per minute is easily reached with practice.

N.B.—The target to be used on miniature ranges representing the " small " 4-foot target is actually larger than that which represents the " large " 6-foot target.

2. **Crossing targets** are useful for practising movement of the rifle.

3. An instructor will supervise and instruct each firer.

4. Marking should be carried out from the firing point by means of field glasses.

5. **Individual battle practices.**—Individual battle practices can be fired, using figures representing men up to 600.

6. **Collective battle practices.**—The necessity for collective fire can be shown, and many useful battle practices carried out, on paper or turf bank landscape targets.

With the aid of these targets, instruction may be given in the description of ill-defined service objects, such as areas of ground, probable enemy positions, &c.

76. *Paper landscape targets.*

1. *Paper landscape targets.*—The frame for landscape targets is 10 feet long and 5 feet high. Landscape pictures in sheets, 5 feet by 2 feet, are pasted on to the lower portion, leaving 3 feet of blank sky-screen above to receive the shots.

The sky-screen should be of brown paper in order to render the bullet holes invisible to the firers.

2. When firing at paper landscape targets, rifles should be given extra elevation so that the bullets will strike the blank sky-screen, even if the aim is taken at an object at the bottom of the landscape ; this necessitates the rifles being harmonised so that they will all shoot to the same height above the point aimed at as follows :—

     Pin or paint aiming marks, at intervals of about 12 in. on a horizontal line at the bottom of the blank sky-screen. (*See* Plate 40.)

     Draw another horizontal line 27 in. higher ; this line must be visible from the firing point. Adjust the *sights* of all the rifles to 1,400 yards. The rifles are then fired with the regulation aim at the aiming marks, and *sights* are adjusted until every rifle hits within 1 inch of the line.

PLATE 40.

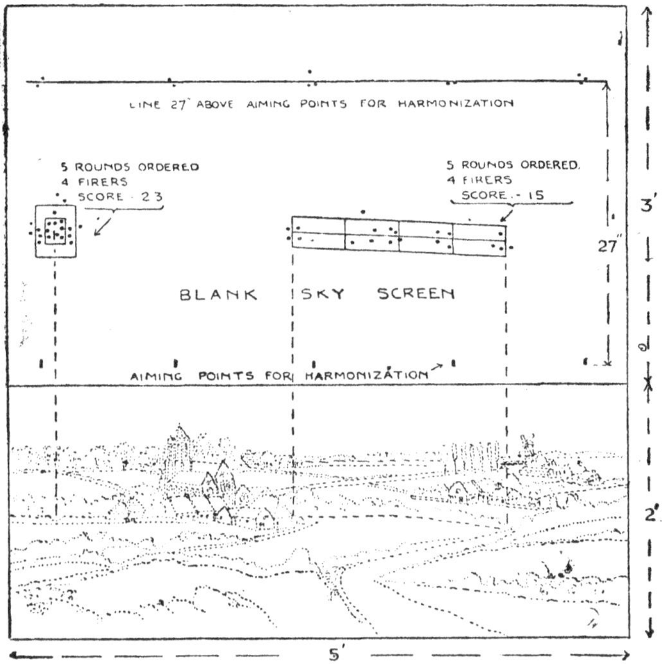

LINE 27' ABOVE AIMING POINTS FOR HARMONIZATION

5 ROUNDS ORDERED
4 FIRERS
SCORE · 23

5 ROUNDS ORDERED.
4 FIRERS
SCORE · 15

3'

27"

BLANK ISKY SCREEN

AIMING POINTS FOR HARMONIZATION

2'

5'

LANDSCAPE TARGET COMPETITION.

The distance 27 in. has been chosen because the landscape is 24 in. high, and the extra 3 inches allows a margin for low shots.

3. A measuring rod 27 in. long is also required. When collective fire has been concentrated on any point on the landscape target, the rod is held vertically, the bottom of it on the point of aim. A mark is then made on the blank sky-screen at the top of the rod ; this mark shows where the centre of the group of shot holes should be.

4. For competitions, two concentric wire rectangles, 5 in. by 4 in. and $2\frac{1}{2}$ in. by 2 in., may be used to determine the score. The centre of the rectangle is placed on the mark with the longest sides of the rectangle vertical ; every shot in the inner rectangle counts two points ; every shot in the remainder of the larger rectangle counts one point.

5. When fire has been distributed between two points on the landscape a mark is made 27 inches vertically above each, as already described ; these two marks are joined by a line parallel to that along which fire has been distributed.

A line $1\frac{1}{2}$ inches above, and another $1\frac{1}{2}$ inches below, are drawn parallel to the first line. The ends of these are joined by vertical lines passing through the two marks, and the large rectangle thus made is again subdivided into equal spaces, one per firer. (*See* Plate 40.)

6. All shots in the rectangle opposite the particular firer (up to the number of rounds given in the fire-order) count 1 point each to the total score of the section which is firing ; any shots in any rectangle over and above the number ordered will not count.

Time limits should be imposed in these competitions.

7. A board should be hung in every miniature range showing the elevation required for each rifle as follows :—

25 Yards Miniature Range.

No. of Rifle.	Elevation for Direct Hits.	Deflection.	Elevation for Paper landscape Targets.
1	300	Central	1,450
2	300	½ division right ...	1,400
3	350	1 ,, left ...	1,500
4	250	Central	1,250

77. *30 yards ranges.*

1. 30 yards ranges have the following advantages over miniature ranges :—

    i. The man uses his own service rifle.

    ii. He learns to shoot with it under easy conditions.

    iii. He becomes accustomed to the shock of discharge. and any tendency to flinch should be eliminated.

    iv. He becomes accustomed to the noise of firing.

    v. Rapid fire with service cartridges can be used.

2. These ranges are very useful at all times, especially when classification ranges are distant, and for training recruits and indifferent shots throughout the year.

3. *Special safety precautions.*—The following special safety precautions will be observed in addition to those referred to in Vol. II, Sec. **11**, 3, 4 and 6 of this manual.

    i. No practice will take place unless an officer or experienced serjeant is present.

    ii. Not more than six rifles or two light automatics are to be fired at the same time on the standard open 30 yards range.

iii. Loading will be carried out with the muzzle of the weapon directed towards the target.

iv. Light automatics will not be cleared by firing the last round. It must be unloaded without firing.

v. Targets must be correctly placed as follows :—

(a) Those representing classification targets in the middle of the sand bullet-catcher and kept 4 feet clear of the sides.

(b) Snapshooting or moving targets in the trench at the bottom of the sand bullet-catcher provided for this purpose.

(c) Approved revolver targets at the bottom of the sand bullet-catcher.

(d) Landscape targets or L.A. instructional targets will be placed on the steps at the end of the ricochet pit so that the sky-screen comes opposite the sand bullet-catcher and the picture directly *below* the bullet-catcher.

vi. **The following types of target are not allowed on the 30 yards range** :—

(a) Steel plates.

(b) Any moving target other than in the trench provided for this purpose.

(c) A.A. targets.

4. Firing revolver.—Practices involving the advance of either the firer or of the target will not be carried out on a 30 yards range.

These practices must be carried out on a classification range or on a specially constructed revolver range.

5. In conjunction with Bayonet Assault Course.— Bayonet assault courses should be built, where possible.

behind the firing point of 30 yards ranges, extending from 80 to 100 yards in depth.

6. **Construction and scale of apparatus.**—Details of construction, target apparatus and list of targets to be maintained for both miniature and 30 yards ranges are given in Small Arms Training, Vol. III.

THE SNIPER RIFLE.

(Pattern 1914, ·303-inch magazine rifle. fitted with 1918 model telescopic sight.)

---

78. *Description.*

1. The rifle is constructed on the *bolt* system, the **breech** being closed by a *bolt* worked by a *lever* on the right side.

2. The *body* is screwed on to the *barrel*. At its front end it forms a *hood* (27), in which are the *recesses* in which the *locking lugs* lie when the *breech* is closed. A *gas escape hole* is provided on the right.

3. The head of the *trigger* is so shaped as to form two *points* (42, 43), which, as the *trigger* is pressed back, bear in turn against the under surface of the *body*, thus giving the double pressure.

4. The *bolt stop* has at its front end a *thumb-piece* (49), and on its inner side a *block* (50), which projects into the *body* and against which the rear face of the *split lug* comes when the *bolt* is drawn back. It is pivoted in the *bracket* on the left of the *body*, and on its outer side is a flat *spring* which keeps the *block* forced inwards.

5. The *bolt stop* contains the *ejector*, which is flat, with a *projection* (51) which enters the body through the *long slit*. When the *bolt* is drawn back this *projection* passes through

the *slot* in the *split lug,* so that the base of the cartridge is
drawn against it. with the result that the case is thrown
out to the right.   The *ejector* is pivoted on the same screw
as the *bolt stop.*

6. The *magazine* holds five cartridges.

7. On the upper surface of the *magazine platform* is a *rib*
which ensures that the cartridges arrange themselves properly
on being forced into the *magazine.*   Moreover, when the

————

PLATE

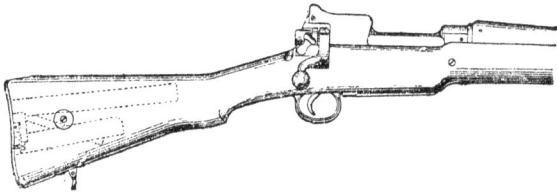

RIFLE, MAGAZINE, ·303·

magazine is empty, the rear end of the *rib* prevents the *bolt*
being closed, thus indicating that it is necessary to recharge
the *magazine.*

N.B.—For drill purposes, to allow manipulation of the bolt
to be practised without dummy cartridges, a *platform depressor*
is provided.   To insert this, place it edgeways right side
down on the *magazine platform,* press down and allow it to
turn over so as to engage under the *body,* thus keeping the
magazine platform depressed and allowing the bolt to pass

freely over it. To remove the *depressor* from the *magazine*,
press it downwards and, the thumb nail being inserted in the
slot, pull the left side upwards until the *depressor* turns on
its edge and can be removed.

79. *Action of the mechanism.*

1. Suppose that a cartridge had just been fired. On raising
the *bolt lever*, the *bolt* is rotated to the left. The *cocking-*

41.

INCH, ENFIELD PATTERN 1914.

piece, being held by the *slot* in the lower part of the *boltway*
in the *body*, cannot rotate with the *bolt*. The *tooth* (19) on
its front end is thus forced by the action of the *sloping surfaces*
to leave the *long groove* (9) in the end of the *bolt* and enter the
short groove (10), thus partially compressing the *mainspring*
and slightly withdrawing the *striker*. As soon as the *locking
lugs* (3, 4) are clear of their *recesses* and the *bolt lever* has left
the recess on the right of the *body*, the *sloping surface* (11)
on the *bolt lever* meets the *sloping shoulder* (35) under the

PLATE 42.

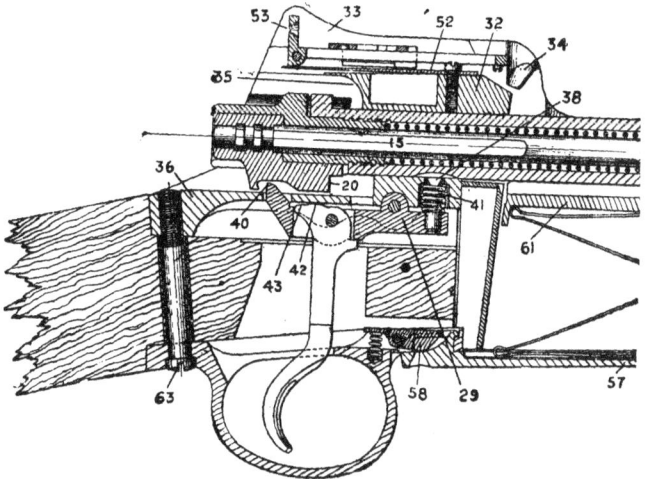

RIFLE, MAGAZINE, ·303-INCH, PATTERN 1914.

Plate 42.

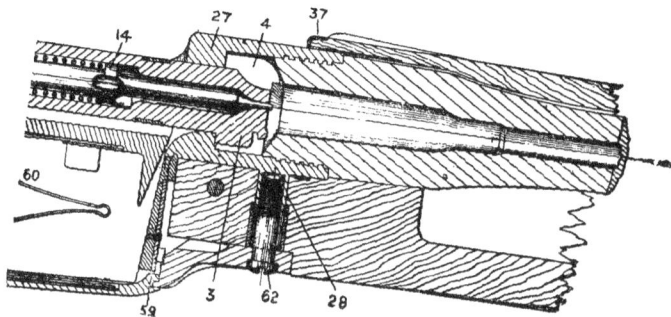

Rifle, Magazine, ·303-inch, Pattern 1914.

Plate 43.

SAFETY CATCH.   LOCKING
                     BOLT.

46   44

B O L

48   47   45

2   6

12

9

4
   5   7   11   10

COCKING-PIECE.   BOLT PLUG.

18   19   17

22   21   20

16   15   STRIKER.   14

43   41
40 SEAR 39
     42   38   54

                                        56
TRIGGER   SIGHT   SLIDE

                                   55

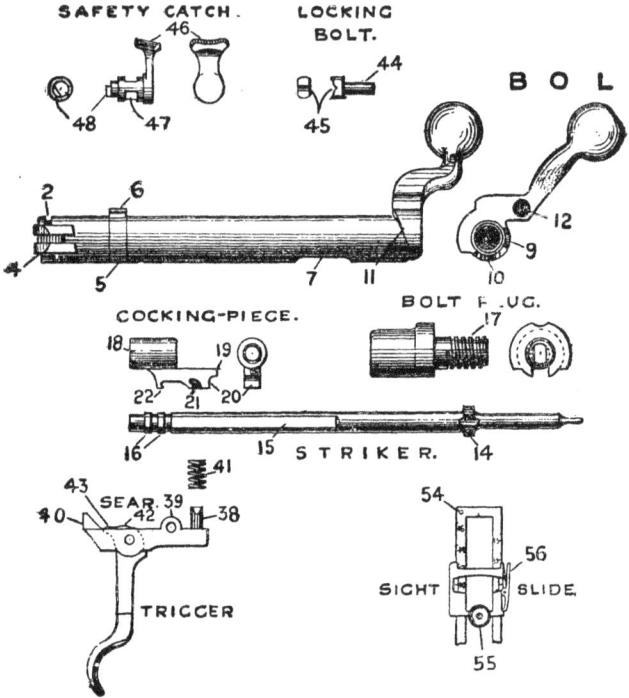

Rifle, Magazine, ·303-inch,

PLATE 43.

EXTRACTOR.

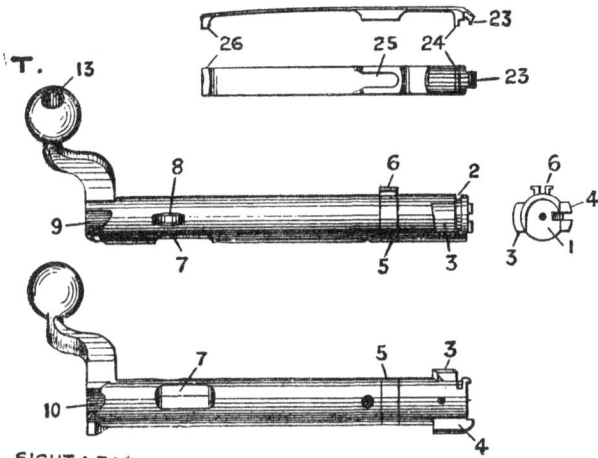

SIGHT LEAF.

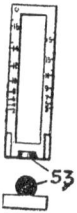

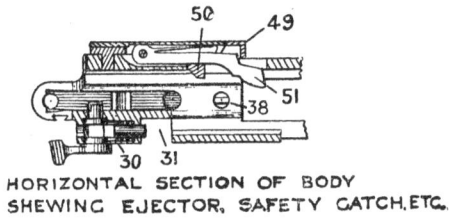

HORIZONTAL SECTION OF BODY
SHEWING EJECTOR, SAFETY CATCH. ETC.

PATTERN 1914.

PLATE 44.

NAMES OF PARTS OF THE PATTERN 1914 ·303-INCH
MAGAZINE RIFLE.

1. Bolt, front face.
2. ,, cannelure.
3. ,, solid lug.
4. ,, split lug.
5. ,, recess for ring.
6. ,, lugs on ring.
7. ,, depression for safety stud.
8. ,, small depression for safety stud.
9. ,, long groove in rear end.
10. ,, short ,, ,, ,,
11. ,, extraction cam on lever.
12. ,, recess in lever for locking bolt.
13. ,, lightening hole in knob of lever.
14. Striker, front collar.
15. ,, flats.
16. ,, collars for cocking-piece.
17. Bolt plug, screw thread.
18. Cocking-piece, cylindrical portion.
19. ,, tooth.
20. ,, bent.
21. ,, recess for safety catch.
22. ,, stripping nib.
23. Extractor, claw.
24. ,, nib.
25. ,, recess for lugs of ring.
26. ,, tail.
27. Body, hood.
28. ,, rib.
29. ,, lugs for sear.

30. Body, housing for locking bolt.
31. ,, recess for bolt lever.
32. ,, backsight bed.
33. ,, wings for protecting backsight.
34. ,, charger guides.
35. ,, extraction cam.
36. ,, tang.
37. Ring, retaining handguard.
38. Sear, safety stud.
39. ,, lugs.
40. ,, nose.
41. ,, spring.
42. Trigger, first point on head.
43. ,, second ,,
44. Locking bolt, plunger.
45. ,, ,, groove.
46. Safety catch, thumb-piece.
47. ,, ,, eccentric stem.
48. ,, ,, half moon.
49. Bolt stop, thumb-piece.
50. ,, ,, stop block.
51. Ejector.
52. Backsight, spring.
53. ,, fixed sight aperture.
54. ,, stop screw.
55. ,, aperture.
56. ,, slide catch.
57. Magazine, bottom plate.
58. ,, catch.
59. ,, undercut rib of bottom plate.
60. ,, spring.
61. ,, platform.
62. Trigger guard, front screw.
63. ,, ,, back screw.

sight bed. This results in the slight withdrawal of the *bolt*
and consequently begins to withdraw the case from the
chamber, effecting primary extraction. During the rotation
of the *bolt* the *extractor* has been prevented by the *groove*
in the front end of the *body* from turning, while the *shoulders*
of the *bolt plug*, resting on the body, have similarly prevented it from rotating.

The *lugs* on the front end of the *bolt* now lie horizontally
and the *bolt* can be withdrawn, the case being withdrawn
by the *extractor.*

2. As the *bolt* begins to travel backwards the *cocking-piece*
rides over the *nose* (40) of the *sear* and depresses it, the *safety
stud* (38) being allowed to rise into the large flat *depression* (7)
on the surface of the *bolt.* When the *cocking-piece* has passed
the *nose* of the *sear* the latter rises under the influence of the
spiral sear spring (41).

3. When the rear face of the *left locking lug* reaches the
ejector (51), the latter is forced inwards into the slot in the
lug (4), and eventually meets the base of the cartridge case,
which is drawn back on to it, and thus thrown out to the
right. Shortly before this occurs, the front end of the *bolt*
passes clear of the rear end of the *magazine*, and the *magazine
spring* is allowed to force another cartridge up so that the
upper part of its base will be caught by the lower part of the
front end of the *bolt* when the latter is again pushed forward.
If there is no cartridge remaining in the *magazine*, the *platform*
itself rises and places the rear end of the *rib* in position to
prevent the *bolt* being closed.

After a short further backward movement of the bolt the
rear face of the *left lug* (4) comes against the *bolt stop* (50), and
the travel of the *bolt* is checked.

4. On pushing the *bolt* forward, if the magazine is empty it is stopped by the rear end of the *rib* on the *magazine platform*. If there is a cartridge in the *magazine* it is pushed forward in front of the *bolt*. As it moves forward the cartridge springs up and its rim places itself under the *claw* (23) of the extractor. It is thus pushed forward into the *chamber*.

5. During the early part of the forward travel of the *bolt* the *ejector* is pushed outwards by the side of the *bolt*. Eventually the *bent* (20) of the *cocking-piece* meets the *nose* (40) of the *sear*. The *striker*, which is attached to the *cocking-piece*. is thus held stationary, while the *bolt* moves on over it. This forward movement compresses the *mainspring*.

6. When the rotation of the *bolt* by means of the *lever* begins, the *locking lugs* work on the *sloping surfaces* leading into their *recesses*, and carry the *bolt* still further forward, completing the compression of the *mainspring*. During the rotation, the *cocking-piece* is prevented by the *slot* in the bottom of the *body* from turning, so that the *long groove* (9) in the bolt is brought opposite to it by the rotation of the *bolt*.

The *bolt* is now securely locked by the two *lugs* having entered their *recesses*, and the *bolt lever* having entered its *recess* (31), the *mainspring* is fully compressed, and the *cocking piece* and *striker* are held back by the *sear*.

7. On pressing the *trigger* the *rounded portion* (42) of its head bears against the bottom of the *body* and slightly depresses the *nose* of the *sear*. The *rear point* (43) of the head of the *trigger* then bears in its turn against the bottom of the *body*, and the *sear nose* is thereby depressed until it frees the *cocking-piece*. The *striker* then flies forward under the influence of the *mainspring*, and, as the *long groove* in the *bolt* is opposite the *cocking-piece*, it is able to go forward sufficiently far for its point to pass through the face of the *bolt*, and strike the cap.

During the depression of the *sear nose* the *safety stud* (38) rises through its hole in the *body* and enters the smaller *depression* (8) in the surface of the *bolt*, and the *spiral spring* (41) which surrounds it is compressed between the *sear* and the top of the *spring seating* in the *body*. If the *bolt* is not fully closed, the small *depression* will not lie immediately over the *safety stud*. Consequently, if an attempt is made to press the *trigger* the *safety stud* will meet the cylindrical part of the *bolt*, and will not be able to rise far enough to allow the *nose* of the *sear* to be depressed sufficiently to free the *cocking-piece*. The *trigger* will thus be inoperative, and the firing of the rifle until the *bolt* is securely closed is made impossible by the action of the *safety stud*.

8. When pressure on the *trigger* is relaxed the *sear spring* forces the front end of the *sear* down, causing the *sear nose* to rise into the *slot* of the *body*.

9. To remove the *bolt* from the rifle, withdraw it to its full extent, pulling outwards the *thumb-piece* (49) of the *bolt stop*, and drawing the *bolt* out of the *body*. To replace the *bolt* in the rifle, press the *magazine platform* down to allow it to pass.

10. *To remove the magazine bottom plate, spring and platform.*—With the point of a bullet press the *magazine catch* (58) inwards, and slide backwards the *magazine bottom plate* (57), when the three parts will come out together. Slide the ends of the *spring* (60) out of the *recesses* in the *bottom plate* and *platform*, raising the bent ends to allow the *spring* to move backwards.

11. *To assemble the magazine bottom plate, spring and platform.*—Replace the ends of the *spring* in the *recesses* in the *bottom plate* and *platform*. That end of the *spring* which engages with the *platform* is slightly narrower than the other,

consequently the *spring* cannot be wrongly assembled. Insert the *platform* and *spring* into the *magazine*, press the *bottom plate* fully home, and slide it forward until the *catch* engages.

80. *Instructions for cleaning.*

1. The instructions in Chapter V will be followed, but paragraphs will be modified as follows to make them applicable to the Pattern 1914 rifle.

2. **The action and outside.**—Thoroughly clean the *bolt*, paying particular attention to the face of the *bolt*, the *striker point*, the *cannelure*, the *claw* of the *extractor*, and the *slot* in the *split lug*. See that there is no dirt in the *grooves* in the rear end of the *bolt*, in the *slot* in the *bolt plug*, or in the *locking bolt hole* in the *lever*, and that the *gas escape holes* are clear. Clean the *safety catch recess* in the *cocking-piece*. The *bolt* should be rubbed over with a piece of oily flannelette before being replaced in the rifle.

3. Wipe the inside of the *body* and the entrance to the *chamber* with a piece of oily flannelette, removing all dirt from the *guide grooves* and from the *lug recesses* in the front of the *body*, and see that the *gas escape hole* is clear. See that there is no dirt in the *recess* for the *bolt lever*. Particular care should be taken that the free play of the fore-end of the *barrel* running through the *nose cap* is not checked by the presence of dirt or grit, as this will affect the accuracy of the rifle, and is likely to cause the sniper to suspect the telescope, when the trouble is only a matter of the care and cleaning of the rifle.

4. Wipe the exterior of the rifle with a piece of oily flannelette, removing all dirt from the *aperture* on the *back-sight*, and from the *notches* for the *spring catch*, and from the *charger guides*.

5. Draw out the *bolt stop* by means of the *thumb-piece*, lightly oil it and the *ejector*; also the *plunger* of the *locking bolt*.

6. Take out the *magazine bottom plate*, and wipe the interior of the *magazine*, the *spring*, *platform*, and *bottom plate* with a dry piece of flannelette.

81. *Telescope.*

1. The mechanism of the telescopic sight is delicate, and the only adjustment which may be made by the user is that for raising or lowering the sighting elevation.

2. The personnel earmarked for training in the sniper rifle should be individually detailed to one particular rifle. Any adjustments necessary to suit their individual requirements, for lateral deflection, must be carried out only by the qualified armourer attached to the unit.

3. The interior or other parts of the instrument must not be touched.

4. The telescope consists of a steel body containing a combination of lenses, with two fittings for attachment to the rifle.

5. When not in use, the telescope should be carried in the waterproofed, canvas-covered case that is provided.

6. Two leather caps, connected by a strap, are provided for protecting the lenses.

7. A small wire brush, for cleaning the fittings of dust, and a cleaning cloth for the lenses, are supplied, and are carried under the flap fitted inside the cap of the case.

8. A telescopic sight eye-piece, consisting of a conical rubber tube, $3\frac{1}{2}$ inches long, beaded at one end, and bevelled

at the other, is supplied with each telescopic sight. The beaded end should be fitted over the eye-piece body of the telescope.

PLATE 45.

FIG. A.

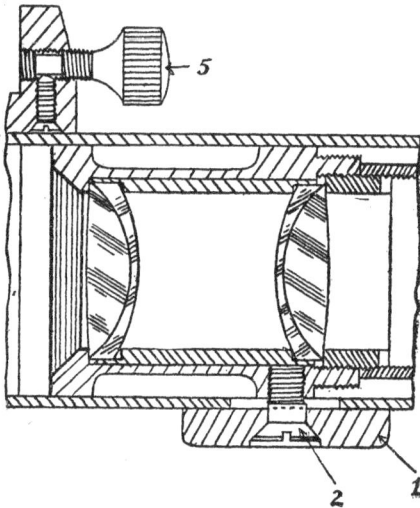

PLATE 45.

FIG. B.

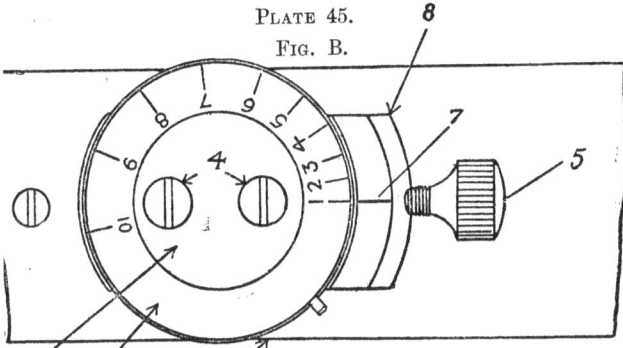

THE SERIAL Nº OF RIFLE IS ENGRAVED HERE
ON SIDE OF TELESCOPE DIRECTLY BELOW THE SADDLE.

FIG. C.

ASSEMBLED VIEW OF TELESCOPE ON RIFLE

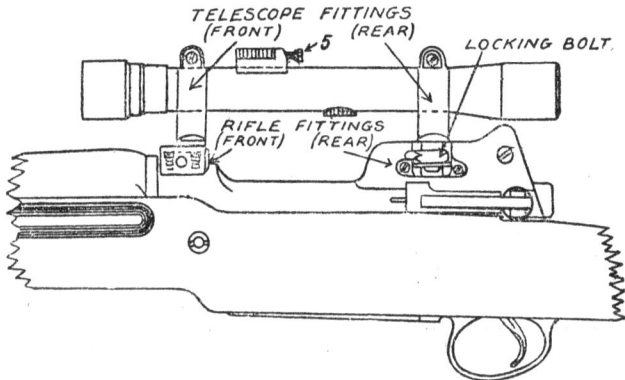

TELESCOPE FITTINGS (FRONT) (REAR)
LOCKING BOLT
RIFLE FITTINGS (FRONT) (REAR)

82. *Detail and sequence of instruction.*

1. Method of attaching the telescope to the rifle.—The *front fitting* of the telescope has two *legs,* which hook into the *front fitting* on the *body* of the rifle. The *rear fitting* on the telescope has a single *leg,* the squared end of which drops into the *rear fitting* on the left side of the *rifle body,* and is secured by a *thumb locking bolt.*

Note.—The number on the telescope must agree with the barrel number of the rifle.

2. Method of focussing—

    i. Remove the telescope from the rifle, and release the screw which clamps the *focussing slide* (2). Holding the telescope steady, look through it as if using an ordinary telescope, with the eye about 4 inches away, and obtain a full field of view.

    ii. Adjust the focus by moving the *slide* (1) backwards or forwards to suit the eye, and tighten up the *clamp screw,* taking care not to disturb the corrected position of the *slide.*

    iii. Replace the telescope on the rifle.

3. Method of loading with the telescope attached.—*Chargers* cannot be used unless the telescope is removed. When the telescope is attached, charge the *magazine* with five rounds singly.

4. Adjustment of the sight.—The telescope is fitted with an adjustable *range scale* mounted on a *drum-head,* and clamped by a *milled-head screw* (5).

This *scale* is marked off in lines numbered from 1 to 10 which figures represent hundreds of yards.

To adjust the *sight*, release the *milled-head screw*, and turn the *scale* with the thumb and forefinger until the line representing the required range corresponds with the zero line (7) on the *saddle* (8). Then tighten the *clamping screw*.

5. **Method of aiming.**—The eye should be about 4 inches from the end of the telescope, close to the rubber eye-piece, which should be adjusted for this allowance.

Aim is taken by obtaining a full field of view through the telescope, so that the *hair-line* across the *pointer* appears horizontal, and the tip of the *pointer* touches the centre of the lowest visible part of the mark, and is in the centre of the field of view (*see* diagram). By looking straight through the telescope this centreing becomes automatic.

Fig. 8.—Correct Aim.

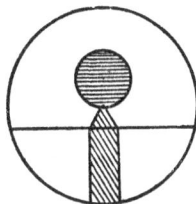

Note.—A floating vision indicates that the eye is either too near or too far from the telescope.

6. **Method for the adjustment of elevation.**—The *drum-head* of the *elevating screw* is fitted with a movable *range scale ring* (3), upon which the *range scale* is engraved. This *ring is*

normally secured by a *washer* (6) and two *fixing screws* (4) to the *drum-head* of the *elevating screw*. If, therefore, at any time it is found that the elevation indicated by the *scale* is wrong for any given range, it can be put right by unclamping the *range scale ring*, adjusting the *pointer* by shooting at a known range, and then turning the *range scale ring* to indicate this range before clamping it once more to the *drum-head* of the *elevating screw*.

THE BAYONET.

83. *General instructions.*

1. Training in the use of the bayonet is an integral part of rifle training.

2. The soldier will be taught and exercised in the use of the rifle and bayonet by one and the same man, *i.e.,* his rifle instructor.

3. *Essential points in bayonet fighting.*—To attack with the bayonet effectively requires *good direction, strength, quickness and endurance* during a probable state of excitement and physical exhaustion. The limit of the range of a bayonet is about 5 feet (between opponents), but more often the combat is at closer quarters, at a range of 2 feet or less, when troops are struggling close together in trenches, darkness or smoke.

4. *An offensive weapon.*—The bayonet is essentially an offensive weapon—go straight at an opponent with the point threatening his throat and deliver the point wherever an opening presents itself. If no opening is obvious, one must be created by beating off the opponent's weapon.

5. *Hand-to-hand fighting.*—Hand-to-hand fighting with the bayonet is individual, which means that a man must think and act for himself and rely on his own resource and skill; but, as in games, he must play for his side and not only for himself. He must be accustomed to place himself under the control and leadership of his section commander and work in his team, because control and a degree of cohesion are essential to the success of the close combat. In an assault all ranks go forward to kill, and only those who have developed skill and strength by constant and continuous training will be able to kill.

6. *The spirit of the bayonet.*—The spirit of the bayonet must be inculcated into all ranks so that in the attack they will go forward with that aggressive determination and confidence which ensures the success of an assault; and which despite danger and exhaustion will hearten the soldier to seek close combat with his opponent.

7. *Continuity of training.*—The essence of bayonet training is continuity of practice.

8. *Recruit's course.*—The recruit's course is divided for convenience into seven lessons.

9. *Trained soldier's course and daily practice.*—Half-an-hour a day, as often as possible, should be devoted by trained soldiers to practice in bayonet training. By this daily practice, accuracy of direction, quickness, strength and endurance are developed, and a soldier is accustomed to use the bayonet under conditions which approximate to actual fighting. Correct action with the bayonet will thus become automatic. This half-hour should be apportioned to (i) pointing at training sticks at varying distances and directions; (ii) parrying training sticks; (iii) dummy work; (iv) counter charges; and (v) the assault practice.

84. *Method of carrying out bayonet training and hints to instructors.*

1. *Development of the individual.*—An important point to be kept in mind in bayonet training is the development of the individual by teaching him to think and act for himself. The simplest means of attaining this end is to make men use their brains and eyes to the fullest extent by carrying out the practices, as far as possible, without words of command, *i.e.*, to point at a shifting target as soon as it is stationary, to parry sticks, &c. The section will, whenever possible, work in pairs and act on the principle of " Master and Pupil." This procedure, in itself, develops individuality, confidence, and leadership. Sharp, jerky words of command which tend to make men act mechanically, will be avoided. Rapidity of movement and alertness are fostered by quickening movements and the introduction of the competitive spirit into the training.

2. *Style.*—To demand from all men of different shapes and sizes exact similarity of poise, balance and style is neither necessary nor desirable—men should rather be encouraged as in boxing to develop the style best suited to their physique and peculiarity of build.

3. *Duration of lessons and practices.*—The technical points of bayonet fighting are simple. Long explanation is unnecessary and makes the work monotonous.

Instruction will be carried out by brief explanation and demonstration on the part of the instructor, followed by practice on the part of the man. It is essential that the men are made to observe each movement of the instructor, so that from the very commencement of bayonet instruction a man is taught to use his eyes and brain.

Words of command should be reduced to a minimum.
Men cannot be " drilled " into becoming good bayonet fighters
any more than they can be " drilled " into becoming good
boxers.

A lesson or daily practice will not last more than half-
an-hour.

Monotony kills interest.

4. The sequence of progress in bayonet training will be to
obtain, first, good direction, and then quickness.

5. *Dress when training.*—Bayonet training should be carried
out chiefly in a " free and easy " kit, but men should be
accustomed to use their bayonets when wearing belt and
pouches ; fighting order may be worn when an efficiency
test is in progress.

6. *Vulnerable parts of the body.*—If possible, the point of
the bayonet should be directed against an opponent's throat,
as the point will enter easily and make a fatal wound on
penetrating a few inches, and, being near the eyes, makes an
opponent flinch.   Other vulnerable and usually exposed parts
are the face, chest, lower abdomen and thighs, and the region
of the kidneys when the back is turned.   Four to six inches
penetration is sufficient to incapacitate and allow for a quick
withdrawal, whereas if a bayonet is driven home too far it is
often impossible to withdraw it.   In such cases a round
should be fired to break up the obstruction.

85. *Upkeep and care of appliances, &c.*

1. The upkeep and repair of bayonet training material
will be in the hands of formations.   The duties of upkeep
and repair will be included in the syllabus for the training of
the instructor.

In the case of assault courses on rifle ranges, the range warden will be responsible for upkeep and repairs.

2. *Sacks.*—Sacks for dummies will be filled with straw in such a way as to afford the greatest resistance without injury to the bayonet.

Dummy sacks should be hung from gallows by a double suspension from the cross-bar to the top corners of the sack and will be weighted or tethered to the ground from the bottom corners.

3. *Aiming marks.*—For practising direction an aiming mark must always be painted on both sides of the dummy. By constantly changing the position of the mark the " life " of the dummies will be prolonged.

4. For the pointing and parrying practices a light stick, 5 feet to 5 feet 9 inches long and $2\frac{1}{2}$ inches to 4 inches in circumference, with ring for thrusting and pad, will be provided for every two men. (*See* Fig. 9.)

5. *Care of weapons.*—*The greatest care should be taken that the object representing the opponent and its support should be incapable of injuring the bayonet or butt. Only light sticks are to be used for parrying practice. Bayonets will be kept sharpened.*

The chief causes of injury to the bayonet are insufficient instruction in the bayonet training lessons, failure to withdraw the bayonet clear of the dummy before advancing, placing the dummies on hard, unprepared ground, and using unsharpened bayonets.

6. *Bayonet fencing with spring bayonets.*—Individual fighting with the spring bayonet is a valuable auxiliary to train men in skill at arms. Weapons for this purpose form part of the

equipment of regimental gymnasia. These will be available for the purpose of bayonet competitions and voluntary instruction.

7. *Standardization.*—The following apparatus for bayonet training is approved and standardized :—

(1) The training stick, 5 feet to 5 feet 9 inches long.
(2) Sack dummies for pointing practice and assault courses.
(3) The " mad minute " course.
(4) The tin ring course.
(5) The assault course.

FIG. 9.—THE TRAINING STICK.

.d made of piece of nvas, stuffed with redded   sacking .d   wired   into roove cut in stick.

A wire ring 3 in. in diameter   covered with string or thin rope.

Nos. 3, 4 and 5 will be made available in the neighbourhood of all barracks at which infantry are quartered.

8. Plates 59, 61 and 63 illustrate the *normal* courses, but these will be modified to suit local conditions.

86. *Bayonet training.*

Lesson 1.

1. *Class arrangements.*—Sections will fall in at " the order " in single rank. The bayonet will be fixed with scabbard on, and the *trigger* action will be " cocked " with *safety catch* applied.

2. On the command " For Bayonet Training—Move," the odd numbers will double forward eight paces, turn about, and cover the even numbers.

3. In uneven sections, the odd man will invariably be given an " opponent " in the opposite rank, *i.e.*, two men point at one man.

4. To guard against accidents during instruction, the men will be at least 5 feet apart laterally.

5. " *On-Guard.*"—Point of the bayonet directed at the base of the opponent's throat, the rifle held firmly and naturally with both hands, *barrel* upright, the right hand over the navel, grasping the small of the *butt*, the left hand holding the rifle at the most convenient position in front of the *back-sight*, so that the left arm is only slightly bent. The legs well separated in a natural position, such as a man walking might adopt on meeting with resistance, *i.e.*, left knee slightly bent, right foot inclined to the right front.

The position should not be constrained in any way but be one of aggression, alertness, and readiness to go forward for immediate attack (*see* Plate 46).

The " On-Guard " position will also be taught with the right foot in front (*see* Plate 47.)

6. " *Rest.*"—Place the *butt* on the ground without moving the feet.

PLATE 46.—" ON-GUARD " (LEFT FOOT FORWARD).

PLATE 47.—" ON-GUARD " (RIGHT FOOT FORWARD).

PLATE 48.—"THE HIGH PORT."

7. " *High port.*"—Bring the rifle to a diagonal position across the body (*see* Plate 48).

This position is suitable for a close formation, minimizes the risk of accidents when surmounting obstacles, and can be maintained with the left hand alone, allowing free use of the right when necessary.

8. When the men have had sufficient practice in the " on guard " and " high port " stationary, they will be practised on the move : first in quick time and then in the form of short controlled charges.

Lesson 2.

9. " *Long point.*"—Grasping the rifle firmly, vigorously deliver the point from the " on guard " position to the full extent of the left arm, *butt* running alongside and kept close to the right forearm. Body inclined forward ; left knee well bent ; right leg braced, and the weight of the body pressed well forward with the fore part of the right foot, heel raised (*see* Plate 49.)

The " long point " is made against an opponent at a range of about 4 to 5 feet from the attacker's eye. In fighting, it is of vital importance to judge this distance accurately.

The power of a " point " is derived from the right arm and rear leg, with the weight of the body behind it, the left arm being used to direct the point of the bayonet. The eyes must be fixed on the object at which the point is directed. In making " points " other than straight to the front, the rear foot should be advanced in the direction in which the " point " is made.

During the later stages of this lesson the men should always be practised in stepping forward with the rear foot when delivering the " point."

PLATE 49.—" LONG POINT."

10. "*The withdrawal.*"—To withdraw the bayonet after a "long point" has been delivered, draw the rifle straight back until the bayonet is clear, and immediately resume the "on guard" position. If the leverage or proximity to the object transfixed renders it necessary, the left hand must first be slipped up close to the *piling-swivel*. When a pupil reaches the stage of delivering a "point" while advancing on a dummy, he will adopt this method (*see* Plate 50).

In the case of a an opponent lying on the ground, the foot will be placed on the body close to the bayonet before withdrawal (*see* Plate 51).

Progression.

11. *Pointing at parts of the body.*—Men should always be made to point *at a target, e.g.*, at a named part of the body of the opposite man : " At the throat " (long pause to commence with), " point " (a pause), " withdraw."

12. As progress is made, the pause between the " point " and the " withdrawal " should be shortened until the men reach a stage when they " withdraw " and come " on guard " directly after making a " point." They should be taught to point at two or more parts of the body, *e.g.*, " First at the throat, then at the right thigh—point." For the purpose of direction, the right or left will be considered to be the right or left of the man " pointing."

13. *Pointing at changing targets.*—The section, working in pairs, with the instructor supervising, should be practised in pointing in various directions at training sticks. The scabbards will be on the bayonets.

This practice should be done without words of command so that **the eye and brain may be trained**.

PLATE 50.—"THE WITHDRAWAL."

14. *Pointing at marks on dummies.*—The men will be taught to bayonet a mark painted on a dummy, first stationary, and then advancing. The advance must be made in a practical and natural way, and should be practised with either foot to the front when the " point " is delivered.

15. The rifle will never be drawn back to make a " long point " in a forward movement. The impetus of the body and the forward punch of the arms supply the necessary force to penetrate.

16. The bayonet will be withdrawn immediately after the " point " has been delivered, and the forward threatening attitude be assumed on the left side of the dummy in anticipation of meeting another enemy.

17. Unless the rifle is firmly gripped it is liable to injure the hand.

18. The principles of this practice will be observed when pointing at dummies in trenches, standing upright on the ground, or suspended from gallows and should be applied at first slowly and deliberately. *No attempt must be made to carry out the assault practice before the men have been carefully instructed in, and have thoroughly mastered, the preliminary lessons.*

Lesson 3.—The right and left parry (scabbards on).

19. Men should be taught to regard the parry as part of an offensive movement, namely, of the " point " or butt stroke which would immediately follow it in actual combat. For this reason parrying must always be accompanied with a slight forward movement of the body.

20. " *Right parry.*"—From the position of " on-guard," vigorously straighten the left arm without bending the wrist,

PLATE 51.—" THE WITHDRAWAL " (USING FOOT).

or twisting the rifle in the hand, and " punch " the rifle forward far enough to the right to beat off the adversary's weapon and, in the same forward movement, deliver a point at any exposed vulnerable part—followed by the " withdraw,". and return " on guard."

21. " *Left parry.*"—From the position of " on-guard " punch the rifle forward to the left to beat off the adversary's point, and step in with the rear foot, swinging the butt horizontally to the jaw. Having knocked the adversary to the ground, deliver the point at any exposed vulnerable part, withdraw immediately and return " on-guard," and continue the former threatening attitude. (*See* para. 35.)

22. To develop the forward " punch " of the rifle, parries will be taught in the following stages :—

    (*a*) Parry and stop (pause). Return " on-guard."

    (*b*) Parry and immediately return " on-guard."

    (*c*) Parry and " kill."

23. The eyes must be kept on the weapon which is being parried.

24. Parries will be practised with the right as well as with the left foot forward.

25. *Parrying with training sticks.*---After the instructor has demonstrated the complete parry, the section will work in pairs, with scabbards on bayonets, one man pointing with the stick and the other parrying. At first this practice will be slow and deliberate without being allowed to become mechani- :ai, and will be progressively increased in rapidity and vigour.

26. After the men have been thoroughly exercised in the above parries, practice should be given them in fending off

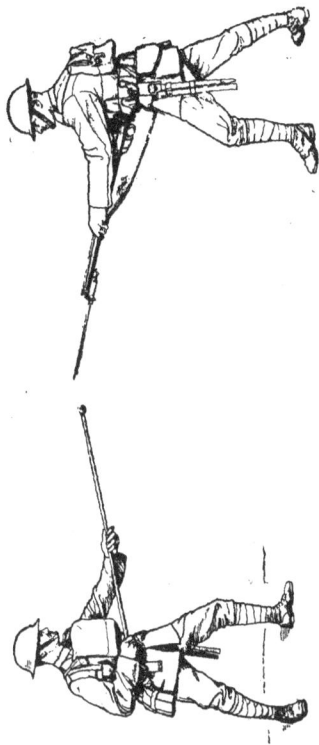

PLATE 52.—" PARRYING " (USING TRAINING STICK).

points directed at their legs. The adversary's weapon will be beaten off by a downward and outward hit either to the right or left; it will be followed immediately by a point, " withdraw " and return to the " on guard " position.

Lesson 4.—The short point.

27. " *Short point.*"—Shift the left hand quickly towards the *muzzle* and draw the rifle back as far as possible, the butt either upwards or downwards according as a low or a high " point " is to be made ; then deliver the " point " vigorously to the full extent of the left arm (*see* Plate 53).

N.B.—The " short point " is used at a range of about 3 feet, and in close fighting it is the natural " point " to make when the bayonet has just been withdrawn after a " long point." If a strong " withdrawal " is necessary the right hand should be slipped above the *backsight* after the " short point " has been made (*see* Plate 54).

28. The combination of a " long point " with a " short point " should be taught at two dummies (one on the ground and one suspended). First a " long point " is delivered, stepping in with the rear foot, the left hand is slipped up to withdraw and then the " short point " is delivered, stepping in with the rear foot.

N.B.—These points can be taught at a single dummy, two separate marks being given.

29. Parries will be practised from the position of the " short point." Unless a decided hit at the adversary's weapon is made from the short point position (either right or left), the parry will not be successful.

PLATE 53.—" THE SHORT POINT."

PLATE 54.—WITHDRAWAL (FROM SHORT POINT).

Lesson 5.—The jab, or upward point.

30. *The " jab," or " upward point."*—From the position of the " short point " shift the right hand up the rifle, and grasp it above or below the *backsight*, according to the range of the target, at the same time bringing the rifle to an almost vertical position close to the body, and, from this position, bend the knees and jab the point of the bayonet upwards into the throat or under the chin of the opponent. In jabbing, the point of the bayonet should be driven home, principally by an upward heave of the legs and body, with only a small movement of the hands and arms (*see* Plates 55 and 56).

31. From the " jab " position men will be practised in fending off an attack made on any part of them by an opponent. When fending off a point at the legs, the position of the right hand may have to be lowered on the rifle to prevent a sweeping movement.

32. When making a " jab " from the " on-guard " position, the right, being the thrusting hand, will be brought up first.

33. The jab can be employed successfully in close-quarter fighting in narrow trenches and when " embraced " by an opponent.

Lesson 6.—Methods of injuring an opponent.

34. It should be impressed upon the section that, although a man's " point " has missed or has been parried, or his bayonet has been broken, he can, as " attacker," still maintain his advantage by injuring his opponent in one of the ways described in the following paragraphs.

PLATE 55.—THE " JAB " POSITION.

PLATE 56.—THE " JAB " POSITION (USING RING.)

35. *Horizontal butt stroke.*—Step in and swing the *toe of the butt* to the opponent's jaw. (*See* Plate 57.)

36. *Forward butt stroke.*—If the opponent jumps back so that the first butt stroke misses, swing the *heel of the butt* back to the jaw.

37. *Slash stroke.*—If the opponent retires still further out of distance, the attacker again closes up and slashes his bayonet at his opponent's face or neck.

38. *Tripping.*—When a man is gripped by an opponent so that neither the point nor the butt can be used, the knee brought up sharply against the fork may make him release his hold, or the opponent can be tripped by forcing his weight on to one leg, and kicking that leg away from under him, or any other wrestler's trip—*e.g.* " back-heel "—may be used.

39. *Practice.*—When the men have been shown the methods of using the butt and the knee, they should be practised on the padded stick.

Lesson 7.—Unarmed defence against attack with rifle and bayonet.

Disarms.

40. *Disarm by gripping forward hand.*—As the opponent makes his " point," fend it off with the left hand (Plate 58, (*a*) and (*b*)), step forward and seize his left hand with both of yours, fingers upwards, and give a sharp twist outwards.

41. *Disarm from outside the guard.*—As the opponent makes his " point," fend it off outwards with the right hand, and, stepping in, seize the opponent's left hand and rifle firmly with your left, and do not relax the grip until he is thrown.

PLATE 57.—"THE BUTT STROKE."

PLATE 58 (a)—DISARM.

PLATE 58 (b).—DISARM

42. From this grip the opponent may be disarmed in three ways, viz. :—

    i. Seize the cloth of his sleeve about his left elbow with your right hand, and jerk his arm over his rifle.

        If this grip fails, your right hand may slip either under or over the opponent's arm.

    ii. If under, seize the rifle at about the point of balance with the right hand, knuckles uppermost, and give a sudden jerk against his elbow with your right arm.

    iii. If over, seize his rifle at about the point of balance with the right hand, knuckles underneath, and jerk it up towards you, so that the *butt* strikes his chin.

43. In each of the above cases the opponent's rifle will be used to kill him.

44. The secret of success in all disarms is " the unexpected."

87. *Recapitulation of progressive steps for the guidance of instructors.*

Lesson 1.

Class arrangements.

Explain hand-to-hand fighting briefly (to inculcate the spirit of the bayonet) and vulnerable parts of the body.

Teach " on-guard," " rest," left and right foot forward, " high port."

Teach how to advance when " on-guard " and at " high port " position.

Short controlled charges (first stage) to be taught and practised concurrently with other lessons.

Lesson 2.

First Practice.

Demonstrate " long point " at dummies.

Teach " long point " slowly in class formation, then quickly, followed by the " withdraw "—left and right foot leading alternately.

Teach " long point " stationary and advancing with either foot forward.

Second Practice. (Pointing at dummies).

Teach " long point " stationary and advancing at dummies.

Teach two " long points " at two dummies.

Practise pointing at dummies in practice trench.

Third Practice. (Section working by eye).

Pointing at ring (always advancing).

Lesson 3.

Demonstrate and explain value of the " parry."

Parry a stick pointed at the breast and stop.

Parry a stick pointed at the breast, and return " on guard."

Parry a stick and " kill."

Parry a stick pointed at the head, body or legs.

Parry a stick pointed in varying order at the head, body or legs.

Parry a point made by an advancing opponent.

Parry a point made by an advancing opponent, and " kill."

Common faults.

(1) Making a wide sweeping parry instead of a close forward parry.

(2) Eyes taken off the weapon to be parried.

Lesson 4.

First Practice.

Demonstrate " short point " with men and with dummies.

At dummies, " long point " and " short point " advancing.

Second Practice.

Varied direct and oblique. Two points—one long and one short—at the training stick.

Practise parries from " short point " position.

Lesson 5.

First Practice.

Demonstrate the " jab " with men and with dummies.

Two dummies " long point," " short point," advancing, and " jab."

" Long point," " short point," and " jab," advancing at two or more dummies.

Second Practice.

Varied " long " and " short " points and " jab " at training stick.

Practise " fend off " from " jab " position.

Common faults.

(1) Rifle drawn backwards and not held upright enough.

(2) " Point " made with sweeping upward action and relaxed muscles.

Lesson 6.

First Practice.

Demonstrate horizontal butt strokes.
Horizontal butt strokes at training stick.

Second Practice.

" Points " and " jabs " at dummies, butt strokes at light
dummies, kicks, &c.

Lesson 7.

No. 1 disarm.
No. 2 disarm.

Repetition of Lessons 1 to 7, as necessary.

88. *The tin ring course*

(Combination of bullet and bayonet.)

1. *Object of practice.*—The object of this practice is to
develop speed, dash, and accuracy of direction with the
bayonet, and to inculcate the alternating use of the bullet and
bayonet.

2. *Method of conducting.*—

i. The firer takes up the " lying " position, and loads
with five blank cartridges.

ii. On the command " Fire," he will fire two rounds at
targets placed 2 feet from the muzzle. (These
targets should be " falling," if possible—corks in
clips are usually suitable.)

iii. Without waiting for further orders the firer advances
at the double, taking the rings while on the move.
The bayonet will not be withdrawn in this exercise
—trans-fixed rings will be shaken off.

STANDING FIGURE
FOR BLANK FIRE

TIN RING

SANDBAG
JUMP

TIN RING

TIN RING

SANDBAGS
TO
REPRESENT
TRENCH

SANDBAG
JUMP

TIN RING

SANDBAG
TRENCH

TIN RING

TIN RING

10 YDS

10 YDS

10 YDS

10 YDS

TIN RING

TIN RING

TIN RING

SANDBAG
JUMP

SCREEN 3' HIGH
FOR FIRE
KNEELING

2 CORKS
FOR BLANK
FIRE

2 KNEELING
FIGURES FOR BLANK FIRE

SANDBAG
FOR PRONE FIRING

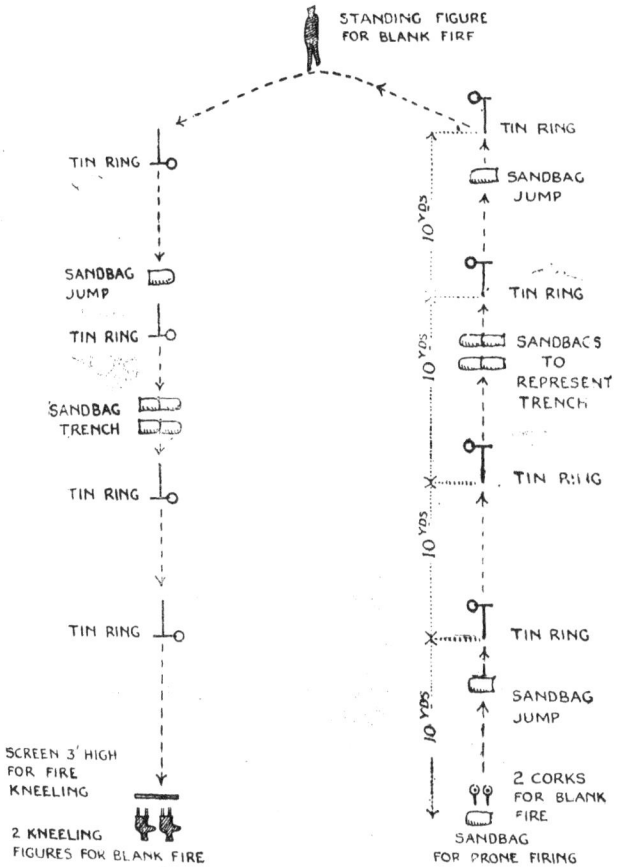

PLATE 59.—TIN RING COURSE

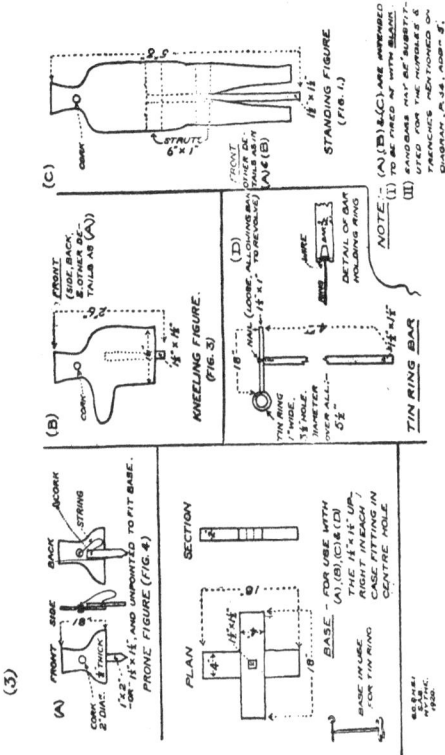

PLATE 60—APPLIANCES FOR "TIN RING" COURSE.

iv. Having bayonetted four rings, the firer will halt
and fire one round at a target, from the " standing"
position.

v. He will then straightway continue down the second
side of the course, transfixing the four remaining
rings.

vi. At the end of the course he will adopt the " kneeling "
position, and fire the remaining two rounds of
blank, at the kneeling figures.

3. *Time.*—This practice should be " timed." The time is
taken from the command " Fire " to the last round being fired.

4. *Marking.*—In order to stimulate the competitive spirit,
the instructor will keep a record of each man's performance,
marking as follows :—

Two points for each target hit with blank.

Two points for each ring transfixed.

One point to be deducted for each second over the
" standard " time for the course.

89. *The "mad minute " course.*

On the completion of the Seven Lessons, the following
speeding-up exercise will be carried out.

Each man will attack a number of dummies, placed
irregularly over a distance of about 50 yards.

The course should be arranged in such a manner as to
include all " points " and " butt strokes." Light dummies
should be used for practice with the butt, in order to avoid
damage. The greater variety in the arrangement of the
dummies the better, the principle being that the soldier
is allowed to go " all-out " for one minute, while at the
same time he must keep sufficiently cool to use his bayonet
with skill.

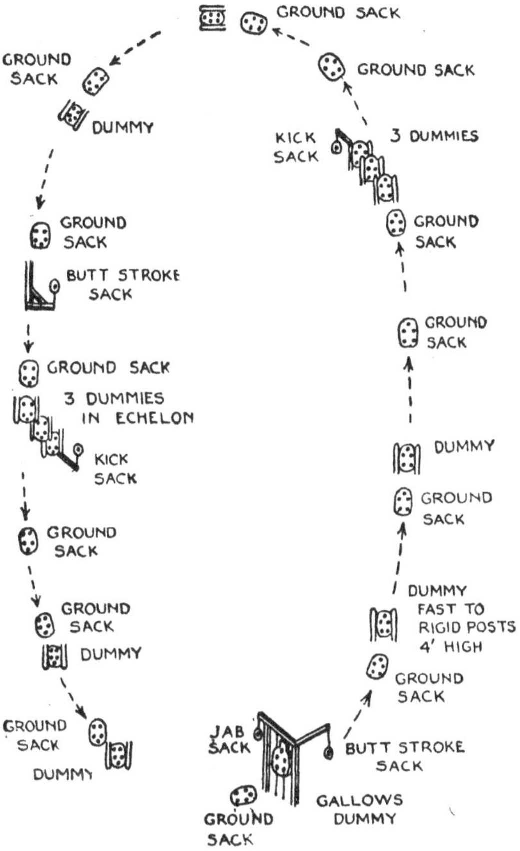

GROUND SACK

GROUND
SACK

DUMMY

GROUND
SACK

BUTT STROKE
SACK

GROUND SACK

3 DUMMIES
IN ECHELON

KICK
SACK

GROUND
SACK

GROUND
SACK

DUMMY

GROUND
SACK

DUMMY

GROUND SACK

GROUND SACK

KICK
SACK

3 DUMMIES

GROUND
SACK

GROUND
SACK

DUMMY

GROUND
SACK

DUMMY
FAST TO
RIGID POSTS
4' HIGH

GROUND
SACK

JAB
SACK

BUTT STROKE
SACK

GALLOWS
DUMMY

GROUND
SACK

PLATE 61.—" MAD MINUTE " COURSE.

90. *The counter charge.*

1. A well-timed counter-assault against an attacking enemy shaken by fire may be productive of far-reaching results.

2. Two parties advancing against each other with the bayonet seldom meet. The party which is possessed with the greater determination and confidence almost invariably causes the other party to waver and turn prior to the actual shock.

3. As proficiency is attained, the following counter-charge exercises will be carried out at the commencement and at the end of each daily lesson.

4. *First exercise.*—Advance and charge towards the instructor in single rank with scabbards on bayonets. Length of advance and charge from 80 to 100 yards.

Points to be emphasised :—

    (*a*) Control while advancing steadily at the " high port."

    (*b*) Dash and determination during the last 20 yards.

    (*c*) Resumption of control and the opening of fire after completion of the charge.

5. *Second exercise.*—Two sections about 80 to 100 yards apart, extended at four paces interval, to advance and charge through one another, passing right arm to right arm.

The same points to be observed as in the first exercise.

6. *Third exercise.*—Assault and counter-assault.

Attackers (one section).

    (i) Advance at the " high port " from about 100 yards off the position to be assaulted.

(ii) After advancing about 50 yards, break into a steady double and commence the assault.

(iii) When within 20 yards of the enemy, charge.

Defenders (one section).

(i) Lying in the open or in a trench. Open fire and continue until the enemy is about 50 yards distant.

(ii) Advance to the front of the position without loss of time, assuming the " on guard " position, and

(iii) Charge the enemy, when the latter are about 25 yards distant, in order to gain a moral advantage.

Points to be emphasised :—

(i) Good fire orders at commencement.

(ii) " Timing " of the counter-charge, *i.e.*, judging the right moment for the defenders to leave cover.

(iii) Control during movement.

7. When carrying out the exercises described above, the following qualities should be developed :—

(a) *Determination.*—Each man as he advances must select an individual opponent to kill, and must concentrate all his thoughts upon that determination. He must keep his eyes upon the selected victim and upon him alone.

(b) *Control.*—While still keeping his eyes upon his victim, each man must develop a " collective sense," which enables him to keep touch with the men on his right and left.

Note.—In addition to being a means of stimulating the man's brain during instruction, counter-charges form an excellent means of developing dash, strengthening the leg muscles, and improving the wind.

91. *Assault practice.*

1. *The assault practice will only be carried out after the men of the section have been thoroughly trained in all the preliminary lessons, and have acquired complete control over their weapons, otherwise injury to rifles and bayonets will result from improper application of the methods laid down in the foregoing instruction.*

2. The assault practice will approximate as nearly as possible to the conditions of actual fighting.

3. For this practice the men should be made to begin the assault or close combat from a trench or from behind a bank or wall, as well as from the open.

4. During the elementary stages it is advisable to use a well-defined enemy position as the objective, with firm ground over which the attacking sections may advance.

5. During the later stages of training, however, sections will be practised to assault over broken ground.

6. The assault practice is not a tactical exercise, but in carrying out the practice the following general principles will be observed :—

    (*a*) Fire should invariably both precede and follow movement.

    (*b*) All members of the attacking party will leave the trench or rise from cover simultaneously.

    (*c*) The first stage of the advance will be steady—not faster than the pace of the slowest man.

Such an advance has a decided moral effect on the enemy, ensures a degree of cohesion on contact, and at the same time allows the assaulting party to reach its objective without undue exhaustion. On the other hand, if the final rush is allowed to develop without control and in a haphazard

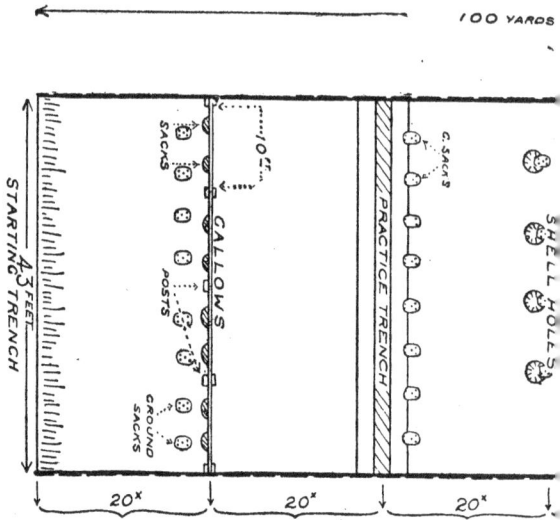

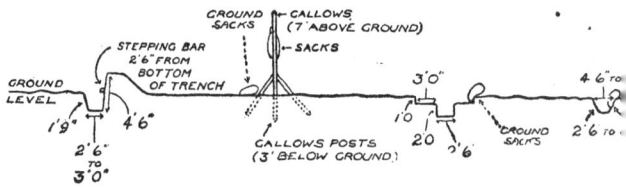

PLAN

SECTION

100 YARDS

STARTING TRENCH
43 FEET

SACKS

GALLOWS

1' 0"

POSTS

GROUND
SACKS

PRACTICE TRENCH

C. SACKS

SHELL HOLES

20ˣ 20ˣ 20ˣ

GROUND LEVEL

STEPPING BAR
2'6" FROM
BOTTOM
OF TRENCH

1'9" 4'6"

2'6"
TO
3'0"

GROUND SACKS

GALLOWS (7' ABOVE GROUND)

SACKS

GALLOWS POSTS
(3' BELOW GROUND.)

3'0"

1'0"

20 2'6"

GROUND SACKS

4'6" TO

2'6" TO

Note.—This course involves digging and the erection of gallows.

(B 27/7)Q

PLATE 62.

ASSAULT COURSE

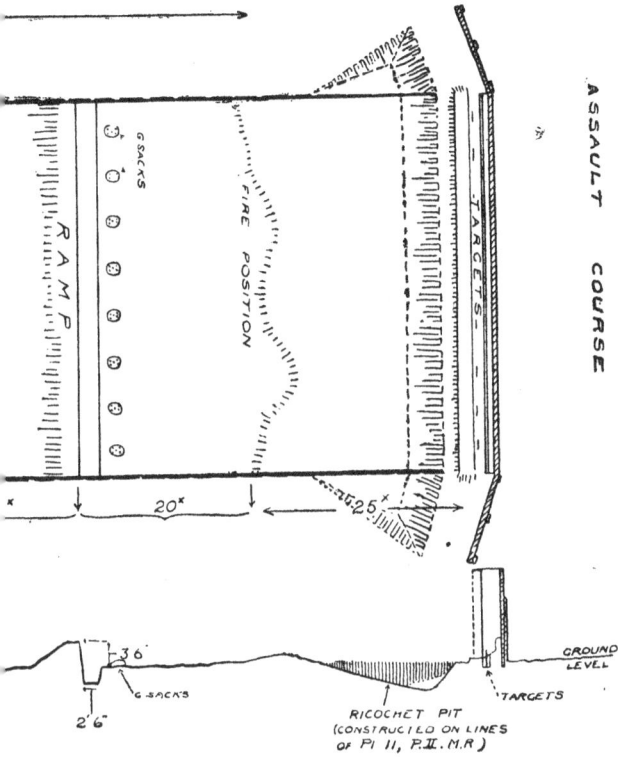

RAMP

G SACKS

FIRE POSITION

TARGETS

20ˣ

ˣ⎵25ˣ

GROUND
LEVEL

3 6

G SACKS

2 6ˮ

TARGETS

RICOCHET PIT
(CONSTRUCTED ON LINES
OF Pl II, P.II. (M.R))

fashion, the moral effect of a seemingly irresistible onset is lost, and the defenders may be given time to dispose of their opponents in detail.

(d) The actual charge or rush in will be made over a distance not greater than 20 paces. Within the last 10 yards, and before closing with the enemy, the rifle will be brought to the threatening, yet defensive, " on guard." Cohesion will, as far as possible, be maintained until actual contact with the enemy occurs.

(e) As soon as the defensive post or locality has been taken and occupied, every precaution will be taken against a counter-attack. The pursuit and repulse of a counter-attack by fire will invariably be practised, with or without ammunition according to the safety area of each assault course. In this way these actions may become second nature.

92. Leadership in the assault.

1. It is essential that leaders, i.e., section commanders should have a thorough knowledge of the tactical application of the bayonet.

2. The importance of discipline and a degree of control throughout the conduct of a bayonet assault or close combat cannot be over-emphasised. It must be remembered that in this, as in all other military operations, success can only be achieved through the closest co-operation of all concerned ; and that, while individual initiative is not to be discouraged, it must be strictly subordinated to the intention of the leader of the assaulting party.

3. Section commanders will regulate the pace and direction of their sections when closing with the enemy. They will also be responsible for deciding the exact instant at which the order to rush in will be given; and for immediately " reforming " their sections ready for a further advance or the repulse of a counter-attack by fire.

4. This control and co-ordination will produce an onset demoralising to the enemy and will assure the maximum shock at the moment of contact and at the same time, the minimum of fatigue to the attackers.

5. The employment of fire during the advance immediately preceding the " rush in " with the bayonet will be practised by sections, part of the section firing and keeping the enemy's heads down whilst others remove or pass through obstacles or wire which impede the advance.

6. A bayonet assault will normally be made under cover of fire, smoke, fog or darkness, and should come as a surprise. In these circumstances the prospect of success is greatest.

7. The bayonet is the best weapon for night operations. On the other hand, confusion is inherent in fighting by night; consequently, the execution of a successful night assault with the bayonet requires considerable and lengthy training. Units and individuals will be frequently practised in night work with the bayonet.

93. *Competitions.*

1. Competition is the spice of training. Bayonet training especially lends itself to competitions, and these should be arranged for individuals and sections, on the " assault course," " tin-ring course," " mad minute course," 30 yards and open range.

2. The details, conditions and paraphernalia suitable for a close combat competition, given below, are framed as a guide for such competitions.

Close combat competition.

3. *Team.*—A platoon commander and 2 sections. Total: 1 officer, 2 N.C.Os. and 12 privates.

4. *Dress.*—Fighting order, all ranks.

5. *Scheme* :—

> i. After delivering fire, to advance from a starting position by successive sections at about 50 paces distance. The officer may be with either section.
>
> ii. Assault with the bayonet four enemy defence posts.
>
> iii. Occupy a final objective and pursue the enemy with fire.

6. *Conditions* :—

> i. Starting position from under cover of trench, parapet, wall, &c., about 3 feet to 5 feet high.
>
> ii. Enemy defence posts. Each post represented by dummy sacks placed according to plan, but irregularly. Two posts will be composed of standing dummies, at each of which a long point and a jab will be delivered. The other two posts will be composed of ground sacks, at which one " point " will be made.
>
> iii. Final objective : Suitable fire position about 10 yards beyond last of enemy posts.
>
> iv. Length of assault course from starting position to final objective to be not less than 60 yards and not more than 80 yards. Distance between enemy posts from about 15 to 20 yards.

DIAGRAM IN SECTION OF ASSAULT COURSE, SUITABLE FOR ERECTION.

Note. No digging is necessary.   (NOT TO SCALE)

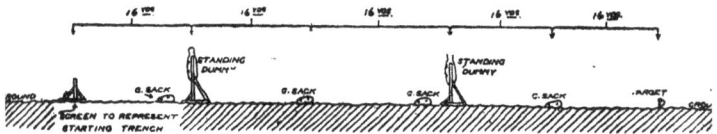

Appliances for Assault Course.

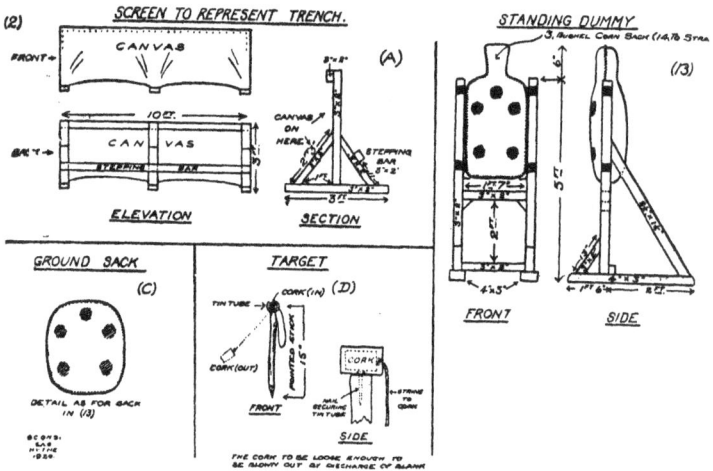

PLATE 63—ASSAULT COURSE.

v. Time for course. To be fixed by preliminary trial according to locality, length of course, and nature of ground.

Time will be counted from the moment when the rear section receive the order to leave the starting position, until the last man of the rear section reaches the final objective. Marks (see para. 7) will be allotted for the fire control and fire discipline before the assault, and at the final objective; but the time taken in delivering and controlling fire at these points will not be taken into account.

vi. Firing: 20 dummy or ball cartridges per man (not leaders) will be carried; pouches and dummies will be inspected immediately before and after each team carries out the competition. At least 10 rounds per man should be fired before the advance to the assault begins, and a further 10 rounds after the assault is completed. This is to allow time for the judges to allot marks for fire control and fire discipline.

7. *Marking*—

(a) For fire control and discipline at starting and final positions, 2 marks per man ... 24

(b) Each enemy " gallows " post, 2 per man ... 48

(c) Each ground " sack " post, 1 per man ... 24

Total marks possible 96

(d) One mark will be deducted for each second over allotted time.

8. *Ties.*—In the event of a tie, the team which completes the course in the shortest time will be adjudged the winner.

9. *Points to be observed—*

   i. Starting position.

      (a) Fire orders, fire control and fire discipline before advance.

      (b) Quickness in getting away.

      (c) Absence of noise—*i.e.,* talking and confusion.

   ii. Charging the enemy dummies.

      (a) Control of the section before contact.

      (b) Dash at the moment of contact.

      (c) Vigour of " point " and " withdrawal."

      (d) Control of the section after contact.

      (e) Absence of noise and confusion.

      (f) Hits on target if ball is used.

10. *Officials—*

   i. There should be a referee, a starter, a timekeeper and a scorer.

   ii. One judge at the starting position, for fire control and fire discipline, who may also judge at the final objective, and one at each post of dummies. Judges should *deduct* marks from the possible total allowed for each post of dummies. The same judges should act throughout at the same positions.

   iii. There should be a sufficient number of orderlies to set up dummies, &c., after each team goes over the course, to collect scores of judges to take to the scorer, and to collect and return ammunition.

11. *Hints to judges—*

    i. Stand in a position so that the whole line can be seen advancing, and at the moment of impact.

    ii. It is easier to count, and deduct a mark for each individual who displays bad fire discipline, loses control, makes a bad " point " or " withdrawal," talks or shouts, than to attempt to give marks for the men who make correct " points."

12. *Material required—*

    i. Dummy sacks, as required five painted marks on each sack.

    ii. Starting screens (*see* plan) and paraphernalia.

    iii. Stop-watch.

    iv. Slips of paper and pencils for officials.

    v. Targets for use with ball ammunition.

CHAPTER III.

LEWIS GUN TRAINING.

GENERAL INSTRUCTIONS ON TRAINING.

94. *Introductory.*

1. The Lewis gun is the principal weapon of 50 per cent. of the fire units of the Infantry ; training in its use must be part of the normal training of the Infantry, equally with any other subject. On no account must the Lewis gun be regarded as a specialist weapon.

2. The principles on which its use in battle are based will be found in Field Service Regulations, Vol. II, and Infantry Training, Vol. II, (*see* especially Infantry Training, Vol. II, (1921) Secs. **10** and **11**).

3. The following sections (**94-124**) set out the detailed instruction for the training of the individual to handle, and the leader to direct the employment, of the weapon in accordance with those principles.

4. The leaders *directly* concerned with the employment of the Lewis gun are the platoon commanders and the section commanders of Lewis gun sections. The Lewis gun is, above all, a platoon weapon.

5. The policy of Lewis gun training for the requirements of battle can be divided into three categories :—

    (a) The training of the private soldier as a skilled man at arms with the weapon, or in any duties connected with serving the weapon.

    (b) The training of the section commander to control and direct the employment of the weapon to the best advantage within the scope of any instructions received from his platoon commander.

    (c) The training of the platoon commander to direct the employment of the weapon in co-operation with the other weapons within his command in such a manner that its powers are exploited to the utmost towards accomplishing the task of the platoon as a whole.

6. Duties in connection with the handling of the Lewis gun are distributed among all the members of the section, differentiated according to their " numbers." Every member of the section must be able to carry out the duties assigned to any particular " number."

7. Amongst the many considerations bearing on the Lewis gun training policy, the characteristics of the weapon itself should be the basis of all. Although it may sometimes be expedient to employ the weapon contrary to the dictates of its characteristics, it will normally exert its full power only when employed in harmony with its characteristics.

The Lewis gun is a shoulder-controlled light automatic weapon, containing delicate mechanism. It is air-cooled and limited to fire action only, being capable of producing rapidly a large volume of highly-concentrated fire.

8. From these characteristics can be deduced the framework of individual training.

9. Owing to the weapon being shoulder-controlled, the degree of accuracy with which its fire is applied to the target is subject to all the normal individual errors of marksmanship. Consequently, the first aim of training is to teach men to hold, aim and fire the gun with accuracy.

10. As the gun fires by automatic action, smooth mechanical working can only be obtained by careful adjustment of the forces which control the automatic action.

11. The number of delicate parts of the mechanism subjected to a great strain during firing give rise to various causes of stoppages. Care of the gun at all times, and especially care in preparing the gun for firing, will minimise to a great extent the frequency of stoppages. A high standard of training in locating the causes of stoppages and applying a remedy quickly is essential to avoid loss of fire power during battle.

12. As the gun is air-cooled and fires at the rate of between six and seven hundred rounds a minute, it is best to fire in short bursts of 4 or 5 rounds, with intervals between bursts. This method not only minimises the risk of defects due to over-heating and continuous strain, but also avoids excessive expenditure of ammunition without compensating effect. For anti-aircraft purposes, however, continuous fire is justified owing to the target being within range for so short a time.

13. The highly concentrated nature of the fire permits of only a very small margin of error in aiming, range estimation,

or allowance for the effect of atmospheric conditions. Training in these subjects, therefore, assumes a place of great importance.

14. The close grouping of the shots, however, favours the chances of observation of fire, thereby giving the firer and the controller a guide as to the alteration in laying necessary to hit the target.

15. The weight of the gun, spare parts, and ammunition supply, require the men of the Lewis gun section to be of good physique, and able after training to carry the extra weight without detriment to their fighting value.

95. *Sequence of training.*

1. In order that a soldier may fulfil his rôle as a Lewis gunner in battle he must be trained to be capable of carrying out the following duties actually concerned with the handling of the gun :—

   (a) To prepare the gun for firing and maintain it in action.

   (b) To carry the gun and get it quickly into action on any type of ground.

   (c) To fire accurately at various rates up to 150 rounds a minute according to the requirements of various types of targets likely to be encountered in battle.

   (d) To observe fire and correct its application accordingly.

   (e) To fire with effect at low flying aircraft.

   (f) To perform the duties assigned to any " number " in a L.G. section.

2. The subjects in which he requires instruction to bring him up to this standard (presupposing that the man has already been trained as a recruit rifleman) are :—

    (*a*) Those concerned with the gun itself (set out in approximately the order in which they should be introduced into a progressive sequence) :—

        Loading and unloading the gun and *magazine*.
        Holding.
        Aiming.
        Firing.
        Elementary handling.
        Stripping (for cleaning).
        Care and cleaning gun, *magazines* and appurtenances.
        Points to be attended to before, during, and after firing.

          Note.—Having learnt the above subjects, the man should be able to pass the tests of elementary training, Standard " A," and fire elementary range practices.

        Advanced handling.
        Duties of Nos. 3, 4, 5 and 6.
        Section handling.
        The mechanical action caused by the forces " Gas " and " Spring."
        Immediate action.

          Note.—Having learnt the above subjects, the man should be able to pass the tests of elementary training, Standard " R." and fire the range practices of Table R.

Stripping component parts.
The remedy and causes of probable stoppages.
Anti-aircraft aiming and handling.
Theory of Lewis gun fire.
The characteristics of the Lewis gun.
Examination of gun.
Packing of limber.

> *Note.*—Having learnt the above subjects, the man
> should be able to pass the tests of elementary
> training, Standard " L," and fire Table L and
> section practices.

(b) Those subjects which go hand in hand with weapon
training irrespective of the particular type of
weapon, viz. :—

Visual training.
Recognition of targets.
Judging distance.
Judging effect of atmospheric conditions.
Fire discipline.
Battle formations.
Use of ground.

The foundations of these subjects should have been laid
during the man's earlier training. When concentrating on
his training as a Lewis gunner it should only be necessary to
amplify them to meet the special requirements of the Lewis
gunner. These subjects should be introduced into the training
programme concurrently with the subjects mentioned in (a)
above.

96. *System of training.*

1. The system of training with the Lewis gun varies according to whether the man is learning a subject or whether he is being exercised in a subject he has already learnt.

The following paragraphs bear on the system to be adopted for teaching.

2. A section under instruction normally consists of eight men. In a 40 minutes period of instruction with only one gun each man gets 5 minutes handling. The system of instruction must therefore be such that all men are learning during the 35 minutes they are not handling the gun.

3. Many unforeseen accidents will happen to the mechanism of the gun in the course of its use in battle. If men are trained to deal with foreseen accidents only they will be unable to deal with the unforeseen when they occur, and the gun may then be out of action at a critical period through some trifling cause. The system of training must therefore be such that it develops the mechanical aptitude of the individual.

4. In the course of a man's military career the design of automatic weapons may change or certain modifications of the existing type may be introduced. If the man has been trained to handle the mechanism in a stereotyped manner he is liable to be confused by the changes. If, however, his training has developed his mechanical aptitude he will quickly adapt his skill to the changes.

5. To meet these requirements the system of teaching is that of appealing to the man's reason rather than to his

memory and is carried out by adhering to the principles set forth in the following paragraphs.

6. The instructor will attempt to draw the information from the man under instruction by putting each point of his lesson to the class in the form of questions. The questions should be such that they will build up point by point the required instruction.

7. If he cannot lead the line of thought of the class to the point at which he is aiming by one series of questions he should try a different line of questions. He should only fall back on the method of demonstration or explanation as a last resort to avoid taking undue time over a minor point. These latter methods appeal to the imitative rather than to the reasoning faculties, and do not develop the mind in the same degree.

8. Having by this process arrived at the correct method of performing any action, the men will each perform the action in turn. The instructor meanwhile questions the remainder as to the correctness or otherwise of each man's execution. In this way he can bring out many minor points bearing on the subject.

9. In some subjects it is unnecessary to use questions prior to calling on a man to carry out an action. In such cases the instructor will simply tell the man to do a certain action, leaving it to the man to think for himself how he will do it. Should the man appear unable to think out a method of doing what is wanted, the instructor should guide his thought by getting suggestions from other men of the class. The instructor must allow the man full latitude to carry out the action in his own way and only interfere if he sees a likelihood of the gun being damaged or undue time taken.

10. The instructor should rarely ask the same man two consecutive questions. As a general rule he should put each question in turn to a different man, always varying the order in which he selects the individual. By this means the same line of thought is kept running through the minds of the whole squad and any inattention is at once exposed.

11. At the end of each period of instruction the instructor will summarise the main points which have been learnt and satisfy himself that no man of the squad is left in doubt about any point of that particular lesson.

12. The instructor must have a thorough knowledge of the subject he is about to teach. He must not attempt to teach too much in any one lesson. A few definite points learnt and understood are better than many points only partly understood. He must be quite clear in his own mind exactly what he is setting out to teach in any lesson and should only be satisfied that he has taught the lesson when he is sure that the students have learnt the matter which he set out to teach.

HANDLING.

97. *Elementary handling.*

1. Training under this heading is designed to teach men to bring the gun quickly into action, correctly mounted in a position suitable for firing.

2. The gun, &c., having been placed in a position suitable for carrying out the exercises, the section falls in. The men form line in rear of the gun and number from right to left.

3. On the order to " **Take post** " being given, No. 1 lies down behind the gun. He at once examines the gun to see that it is ready for action, looking especially to : *Barrel mouthpiece, clamp ring, gas regulator key, mounting adjustment, sights, feed mechanism, bolt* and *piston rod.*

4. No. 2 simultaneously lies down about two paces to the left of No. 1. He slings the *spare parts bag* over his left shoulder and examines all the *magazines* in the *carrier* to ensure that they are correctly filled and undamaged. He also examines the *spare parts* to see that they are ready for use when required.

5. On completion of his examination he reports to No. 1 " Ammunition and *spare parts* correct," or otherwise, and hands a *magazine* to No. 1.

6. No. 1 places the *magazine* on the gun and reports " Ready " to the instructor.

(Henceforth No. 1 will repeat all orders given by the instructor.)

7. The instructor will then indicate certain aiming marks on the landscape target and give them brief titles.

8. On the command " **Range** "—" **Aiming Mark** "— " **Action,**" No. 1 will rise and carry the gun forward, holding the field mount with his left hand (back of the hand to the rear) and the *small of the butt* with his right hand.

9. On reaching the position indicated by the instructor, he will mount the gun by placing the feet of the *field mount* on the ground. After the feet of the *field mount* have reached the ground he transfers his left hand to the *small of*

the butt, releasing his right hand, which he places on the ground palm downwards. Using his right hand as a support he drops into the lying position straight behind the gun, at the same time lowering the *butt* gently to the ground.

10. He then loads, adjusts the *sights,* holds the gun in the firing position, and aims at the mark indicated.

11. No. 2, carrying the *magazines* and *spare parts,* will advance with No. 1 and drop down on the latter's left. He must lie in such a position that he can readily assist in changing *magazines* or supply *spare parts* when wanted, whilst at the same time he offers the minimum possible target surface to the front.

12. When in position, No. 2 will take a *magazine* from the *carrier* and hold it in readiness for use. He will also place the *spare parts bag* in a position of readiness.

13. When No. 1 is ready to open fire he calls out " On " to No. 2, who will raise his right hand over the shoulders of No. 1, and at the same time watch the section commander for signals.

14. On the command, " **Fire,**" No. 2 will shout " Fire," whereupon No. 1 will press the *trigger* and fire in short bursts of about one second's duration, pausing to observe fire and to relay his aim between bursts.

15. On the command " **Change** " (*magazine*), No. 1 (keeping the *butt* in his shoulder) will press the *catch* of the *magazine* to the right with the thumb of his right hand. At the same time No. 2 will press upwards the *centre block* of the *magazine.*

PLATE 64.

Fig. A.

" CHANGE "—1ST PHASE.

Fig. B.

" CHANGE "—2ND PHASE.

16. Having removed the *magazine* from the *magazine post*, No. 1 will pass it, with the open side upwards, under the gun to No. 2.

17. No. 2 places another *magazine* on the gun, and No. 1 loads and continues firing.

18. On the command " **Stop,**" No. 1 will pull back the *cocking handle* (if forward) and, assisted by No. 2, change *magazines*. He will then place the *butt* on the ground and await a further command.

19. On the command " **Unload,**" No. 1 will remove the *magazine*, press the *trigger*, pull back the *cocking handle*, press the *trigger* again, and lower the *leaf* of the *backsight*. No. 2 replaces all *magazines* in the *carrier*. (Note.—When practising with dummy cartridges, the *cocking handle* should be pulled back to simulate the position in which it would be when firing ball.)

20. Both No. 1 and No. 2 will then rise from the gun, and No. 1 reports " No. — gun clear."

21. On the command " **Unload without firing,**" the action will be as for the command " Unload," with the exception that, after removing the *magazine*, No. 1 will remove the round in the *feed-way* without firing it (*see* Section 101 (5)).

22. On the command " **Cease firing** " No. 1 unloads the gun,* (leaving the *cocking handle* forward), No. 2 then places a new *magazine* on the gun while No. 1 lowers the *leaf* of the *backsight*. No. 1 then carries the gun to the " cease firing " position, and No. 2 replaces the *magazines* in the *carrier* and moves to the " cease firing " position (*see* special note 1).

---

* Under certain circumstances, such as leaving an "action" position without having opened fire prior to the command "Cease firing," the gun should be unloaded without firing the round in the *feedway*.

23. **Signals.**—The following signals will be used :—

" **Action.**"—Both arms raised and lowered in line with the shoulders.

" **Ready to open fire.**"—No. 2 raises his hand over the shoulders of No. 1.

" **Stand by, ready to fire.**"—Hand raised.

" **Fire.**"—Hand lowered to side.

" **Stop.**"—Hand waved horizontally.

" **Cease firing.**"—Arm circled from shoulder.

NOTES FOR INSTRUCTORS.

Preliminary.—In teaching elementary handling the subject should be divided progressively into stages which gradually work up to the stage at which the handling actions are carried out by word of command and signals.

Subjects.—The progressive stages should be :—

Working up to—	Progressive Stages.
I.—Take Post ...	i. Class arrangements (falling in and number-ing off, &c.). ii. Action of No. 1. iii. Action of No. 2. iv. Carry out by word of command.
II.—Action	i. No. 1 carrying forward and placing the gun in position. ii. Position of No. 2. iii. Repeat i. and ii., adding loading. iv. Repeat iii., adding adjustment of *sights* and aiming. v. Repeat iv., adding firing. vi. Carry out by word of command.

Working up to—	Progressive Stages.
III.—Change Magazines	i. Each action of Nos. 1 and 2. ii. Carry out by word of command.
IV.—Stop	i. Each action of Nos. 1 and 2. ii. Carry out by word of command.
V.—Unload	i. Each action of Nos. 1 and 2 when unloading by firing. ii. Each action of Nos. 1 and 2 when unloading without firing. iii. Carry out i. and ii. by word of command.
VI.—Cease firing ...	i. Each action of Nos. 1 and 2 in preparing the gun for movement. ii. Each action of Nos. 1 and 2 in moving to the " cease firing " position. iii. Carry out by word of command.
VII.—Signals	i. Teach the signals and test recognition. ii. Carry out Elementary Handling, substituting signals for words of command.

SPECIAL NOTES.

1. Training in this subject should be carried out on level ground, and the distance between the " Action " and the " Cease firing " positions should be about 5 yards.

2. From the time the recruit has learnt how to carry out the actions required for elementary handling he should receive constant practice, so as to ensure that he instinctively carries out the correct action on any given word of command. This practice comes under the heading of " Handling exercises."

As the man's training progresses, the exercises should include
any further stages of manipulation which have been learnt,
such as immediate action and stoppage remedying.

3. In timing the pace of these exercises the instructor
should gradually shorten the interval between his words of
command to conform to the increased efficiency of the section.
At the same time, he should be careful to balance the claims
of speed with those of accuracy of manipulation.

98. *Advanced handling.*

1. Advanced handling consists of exercises for the purpose
of teaching the Nos. 1 and 2 to make the best use of ground
features when occupying fire positions, in order to secure
the maximum cover consistent with the full use of the gun
for fire action.

2. The use of both natural and artificial cover will be
practised in mounting the gun for action.

3. The way in which the gun should be mounted will be
determined in every case by the shape of the ground.

4. Suitable exercises include :—

    (a) *Mounting the gun for firing over or round cover of varying*
        heights, such as breastworks, trench parapets,
        banks, shell-holes, minor undulations, hedges or
        undergrowth giving cover from view. The types
        of position selected should be such that sometimes
        the *field mount* is used and at other times not used.

    (b) *Firing from behind the crest of a gentle slope.*

    (c) *Mounting the gun on uneven ground* which necessitates
        adjustment of the length of the legs of the bipod.

PLATE 65.

LINE OF FIRE

SECTION OF GROUND

FOLD IN THE GROUND.

PLATE 66.

SECTION OF GROUND

BIPOD LEGS OUT TO FULL EXTENT.

PLATE 67.

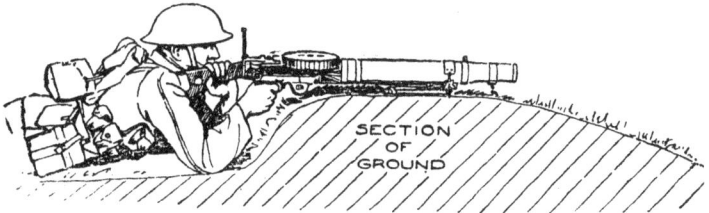

SECTION OF GROUND

BIPOD FOLDED—GUN RESTED ON GROUND.

PLATE 68.

FIRING THROUGH "V" IN BANK—LOWEST POSITION.

PLATE 69.

FIRING OVER PARAPET OF TRENCH—LEGS CLOSED.

(d) *Methods of crawling with the gun.* As crawling is
fatiguing and slow, it should be limited normally
to movement over the last 2 or 3 yards on to a fire
position, or to crossing short exposed stretches in
an otherwise concealed line of approach.

Crawling should only be employed when other
forms of movement would spoil the chance of
surprise by disclosing the movement.

*Nos. 1 and 2 carrying the gun together, moving behind
cover,* which affords concealment only to a man in
a crouching attitude.

99. *Duties of Nos. 3, 4, 5 and 6.*

1. The actions of Nos. 1 and 2 alone are legislated for in
elementary and advanced handling. Before the section can,
however, work as a team the duties of the other numbers
must be understood by every member of the section.

2. All members of a section must be able to undertake
the duties assigned to any particular number. As the
number of men in a section at any particular time may
vary, the allocation of duties must be sufficiently flexible to
meet any variation in strength.

3. The remainder of the section, exclusive of Nos. 1 and 2
who are required to fire and feed the gun, have alternative
duties, the main ones being :—

(a) To carry and replenish the ammunition supply.
(b) Protective duties.
(c) As riflemen.

4. The normal allocation of duties would be :—
No. 3 responsible for maintaining the chain of ammunition supply between the No. 2 and the other members of the section.

Nos. 4, 5 and 6 as ammunition carriers, riflemen, and for protective duties.

5. The subjects to be taught under this section are therefore :—

i. Methods of carrying the ammunition.

ii. Transfer of full and empty *magazines* between Nos, 2 and 3.

iii. Methods by which No. 3 collects the full *magazines* from other numbers and disposes of the empty *magazines*.

iv. Protective duties.

6. The amount of ammunition taken into action by the section will vary with the nature of the operation. For training purposes the following scale will be considered the normal :—

Carried by the Section Commander					1 *magazine.**
„ „ No. 1	...	...	...		1 *magazine* on the gun.
„ „ No. 2†	...	...	...		2 *magazines* in pouch equipment.
„ „ No. 3†					
„ „ No. 4		each	...	...	4 *magazines* in
„ „ No. 5					pouch equipment.
„ „ No. 6					

Total—20 *magazines*, each containing 47 rounds = 940 rounds.

---

* This *magazine* will be carried in *pouch* suspended to belt on the left end piece on the waist belt.

† No. 2 will carry his 2 *magazines* connected by the brace and hung round the neck with both *magazines* in front.

Nos. 2 and 3 will each carry an empty *magazine carrier* in addition.

No. 1 carries a revolver and 36 rounds of revolver ammunition.

No. 2 carries the *spare parts*, a revolver and 36 rounds of revolver ammunition.

7. No. 3 will take up a position in the neighbourhood of the gun, under cover if possible, and will transfer his *magazines* from his *pouches* into his *magazine carrier*. He must avoid making the gun position conspicuous. Unless there is adequate cover, if he is too close to the gun he will increase the target, while if he is too far away he will draw attention to the gun by undue movement when handing up ammunition.

8. When No. 2's supply of ammunition has been expended, No. 3 will hand over his *carrier* to No. 2, and take away No. 2's *carrier* into which the latter has placed the empty *magazines*.

9. No. 3 then goes to the nearest remaining " number," takes off him four full *magazines* with which he fills his own *carrier*, and substitutes the empty *magazines* in the other's pouches. If a further supply of ammunition is at hand, the empty *magazines* will be refilled.

10. The individual training for protective duties comprises:

    (a) Development of an eye for ground for the purpose of :—

        i. Selecting the best lines of advance.

        ii. Recognising ground features suitable for the next bound of the section.

        iii. Selecting suitable fire positions.

    (b) Methods of keeping in touch with the section and reporting information by signal.

    (c) Two men, working as a pair, reconnoitring areas of ground without undue delay. (See Infantry Training, Vol. I, (1922) Sec. **138**.)

(d) Observation. When the gun is in action the section commander is fully occupied in observing and directing the fire and will need to employ other men of the section to assist him in looking out for :—

    i. The action of neighbouring sections and of platoon headquarters.

    ii. Fresh targets.

    iii. Location of enemy posts or snipers.

100. *Section handling.*

1. A Lewis gun section can manœuvre successfully as a unit only if the members of the section carry out their individual rôles intelligently and in harmony with the mission of the section as indicated briefly by the section commander.

2. When the individual rôles have been carried out by all men of the section in " Elementary Handling," "Advanced Handling " and " the duties of Nos. 3, 4, 5 and 6," the foundations of team work have been laid. The next requirement of training is to combine these individual roles into collective action as a unit.

3. The section will first be exercised in " Section Battle Formations ; " the amount of practice necessary will depend on the previous training which the men have had in the subject.

4. The next stage is to set exercises to practise the section in :—

    i. Making a bound from one fire position to another.

    ii. Occupation of a fire position and working the chain of ammunition supply.

   iii. Making a long advance by successive bounds, coming
into action at the end of each bound.

   iv. Occupation of a post in a defended locality.

   v. Handling in the dark.

Preliminary Training.

(With Notes for Instructors).

*****

101. *Loading and unloading.*

1. To load the magazine :—

   i. Place the *magazine*, bottom upwards, on a flat surface.

   ii. Insert the *loading handle* in the *socket*, and press it
fully home.

   iii. Place the cartridges in succession, so that the rim
of the cartridge is behind the *retaining plates* of
the *magazine*, and the bullet between the *separating pegs*.

   iv. After inserting each cartridge, rotate the *centre
block* or *pan* so that the lip of the *bullet groove* in
the *centre block* engages the cartridges and leads
them into the *groove*.

2. To empty a magazine.—Insert the *loading handle*
into the *socket* in the *centre block* and rotate it slowly, removing
each cartridge as it becomes disengaged from the *bullet groove*
in the centre.

3. To load the gun :—

   i. See that the *cocking handle* is fully forward.

   ii. Place a *magazine* in position on the *magazine post,*
seeing that the *thumb piece* of the *spring catch* is to

the right. (In those *magazines* which have one half of the surface of the *centre disc* painted white, the painted portion should be to the rear.)

iii. Press the *magazine* down gently (rotating it slightly, if necessary, in both directions) until the *hook* of the *magazine catch* engages under the *internal cone* of the *magazine post*.

iv. Rotate the *magazine* as far as it will go in the feeding direction and then pull back the *cocking handle*. The gun will then be loaded, with a round in position in the *feedway* ready to be moved to the *chamber*.

4. To unload the gun.—If the *magazine* can be rotated by hand in the feeding direction when the *cocking handle* is forward, it indicates that the *magazine* is empty. If it cannot be rotated by hand, it still contains cartridges.

i. Press the *magazine catch* over to the right with the thumb, and lift off the *magazine*.

ii. If the *cocking handle* is in the forward position pull it back and then press the *trigger*, but if the *cocking handle* is in the backward position fire the round in the *feedway*, pull back the *cocking handle* and press the *trigger*. This latter action is necessary to make sure the gun is clear.

5. To unload the gun without firing the round in the feedway :—

i. Remove the *magazine* as before.

ii. With the point of a live round or the end of an empty case, depress the base of the round under the *tongue*.

    iii. Seize the bullet of the latter round in the left hand and draw it forward until the point of the bullet is resting on the front of the opening in the *feed-arm.*

    iv. Holding the *cocking handle* with the right hand, press the *trigger* and allow the *cocking handle* to go forward slowly until the point of the bullet turns over to the right.

    v. Draw back the *cocking handle.*

    vi. Remove the round with the left hand and then allow the *cocking handle* to go forward.

NOTES FOR INSTRUCTORS.

Subject.—The sequence of teaching the above subject should be :—

    I.—Loading the *magazine.*

    II.—Unloading the *magazine.*

    III.—Placing the *magazine* on the *magazine post* and rotating it.

    IV.—Completing the loading motion.

    V.—Unloading the gun by firing the round in the *feedway.*

    VI.—Unloading the gun without firing the round in the *feedway.*

Note.—Each of these subheads should be learnt and practised by every member of the class, before the instructor proceeds to teach the next subhead.

SPECIAL NOTES.

In the course of the instruction the instructor should impress on the recruit :—

1. The object of the *loading handle* and the necessity for it to be pressed fully home into the *socket* of the *magazine*.

2. The consequences, if the rim of any one cartridge is not placed behind the *retaining plates* of the *magazine*.

3. To avoid leaving any spaces in the *magazine*.

4. That damage may occur if undue pressure is applied when placing the *magazine* on the *magazine post*.

5. That the position of the cartridge when the gun is loaded differs from that of a rifle. In the rifle the cartridge is in the chamber, whereas in the Lewis gun it is in the *feedway* and the *bolt* is open.

6. That the gun is not loaded unless the *magazine* is rotated before pulling back the *cocking handle*.

Kit required.—Gun, *magazines, loading handles*, drill cartridges Mk. VI, ground sheets.

102. *Holding, aiming and firing.*

A.—**Holding**.

1. To hold the gun in the firing position, the firer lies in a straight line behind the gun with both elbows on the ground.

2. He holds the *pistol grip* with his right hand, the forefinger reaching round the *trigger*, whilst the remaining three fingers clasp the *pistol grip* (the second finger being close up

under the *trigger guard*). He uses his thumb to secure the grasp by pressing on the left side of the *pistol grip*.

3. By a steady backward pressure with his right hand, the *butt* is held tight against his shoulder, and the hold locked by a steady downward and backward pressure with the left hand which grips the *small of the butt*, with the fingers passing over the top and the thumb passing underneath.

4. The *bipod legs* supporting the gun at its forward end should be firmly fixed into the ground with the *shoes* towards the firer.

B.—Aiming.

5. Adjustment of *sights*.—To adjust the *backsight* elevation, rotate the *milled head* until the line on the *slide* is level with the line on the *leaf* immediately below the figure indicating the elevation for the distance named.

6. The principles of aiming with the rifle *sights* apply equally to aiming with the Lewis gun *sights*, except that the *backsight* of the Lewis gun is fitted with an *aperture*.

7. The rules for aiming are therefore :—

    i. Keep the *sights* upright.

    ii. Keep the disengaged eye closed.

    iii. Aim will be taken by aligning the *sights* on to the lowest central portion of the aiming mark, the tip of the *foresight* to be in the centre of the *aperture* of the *backsight*.

C.—Firing.

8. In order not to disturb the aim, the gun must be fired by a steady pressure of the forefinger on the *trigger*, whilst maintaining a firm hold of the gun.

Correct Hold.
Plate 70.

Fig. A.
Holding.

Fig. B.
Holding.

9. The *trigger* should be held back for about half a second
and then released, as by this means the rate of fire is regulated
in short bursts of 4 or 5 rounds at a time. Simultaneously
with releasing the *trigger*, the firer should observe the result
of his fire by looking over or round the *sights* towards the
target.

PLATE 71.

LEWIS GUN—CORRECT AIM.

10. The firer must always relay his aim between the time of releasing the *trigger* and pressing it again.

NOTES FOR INSTRUCTORS.

Subjects.—Instruction in holding, aiming and firing can normally be combined in the same lesson period and must be taught in that sequence.

SPECIAL NOTES.

1. Although there is no appreciable shock of recoil to " hold " against, the vibrations set up when the automatic action of the gun is in play are such that unless countered, they will throw the gun completely off its alignment.   A firm hold is therefore the essential foundation of accurate shooting. Any tendency to loose holding, even during some part of instructional training when live ammunition is not being used, is sowing the seeds of failure in marksmanship.

Aiming.

2. Men should be taught to adjust the *backsight* elevation before they are taught to aim.

3. Aiming is best taught as follows :—

First, by explanation of correct and incorrect aims by diagrams.

Secondly, the instructor lays the gun (rested in any convenient way) with a correct aim, and lets each recruit see that aim ; then the recruit lays an aim and the instructor checks.

Thirdly, the recruit aims at the eye disc which is held by the instructor about one yard from the *muzzle* of the gun.

Note.—Before doing this the instructor must satisfy himself by personal inspection that the gun is unloaded.

4. Although some form of bull's-eye aiming mark can be used in the first stages, the subject cannot be considered to be learnt until the instructor has satisfied himself that the recruits can aim correctly at landscape aiming marks. Thereafter, the landscape aiming marks should be used for all future training.

Firing.

5. The recruit should be taught to observe his fire by developing the habit of looking at the target over or round the *sights* every time he releases the *trigger*. The sequence of acts being—Aim--press *trigger*---release *trigger*—look—relay aim—and so on.

6. Instruction in aiming and firing should include changing the point of aim along a linear target by, approximately, a width of the foresight.

Kit required.—Gun. Aiming diagrams. An aiming mark. An eye disc. A landscape target. *Magazine carrier* or some other form of rest for the gun when laying an aim.

103. *Stripping and assembling.*

1. When provided, the *combination spring balance* should be used for stripping. In its absence a dummy cartridge may be used.

(*Note.*--**Ball** ammunition must never be used for instructional purposes except on the ranges).

2. By these means the whole of the gun can be stripped with the following exceptions :—

> (*a*) The *gas chamber* and *barrel mouthpiece* (or *flash eliminator*) for which the special spanner has to be used.

(b) The *clamp ring screw*, which is unscrewed with a screw-driver or the *gas regulator key*.

3. **To strip the gun.**—The gun is stripped in the order set forth in the succeeding paragraphs.

4. 1st, **Butt.**—With the *cocking handle* in the forward position, insert the point of a bullet behind the *No.* 1 *catch* and press it upwards to disengage the *catch*. With the *No.* 2 *catch* press the *thumb piece* forward. Then rotate the *butt* one-eighth of a turn, underside of the *butt* to the right, and withdraw it.

5. 2nd, **Body cover.**—See that the *feed arm* is over to the right. Then draw back the *body cover* until it is clear of its *retaining ledges* on the *body*. Then lift off the *body cover*.

6. 3rd, **Feed arm.**—With the point of a bullet press forward the *latch*. Turn the *feed arm* until the *key way* in the *axis hole* clears the *key* on the *magazine post*. Then lift off the *feed arm*.

7. 4th, **Trigger guard and pistol grip.**—Press the *trigger* in order to disengage the *sear nose* and *plunger* from their holes in the bottom of the *body*. Slide the *guard* back until it is clear of the body. (It should not be completely withdrawn until the *pinion casing, bolt* and *piston rod* have been removed.)

8. 5th, **Unhook the pinion casing.**

9. 6th, **Bolt and piston rod.**—Draw back the *cocking handle* to its full extent, and withdraw it from the *piston rod* by pulling it outwards. Draw out the *bolt* and *piston rod*.

10. 7th, **Body.**—With the point of a bullet, press back the *body locking pin*. Unscrew the *body* from the *barrel*. In the event of the body being so tightly breeched up that it cannot be turned by hand, the operation should be undertaken only

by the armourer, who will use his raw-hide mallet and strike the *body* on the left side, near the bottom joint of the *locking piece*.

After the rear face of the *barrel* is removed from the protection afforded by the *body*, great care must be taken to preserve the projections on it from damage. The *barrel* and *radiator* should never be stood *muzzle* upwards on any hard surface.

11. 8th, **Clamp ring and front radiator casing.**— Unscrew the *No.* 1 *clamp ring screw* and remove the *clamp ring* and *front radiator casing*. The *No.* 2 *screw* will only be unscrewed so far that the screw is flush with the outside of the left wing of the *clamp ring*.

12. 9th, **Mounts, field.**—Unscrew the *band* and withdraw. If withdrawn forward—turn it so that the opening passes the *gas regulator*, then turn it again, so that the opening passes the *foresight*.

13. 10th, **Gas regulator.**—With the point of a bullet, lift the *key* until the *stud* on its end is clear of the hole in the *radiator casing*. Remove the *key* and unscrew the *gas regulator*.

14. 11th, **Rear radiator casing.**—Slide the *casing* off to the rear.

15. 12th, **Gas cylinder.**—Insert the *piston rod* until about half of the *rack* has entered the *cylinder*. Then, using the *piston rod* as a wrench, unscrew the *gas cylinder*. Take care not to use such force as would fracture the rear end of the *gas cylinder*.

16. 13th, **Gas chamber.**—Using the spanner, unscrew the *gas chamber*.

17. 14th, **Barrel mouthpiece.**—Using the spanner, un-screw the *barrel mouthpiece.* This has a left-handed thread and must be turned as when screwing up an ordinary screw.

When a *flash eliminator* is fitted, the *projections* on the *locking collar* which engage with the *eliminator* must be pressed upwards before the *eliminator* can be unscrewed.

18. 15th, **Radiator** :—

(a) Using the *jack screw,* withdraw the *barrel* from the *radiator.*

(b) If the *jack screw* is not available, use a *wooden drift* to drive the *barrel* out of the *radiator* to the rear. This operation is facilitated if the *radiator* is first heated with boiling water. The utmost care must be taken to avoid damaging the *muzzle* of the *barrel.*

For the method of using the *jack screws, see* Appendix II, Section 3 (5).

19. 16th, **Band.**—When the *barrel* comes away, the *band* is left in the *radiator* and can be removed.

20. **To assemble the gun.**— *Reverse the operations.*

21. In replacing the *barrel* and *radiator* in the *rear casing* great care must be taken to avoid damaging the *projections* on the rear face of the *barrel.* Similar care must be exercised in replacing screwed portions, particularly the *gas chamber, cylinder* and *barrel mouthpiece.*

22. When it is not found possible to screw the *body* home to position by hand, it should be assembled only by the armourer, who will use his raw-hide mallet and strike the *body* on the right side, near the bottom joint of the *locking piece.*

23. When assembling the *clamp ring* with the *No.* 2 *screw* place the *clamp ring* on *rear radiator casing*, and insert the lower part of the *flange* of the *front radiator casing* into the recess in *clamp ring*. Then press the upper part into place, keeping the *slot* in the *casing* in line with the *stud* under the *foresight block*. See that the *clamp ring* lies evenly around the *flanges* on the *radiator casings* ; then tighten the *screw* until there is no perceptible shake.

24. Before replacing the *bolt*, see that the *feed arm* is over to the left, in order to allow the *feed arm actuating stud* to engage ; also see that the rear end of the *ejector* is clear.

104. *Stripping component parts.*

1. To remove an **extractor**, raise the *hook* until the *stud* is clear of the *recess in the bolt*, and push the *extractor* out. Take care not to strain the *extractor* by lifting it more than is necessary. The *Mark* III *extractor* is removed in a similar manner, the *spring* being subsequently removed by pressing the point of a bullet between the end of the *slot in the bolt* and the *groove* in the end of the *spring*, and then withdrawing the latter.

2. To remove the **magazine stop pawls**, force the *stud* on the *pawls spring* out of its seating and lift the *pawls* off their *studs*. Note that the *studs* and *pawls* are marked 1 and 2, so as to ensure that they are reassembled in the right order.

3. To remove the **feed arm pawl** and **spring**, press the *pawl* towards the *spring*, and raise.

4. To remove the **cartridge guide**, press the *stud* down and slide it out.

5. To remove the **ejector**, raise the rear end of the *ejector cover*, and slide it to the rear. With the *bolt* half way to the rear, and the *feed arm* to the right, raise the *ejector* by placing the nose of a bullet in the hole which is provided for this purpose on the left underside of the *body* below the *ejector*. Lift the *ejector* out.

6. To strip the *pinion group*, press the *pinion pawl* to lower the tension on the *return spring*, then remove the *tension screw*; withdraw the *return spring*, and then remove the *hub*. With a *punch*, knock out the *pinion pawl axis pin*, and remove the *pinion pawl* and *spring*.

7. To strip the *trigger* and *sear*.—With a *punch*, knock out the *trigger* and *sear axis pin*, and remove the *trigger* and *sear*, taking care not to lose the *plunger* or *spring*.

Notes for Instructors.

1. **Preliminary**.—This subject should be dealt with under two distinct headings :—

    i. *Stripping necessary in order* to clean the gun and to keep it in good order.

    ii. *Stripping the component parts* which might break when firing, so that they may be exchanged for spare parts quickly. Only those parts which it is absolutely necessary to move should be stripped when changing a damaged part.

2. Sequence of lessons :—

    i. Stripping and replacing each part as far as the removal of the *body* from the *barrel*.

    ii. Practice.

    iii. Stripping and replacing each part as far as the *gas chamber*.

iv. Practice.

v. Stripping component parts.

Subjects.—A sequence is necessary during the early lessons in stripping the *body* and *barrel* groups, so that the reasons for certain precautions may be impressed upon the man. When, however, he becomes proficient it does not greatly matter in which order the parts are removed, provided that there is no chance of the gun being damaged.

Sequence of Stripping.

I.—**Body group.**—*Butt, cover, feed arm, pistol grip* drawn back and the *pinion casing* removed, *bolt* drawn back and the *cocking handle* removed, *bolt* and *piston rod, pistol grip, body locking pin* and *body.*

II.—**Barrel Group.**—*Clamp ring, front radiator casing, bipod, gas regulator key and regulator, rear radiator casing, cylinder and gas chamber, barrel mouthpiece.*

Except as an original demonstration by the instructor, the barrel should only be removed if it is necessary to change it.

III.—**Component parts.**—These include the *cartridge guide, ejector* and *extractors, pinion* from its *casing, feed arm actuating stud, feed arm pawl* and *spring, stop pawls* and *spring.*

The stripping of the *pinion pawl*, the *trigger* and *sear* should be shown as a demonstration only by the instructor.

The *striker, butt catch* and *spring* should only be removed by a qualified armourer.

Special Notes.

1. The greatest value will be gained from the instruction by allowing the man to try to remove certain parts without any assistance. The instructor should not interfere except

to prevent damage to the gun or offer suggestions if the man finds his task difficult or impossible.

2. Each part of the gun should be removed and replaced in turn by the whole section before going on to the next. For each part, a different man should be selected as the first to attempt it.

Kit required.—Gun complete with spare parts.

105. *Cleaning the gun.*

1. **When a screw thread is found to have seized, no attempt should be made to unscrew the part by force. The joint should be thoroughly soaked in mineral ːrning oil** (paraffin), **which will loosen it.***

2. **When to clean the barrel.**—When ball ammunition has been fired, daily cleaning of the *barrel* is necessary for at least ten days afterwards.

3. Subsequent cleaning must depend on the discretion of the officer in charge of the gun ; in a dry climate once a week should be sufficient, but in situations where a *barrel* is exposed to a moist atmosphere daily cleaning may be necessary.

4. **The gas chamber must be cleaned** with the same frequency as the *barrel.* In order to avoid loosening the joint between the *gas chamber* and the *barrel* by constant stripping, the *gas chamber* will not be removed but will be cleaned while in position on the *barrel.*

5. The *gas cylinder*, the *gas regulator* and the *piston rod* will also be cleaned with the same frequency as the *barrel.*

---

* G.S. lubricating oil only is to be used for lubricating purposes. Where mineral burning oil is used either separately or mixed with G.S. lubricating oil for cleaning and other purposes, it must be thoroughly removed and the parts dried before the G.S. oil is applied.

6. After cleaning, all parts must be left lightly coated with G.S. oil

7. **How to clean the barrel.**—Normally the gun should be stripped in order to clean the *barrel*. If it is impracticable to strip the gun, proceed as follows :—

    i. Pull the *cocking handle* back until the *sear* engages.

    ii. Place a piece of flannelette, about 4 inches by 1½ inches, in the *eye* of the *cleaning rod, taking care to surround the metal of the cleaning rod with the flannelette*, which must be well oiled.

    iii. Insert the *rod* into the *muzzle* and pass it up and down the *bore* until all fouling has been removed.

    iv. Then replace the oily flannelette with dry pieces and pass through.

    v. Finally pass freshly oiled pieces through, leaving the *barrel* well oiled with G.S. oil.

Note.—If the flannelette is tight and is pushed through the breech it must be reversed before pulling it back, otherwise it will jam.

8. If the *chamber* has not been properly cleaned by the above process, remove the *butt*, draw back the *pistol grip* sufficiently far to release the *pinion*, and remove the *piston rod* and *bolt*. Then place a larger piece of flannelette in the *front eye* of the *cleaning rod*, insert the rod from the *breech* end and clean the *chamber*, first with oiled and then with dry flannelette.

9. **Method of using the double pull-through.**

    i. If rust or metallic fouling is present in the *barrel,* remove the *body*.

    ii. Thoroughly oil the gauze on the pull-through, and drop the *weight* through the *bore* from the *breech.*

    iii. Ensure that the *barrel* is held horizontally, and then, with the assistance of another man, pull the cord backwards and forwards until the rust or fouling is loosened.

    iv. The *barrel* can now be cleaned with the cleaning rod and flannelette as already described.

10. When the gauze fits too loosely to clean the *grooves* of the *rifling*, its diameter can be increased by inserting narrow strips of flannelette under each side. When the gauze is worn out it should be replaced by one of the spare pieces.

11. To clean the gas cylinder.

    i. Join up the *cylinder cleaning rod* and screw on to it the *wire brush.*

    ii. Insert the rod into the *gas cylinder* and work it backwards and forwards a few times.

    iii. Then remove the *wire brush,* replace it with the *mop,* and clean the *cylinder.* Care should be taken that the extreme front end of the *cylinder* is reached by the brush and thoroughly cleaned, for it is at this point that the fouling collects most thickly.

11. If the *cylinder* is found to be a very tight fit on the *gas chamber*, no attempt should be made to force it, but the joint should be first saturated with " oil, mineral, burning " (paraffin) for a time to loosen the rust. On no account should emery be employed to clean the *cylinder*, as this would enlarge the *bore*, and so cause an excessive leakage of gas beyond the *piston head.*

12. **To clean the mechanism.**—A mixture of equal parts of G.S. oil and mineral burning oil should be used. If any parts are clogged with dried oil, mineral burning oil (paraffin)

should be used to remove it. After cleaning each part it should be thoroughly dried and slightly oiled with G.S. oil. Very little oil should be used for this purpose, as it is apt to catch the dust and clog. A little oil should be applied to the *magazine catch*, and round the exterior of the *centre disc*.

The exterior of the gun and the exterior and interior of the *magazines* should be rubbed over with a slightly oiled rag. Any excess of oil in the interior of the *magazine* is likely to be carried into the *chamber* and clog it.

106. *Protection of the gun from the effects of gas attacks.* (Chlorine gas only : mustard gas does not affect the gun.)

1. The gun must be kept carefully cleaned and well oiled with G.S. oil.

2. The effects of corrosion on ammunition are even more serious than the direct effect of gas upon the gun. *Magazines* should be kept in some form of box, the joints of which can be made gastight by inserting strips of flannelette.

3. Occasional short bursts of fire will lessen the chance of guns jamming from the action of gas during a gas attack.

4. After a gas attack the gun must be cleaned and re-oiled at once. At the first available opportunity it should be stripped, and all working parts cleaned in boiling water containing a little soda.

NOTES FOR INSTRUCTORS.

Sequence of lesson—
    I.—Daily cleaning of the *mechanism* and of the *barrel* when necessary.

    II.—Cleaning after firing.

    III.—Use of the *double pull-through* to remove fouling.

IV.—Cleaning *magazines.*

V.—Protection of gun from the effects of gas.

Kit required.—Gun, spare parts, cleaning accessories.

107. *Points to be attended to before firing.*

1. Examine the gun to see that no part is deficient, and that the mechanism works freely.

2. Remove the oil, and examine the *bore* to see that there is no obstruction in it.

3. Thoroughly oil, with G.S. oil, all working parts and surfaces of the mechanism which lie within the *body*, especially the *cam slot* and exterior of the *bolt*, and the *striker post* on the *piston rod*. In order to avoid fouling or smoke, which would disclose the gun position, parts which lie in front of the *body* should have the oil removed from them.

4. Having replaced the parts in the gun, test the weight of the *return spring* (and spare *return spring*) by applying the *spring balance* to the *cocking handle*, which must be in the forward position. The weight required to move the handle should, in normal circumstances, be from 13 to 15 lbs. This should be tested when the *gas cylinder* and *piston head* are clean.

The weight specified is that which is required to hold the *cocking handle* steady just after it has started to move back.

5. **To alter the tension of the spring**, remove the *butt* and draw the *trigger guard* back sufficiently far to disengage it from the *pinion casing*.

(*a*) **To increase the tension of the spring**—

    i. Press up the *pinion casing* with the left hand to keep the *pinion* in engagement with the *rack*, and draw back the *cocking handle.*

    ii. When the *cocking handle* has been drawn back to such
        a distance as will give the required increase of
        tension, allow the *pinion casing* to drop so that the
        pinion is out of engagement with the *rack*.

    iii. Then push the *cocking handle* fully forward, raise the
        pinion casing, slide forward the *trigger guard*.

    iv. Replace the *butt*.

  (*b*) **To decrease the tension of the spring—**

    i. Allow the *pinion casing* to fall so that the *pinion* is
      not engaged with the *rack*, and draw back the
      cocking handle.

    ii. When the *cocking handle* has been drawn back to such
      a distance as will give the required decrease of
      tension, press up the *pinion casing* with the left
      hand to engage the *pinion* of the *rack*, and slide
      forward the *trigger guard*.   This action will cause
      the *cocking handle* to fly forward.

    iii. Replace the *butt*.

6. Place an empty *magazine* on the gun and work the
cocking handle to see that the *feed mechanism* is working correctly.

7. Before filling, examine each *magazine* to see that the
separating pegs are not broken or bent, and spin the *magazine*
on the *loading handle* to ascertain that the *pan* is not distorted,
and that it rotates freely.

8. See that the *magazines* are carefully loaded. If the
cartridges jam while passing into the *magazine*, the latter
should be emptied and examined to ascertain the cause.

9. See that all the spare parts and tools are in the *spare
parts bag* and *gun chest* respectively.

10. See that the *oil can*, the *oil bottle* in the *butt*, and where it is fitted, the *oil receptacle* in the *spade handle grip*, are full of oil.

11. Examine the *field mount*, and see that the *legs* are stopped effectively when in their forward position.

12. See that the *gun, magazine,* and *spare parts bag* are properly secured to avoid loss or damage in transit.

108. *Points to be attended to during firing.*

1. The *magazines* should be kept in their pouches or *carriers* until they are required, and empty *magazines* should be replaced in the *carrier* as soon as possible. Great care should be taken to prevent any damage or distortion of the *rim* of the *magazine* which would cause a fault in the *feed,* and also to avoid the entry of dirt or grit into the *bullet grooves* in the *centre block*.

2. During a temporary cessation of fire, if time permits, the gun should be unloaded, and the *bolt* and *striker post* oiled. The weight of the *spring* should be tested and any necessary adjustment made. The *spring* tends to lose strength as it becomes heated. It should not in normal circumstances be allowed to fall below 12 lbs., otherwise the violence of the backward movement is likely to break the moving parts.

3. A partially emptied *magazine* should be replaced by a full one when fire ceases temporarily. Empty or partially empty *magazines* must be filled without delay, provided ammunition is available.

4. In cold weather the amount of oil used for lubrication should be reduced to a minimum, as it is likely to congeal, and affect the working of the mechanism.

5. When the gun ceases firing, and on opening the breech it is found that a cartridge case has been withdrawn from the *chamber*, the case must be carefully examined to see if the propellant has been ignited ; if not, the bullet will most likely be found in the *bore* near the *breech end*, and should be removed by means of the *cleaning rod* inserted from the *muzzle*. In all cases the *reflector mirror* should be used to see that the *bore* is clear before firing is resumed.

109. *Points to be attended to after firing.*

Immediately after firing.

1. See that the gun is unloaded (*see* Vol. II., Sec. **11, 4**).

2. See that the *bore* and *chamber*, and also the *gas cylinder* and *piston rod* are well oiled immediately firing has finished.

3. See that the *return spring* is eased. The *cocking handle* will be in its forward position when this has been done.

4. See that any live cartridges which may be among the empty cases are collected.

On return to quarters.

5. See that the gun is thoroughly cleaned, without delay. All parts of the *mechanism*, as well as the *magazines*, must be examined at the same time to see that they are in good order.

6. See that any repairs to the gun which may be necessary are carried out by the armourer, and that the unserviceable parts which have been replaced from the spares are exchanged for serviceable parts from store to complete the spare equipment.

7. Reduce the weight of the *return springs* to about 4 lbs.

MECHANISM AND STOPPAGES.

110. *Mechanism, gas and spring.*

A.—Action of the gas.

1. When a round is fired the gases force the bullet up the *bore*, and when it has passed the *gas vent* in the *barrel* a portion of the gases rush with great force through the *vent* into the *gas chamber*, and thence through the *hole* in the *gas regulator* on to the *head* of the *piston rod*, driving it back.

2. The *rack* on the *piston rod* rotates the *pinion* and so winds the *return spring*.

3. During the first $1\frac{1}{4}$ inches of travel the *bolt* and the *feed arm* remain stationary, but then the right side of the *striker post*, working against the face of the *cam slot* in the *bolt*, rotates the *bolt* to the left so that the *lugs* are clear of their *recesses* in the *body* and in line with the *guide grooves*.

4. The *rear* of the *striker post* then comes against the *rear end* of the *slot* and the further backward travel of the *piston rod* carries back the *bolt*.

5. As the *bolt* moves back, the *extractors* withdraw the empty cartridge case from the *chamber*.

6. The *boss* on the *feed arm actuating stud*, working in the *groove* in the underside of the *feed arm*, carries the latter over to the left.

7. The *feed arm pawl*, which is engaged behind one of the *projections* of the *magazine pan*, carries the *magazine pan*

around with it, and a cartridge is thereby forced down the slope in the *magazine centre block* until the bullet is free, when it drops into the *cartridge opening* in the *feed arm*.

8. The *tongue* of the *body cover* ensures that a cartridge is made to fall clear of the *centre block* of the *magazine* if it does not drop by its own weight.

9. The cartridge is then carried to the left by the *separating pegs* and the *indentations* of the *magazine*, aided by the right side of *cartridge opening* in the *feed arm*, until it reaches the *cartridge opening* in the *body*, by which time it has been forced under the *cartridge guide*, and is clear of the *pegs* and *indentations* of the *magazine*.

10. During this motion the *spring retaining stud* on the *feed arm* passes over to the left and releases the pressure on the *No.* 2 *right stop pawl*, which is then pressed forward by its *spring* and engages the *magazine*. This prevents the *magazine* rotating too far.

11. When the *lug* on the left side of the *feed arm actuating stud* reaches the *tail* of the *ejector* it forces it out of the *bolt way*, thus forcing the *head* into the *bolt way* and ejecting the empty cartridge case.

12. As the end of the travel of the *piston rod* is neared, the *bent* in rear of the *rack* rides over the *nose of the sear*, depressing it.

13. When the *bent* has passed, the *nose of the sear* rises by the influence of the *trigger spring*.

14. The *rod* and the *bolt* now come up against the *butt cap* and can go no further back.

15. The *feed arm* has then been brought over the *cartridge opening* in the top of the *body* into which the *cartridge* has been forced by *cartridge guide*.

16. The *No.* 1 *left stop pawl*, which has been pressed back by the rotation of the *magazine*, springs forward again and is ready to prevent any rotation of the *magazine* in a contrary direction.

17. During the whole of the backward movement of the *piston rod* the *rack* has caused the rotation of the *pinion* and consequent tension on the *return spring*.

B.—Action of the return spring.

18. The actions caused by the force of the gas cease when the *piston rod* is arrested in its backward travel. The *spring* then comes into play and moves the *piston rod* forward until the *bent* is caught and held up by the *nose of the sear*.

19. If the *trigger* is now pressed, the *nose of the sear* is lowered and released from contact with the *bent* of the *piston rod*. The *return spring* coming into play rotates the *pinion*, thus forcing the *piston rod* forward.

20. The *striker post* now being lodged in the *recess* at the rear of the *slot in the bolt*, and the *bolt* not being allowed to turn by reason of the *guide grooves* in which the *lugs* work, the *bolt* is carried forward with the *piston rod*. The *feed arm actuating stud* is carried forward with the *bolt*, forcing the *feed arm* over to the right.

21. During this movement the *feed arm pawl* passes over the *projection* on the *magazine pan* and engages behind it, whilst the *spring retaining stud* on the *feed arm* presses back the *No.* 2 *right stop pawl* out of the path of the *magazine*.

22. The *No.* 1 *left stop pawl* prevents the *magazine* from rotating backwards during this movement.

23. During the forward movement of the *bolt* the *top extractor* meets the base of the cartridge in position in the *feed way* and pushes it into the *chamber*. The *cartridge guide*, the *cartridge stop*, and the *small depression* on the *feed arm* control the cartridge during the movement.

24. The front of the *bolt* pushes the *head* of the *ejector* out of the *bolt way* and the *tail* swings in.

25. The *extractors* spring over the rim of the cartridge when it is home in the *chamber*; the *bolt*, which is now fully forward, has its *lugs* clear of the *grooves* and is able to turn, and the *striker post*, bearing on the *cammed portion* of the left side of the slot, rotates the *bolt* to the right and causes the *lugs* to turn into the *locking recesses* in the *body*, thus locking the *bolt*.

26. The *piston* still continues to travel forward, and carries the point of the *striker* on to the cap of the cartridge, igniting the charge.

C.—Continuous fire.

27. If pressure is maintained on the *trigger* the *nose of the sear* is kept depressed, and there is nothing to prevent the *piston rod* and *bolt* flying forward, so that the backward and forward movement, with the firing of a cartridge at the end of each forward movement, is not interrupted until the *trigger* is released or the *magazine* is empty.

28. When the *trigger* is released, the *nose of the sear* rises, and so intercepts the *bent* in the rear of the *rack* the next time

it is moving forward and holds the *piston rod* and *bolt* in their backward position.

D.—To apply the safety catch.

29. Should it at any time be necessary to apply the *safety catch* with the *cocking handle* in the fired or cocked positions, press up the *safety catch plate* on the side on which the *cocking handle* is, until the *recess* on the *plate* passes over the *shank* of the *handle* and prevents any movement of the moving portions of the mechanism.

Note.—The *plate* on the side opposite to the *cocking handle* should always be kept raised to prevent the entry of dirt into the *body*.

30. *To disengage the safety catch.*—Press down the *plate* until the *recess* is clear of the *cocking handle*. If the *trigger* has been pressed while the *plate* is up, it will be necessary to pull back the *cocking handle* to disengage the *shank* from the *undercut* in the rear *recess*.

NOTES FOR INSTRUCTORS.

1. **Preliminary.**—Knowledge of the mechanical actions caused by the two forces " gas " and " spring " is the foundation of a man's line of thought in detecting the cause of any stoppages and so grasping the action necessary to remedy it.

2. He must, therefore, have a clear mental picture of the mechanical actions caused by each of these forces.

Although aids to establish this picture in the man's mind, such as models, cut guns, diagrams and cinema pictures, are a great help, a good instructor can show it quite clearly by using a gun with certain removable parts detached.

Sequence of lesson.

Gas :—

    I. How a portion of the gases operate the *piston rod*.

    II. The way in which the *rack* puts tension on to the *return spring*.

    III. The *striker post* unlocks the *bolt* and moves it back.

    IV. The *feed arm actuating stud* moves the *feed arm* to the left.

Spring :—

    V. How the *return spring* actuates the *piston rod*.

    VI. The *striker post* carries forward and locks the *bolt*.

    VII. How the *feed arm* is moved over to the right.

    VIII. How the *bent* of the *piston rod* is caught by the *nose of the sear*.

    IX. On pressing the *trigger*, how the *nose of the sear* is released from the *bent* of the *piston rod*.

Kit required.—Gun, spare piston, spare pinion group, spare gas cylinder.

111. *Stoppages.*

1. It is essential to train men to remedy stoppages in the automatic action of the gun when firing. The aim must be to teach the men to detect the cause of the stoppage quickly and to rectify it without delay.

2. Some causes of stoppages will occur with marked frequency whilst others may never occur within the experience of numerous individuals. For training purposes, therefore, the causes of stoppages can be considered in two categories— (*a*) **Probable**; (*b*) **Possible**.

[*To face page* 304.

PLATE 72.—GUN ASSEMBLED FOR TEACHING, "Gas AND Spring."

3. The greater part of the instruction in stoppage remedying must be devoted to ensure speedy and correct action in dealing with probable causes, whilst only a limited proportion of the available time should be spent on possible causes.

4. A large proportion of stoppages are remedied by certain actions on the part of the firer which can be learnt as a drill and carried out instinctively whenever the gun stops firing. These actions are termed " Immediate Action," and the stoppages cured by their employment are classified as " Immediate Action Stoppages," whilst those which require a further action for their remedy are classified as " Additional Stoppages."

Whenever a stoppage occurs the first action on the part of the firer must always be to perform " Immediate Action."

5. For the purpose of grouping stoppages, three distinct categories are obtained from the position of the *cocking handle* when the gun stops, viz. :—

A " first position " stoppage is one which occurs when the *cocking handle* is forward.

A " second position " stoppage is one which occurs when the *cocking handle* is over the *thumb piece* of the *safety catch*.

A " third position " stoppage is one which occurs when the *cocking handle* is behind the *thumb piece* of the *safety catch*.

6. When a stoppage necessitates stripping to change any part of the gun *it must be cleared of rounds beforehand*.

7. The use of the strap of the *spare parts bag*, or the *double pull-through* will sometimes be necessary to enable the firer to pull back the *cocking handle*, **but in no case may the** *cocking handle* **be hammered back.**

STOP

This TABLE should be read from left to right in each horizontal the remedy shown in the horizontal column next below will be tried.

(Whenever the gun stops firing, with the *trigger* pressed, the first

If the *cocking handle* is in the 1*st position* :—			
A. TRY TO RO-TATE THE MAGAZINE.	If the *magazine* rotates.	**CHANGE THE MAGAZINE, RELOAD, RE-LAY AND FIRE.**	—
B.	If the *magazine* does not rotate.	**PULL BACK THE COCKING HANDLE, RE-LAY AND FIRE.**	—
C.	—	If on pressing the *trigger*, gun does not fire,	**CHANGE THE MAGAZINE, RELOAD, RE-LAY AND FIRE.**
D.	—	—	If on pressing the *trigger*, gun still does not fire,
E.	—	—	—
F.	—	If on pressing the *trigger*, gun fires one round and stops again in the 1st position,	UNLOAD, CHANGE THE LEFT STOP PAWL, RELOAD, RELAY AND FIRE.

PAGES.

column, A., B., &c. If the remedy given does not cure the stoppage,
Thus the table will be read across and down the page diagonally.
action of the firer is to feel for the position of the *cocking handle*.)

A. —	—	**Cause :**—Empty *magazine.*
B. —	- -	**Cause :**—Missfire.
C. —	—	**Cause :**—Damaged *magazine.*
D. UNLOAD AND TEST THE FEED ARM PAWL OR FEED ARM PAWL SPRING TO SEE IF BROKEN. If either is defective :—	CHANGE IT, REASSEMBLE, RELOAD, RELAY AND FIRE.	**Cause :**—Damaged *feed arm pawl* or *spring.*
E. If neither is defective :—	CHANGE THE PISTON ROD, REASSEMBLE, RELOAD, RELAY AND FIRE.	**Cause :**—Broken *striker.*
F. —	—	**Cause :**—*Left stop pawl* worn.

If the *cocking hand le* is in the. *2nd posi ion* :—			
G. **PULL BACK THE COCK-ING HANDLE, RELOAD, RELAY AND FIRE.**	—	—	—
H.	If the gun fires a few rounds and stops again in the 2nd position.	UNLOAD, STRIP DOWN, CLEAN AND OIL. If it is undesirable to delay for the prolonged period required for this remedy, try the following expedients :— (*a*) Unload, lower the tension of the *return spring* by about 3 lb., reload, relay and fire. (*b*) If the stoppage recurs, unload and oil without stripping the gun, reload, relay and fire. If these expedients are tried the gun must be stripped, cleaned and oiled at the first opportunity, and the tension of the *return spring* readjusted to normal.	—
I.	If on pressing the *trigger*, the gun does not fire,	UNLOAD WITHOUT FIRING, CALL FOR THE CLEARING PLUG AND REMOVE THE PORTION OF CASE IN THE BARREL, RELOAD, RELAY AND FIRE.	
If the cocking han dle is in the *3r d position* :—			
K. **PULL BACK THE COCK-ING HAND-DLE, RE-LAY AND FIRE.**	—	—	—

G. —	—	**Cause** :—Hard extraction.
H. —	—	**Cause** :—Friction due to dirt in the *gas cylinder, body* or *chamber.*
I. —	—	**Cause** :—Separated case.
K. —	—	**Cause** :—Slight fault in feed.

L.	If the gun fires a few rounds and stops again in the 3rd position.	**PULL BACK THE COCKING HANDLE, REMOVE THE MAGAZINE, FIRE THE ROUND IN THE FEEDWAY, CHANGE THE CARTRIDGE GUIDE, RELOAD, RELAY AND FIRE.**	—
M.	If on pressing the *trigger*, gun does not fire.	PULL BACK THE COCKING HANDLE AND REMOVE THE MAGAZINE. If there are 2 rounds trying to be fed into the gun,	REMOVE THE TOP ONE, CHANGE THE MAGAZINE, RELAY AND FIRE.
		If this stoppage recurs,	UNLOAD AND CHANGE THE RIGHT STOP PAWL.
N.	—	If the feeding is normal,	EXAMINE THE EJECTION OPENING AND CHAMBER. If there is an empty case in the *chamber* and a live round in the feedway.

L. —	—	**Cause :**—Weak *cartridge guide spring.*
M. --	—	**Cause :**— *Magazine* rotated too far owing to the *magazine* being slightly damaged.
—	---	**Cause :**—*Right stop pawl* failing to stop *magazine* rotating too far.
N. UNLOAD WITHOUT FIRING, CHANGE THE BOLT, REASSEMBLE, RELOAD, RELAY AND FIRE.	—	**Cause :**—Broken *extractor.*

0.	—	—	If there is an empty case lying in the bottom of the *bolt-way*, with a live round in the *feed-way*,

Note.—If a stoppage has been caused by a breakage of some part, the broken to stop in any position and prevent the *cocking handle* from being moved. and then pull back the *cocking handle* before trying to clear the gun.

SOME POSSIBLE STOPPAGES.

Any position, i.e., the *cocking handle* may be in the 1st, 2nd or 3rd position, and no weight felt on the *return spring.*	CHANGE THE PINION GROUP.	**Cause :**—Broken *return spring.*
3rd position	EXAMINE THE EJECTION OPEN-ING AND CHAM-BER.	—
If there is only one round in the *feedway* and nothing in the *chamber,*	CLEAR GUN, CHANGE THE CARTRIDGE GUIDE, RE-LOAD, RELAY AND FIRE.	**Cause :**—Broken *cartridge guide*

If on reassembling the gun it is found impossible to load, remove the *magazine* and correctly reassemble the *stop pawls* or the *ejector cover.*

    Cause :—*Stop pawls* wrongly assembled or *ejector cover* not quite home.

O. CLEAR GUN, CHANGE THE EJECTOR, RE-ASSEMBLE, RELOAD, RELAY AND FIRE.	—	Cause :—Broken *ejector*.

part is liable to fall into the *bolt* or *piston way* and so cause the *cocking handle*
In this case it is advisable to turn the gun over and shake it gently
Undue force must not be used to pull back the *cocking handle.*

NOTES FOR INSTRUCTORS.

1. For instructional purposes this subject should be divided into the two distinct parts, *i.e.,* "Immediate Action" and "Additional Stoppages."

2. The instinctive procedure termed "Immediate Action" should be taught first. When the recruit is proficient in performing "Immediate Action," he can be taught the causes of those stoppages which are cured by this "Immediate Action." (These are printed in thick type in the foregoing table.) Then later the recruit comes to the Additional Stoppages, reasoning from the point where the "Immediate Action" failed.

3. It is unnecessary for men to know every detail of the mechanism of the gun, but they require to know the action of certain parts in order to be able to locate the cause of stoppages. Consequently, teaching of mechanism should be confined to that which is concerned with each stoppage taught.

4. The following table gives the mechanism that should be taught with each particular stoppage. (The letters refer to the stoppage given in the preceding table.)

Stoppage.	Mechanism.
C	Action of the *feed arm pawl*.
F	Action of the *left stop pawl*.
G	Action of the *magazine centre block* and feeding of rounds from the *magazine*.
L	Action of the *cartridge guide*, and the control of the round during its forward movement to the *chamber*.
M	Action of the *right stop pawl*.
N	Action of the *extractors* (extraction and feeding).
O	Action of the *ejector*.

5. As the *sights* are thrown off the target when a stoppage is remedied, the instructor should insist on the importance of relaying the gun after every stoppage. To inculcate this procedure he should always give an aiming mark when teaching stoppages and their remedy.

6. Possible stoppages should only be dealt with when the soldier can remedy the probable stoppages efficiently. Moreover, the object of such instruction will rather be to make him thoroughly conversant with the working of the gun under all circumstances, than to teach him definite remedies.

7. In quarters, when teaching stoppages the gun must be set up to simulate what would be the condition of the gun when the stoppage actually occurs (*see* Section 112, Setting up Stoppages).

Kit required.—Gun and spare parts, complete. Dummies, damaged *magazine*, cut dummies, portion of separated case. Instructional landscape target.

112. *Setting up stoppages.*

1. This subject need only be taught to instructors.

2. It is important that the gun should be made to stop under as nearly as possible the same conditions as would occur if firing live ammunition. When the instructor wishes to convey to the firer that " Immediate Action " has failed, he should say " Gun does not fire," or " Gun fires a few rounds and stops again."

3. Some stoppages cannot be set up, but most of the probable ones are easily arranged. The following table is a guide :—

Cause.	In Barracks.	On the Range.
1st Position.		
A.—Empty *magazine*	Use a *magazine* with a single round in it	Occurs automatically.
B.—Missfire ...	Allow the firer to begin firing, and then say "Gun stops"	Place a dummy round in the *magazine*.
C.—Damaged *magazine*	Use a slightly damaged *magazine*	Place 2 dummy rounds in *magazine*.
D.—*Feed arm pawl* or *spring*	Remove the *feed arm pawl* and *spring*	Place 2 dummy rounds in the *magazine*, and one dummy as the first round in the *magazine* used on "changing."
E.—Broken *striker*	As for missfire and when the complete "I.A." has been performed instructor says "Gun still does not fire," and indicates that the *feed arm pawl* is correct	
F.—*Left stop pawl*	As for missfire, and when firer has performed the first "I.A." instructor says, "Gun fires one round and stops again"	Two alternate rounds, with alternate spaces in the *magazine*.

Cause.	In Barracks.	On the Range.
2nd Position. G. & H.—Friction	Withdraw the *cocking handle* to eject the empty case, but not far enough to feed a fresh round	As in barracks.
J.—Separated *case*	Use a portion of a separated case	Ditto.
3rd Position. K. & L.—Slight fault in feed	Press the *trigger*, and allow the *bolt* to go forward gently	As in barracks.
M.—Double feed. *Right stop pawl* defective	When pulling back the *cocking handle* to load, hold the *pawl* back with a thin strip of metal, and rotate the *magazine* until a double feed is caused. The instructor should hold the *magazine* to prevent it from rotating when the *trigger* is pressed	Do not attempt to set up this stoppage unless a decidedly worn *right stop pawl* is available.
N.—Broken *extractor*	Load, and place an empty case in the *chamber*	As in barracks.
O.—Broken *ejector*	Load, and place an empty case in the *bolt way* in front of the *bolt*	Ditto.

NOTES FOR INSTRUCTORS.

Preliminary.—In setting up stoppages, the gun should first of all be firing normally, *i.e.*, the firer should be made to load and fire.

I. The stoppages should be set up while the class, including the firer, have their heads turned away from the gun. Thus,

in " A," the firer loads and fires, thus removing the single
round from the *magazine*. Again, in " N," he loads, fires and,
after pressing the *trigger* to represent a number of bursts,
he should be told to pull back the *cocking handle*, and turn his
head away ; the instructor then inserts the empty case, and
orders the firer to continue firing, saying " Gun stops " when
the *trigger* has been pressed, and " Gun does not fire " when
the " I.A." has been performed.

113. *Examination of the gun.*

1. The following are the principal points to which attention
must be paid in examining the gun. Except for the replacement of damaged parts from the parts provided as spare,
repairs cannot as a rule be carried out by the section. The
repairs, as well as the tests to be made by means of gauges,
will be undertaken only by a qualified armourer.

2. **Barrel.**—See to the condition of *bore, rifling, lead,*
exterior and *gas vent*, and that the *projections* on the rear
face and the thread on the *muzzle* are not damaged. The
barrel should only be removed from the *radiator* for examination at infrequent intervals.

3. **Barrel mouthpiece.**—See that it screws up tightly to
the *barrel*, and that the threads have not been crossed.

4. **Radiator.**—Examine this for indentations in the
flanges, and see that the *barrel* fits properly.

5. **Rear radiator casing.**—Examine this for indentations
and wear, especially at its forward end.

6. **Front radiator casing.**—Examine this for indentations, and that it fits into the *clamp ring* correctly ; *sling
swivel* not too loose.

7. **Clamp ring**.—See that it is firmly screwed up, and that it holds the *front radiator casing* rigidly.

8. **Foresight**.—See that it is in good condition and not loose.

9. **Gas regulator and gas chamber**.—Examine these for erosion and carbon deposit ; see that they are not stuck. If they are, apply a little paraffin at the joint, and allow it to soak in to loosen the fouling or rust.   If fouling has accumulated inside the *regulator*, it should be removed by means of the *gas regulator cleaner*.

See that the *gas chamber* is closely and firmly seated to the barrel ; that the *screw threads* have not been overstrained ; that the *gas holes* are not choked.

10. **Gas cylinder**.—See that the interior is clear of fouling and carbonised oil, and that the rear end is not cracked or split.

Examine the *screw thread* to see that it is not damaged, and the *bore* to see that it is not distorted or excessively enlarged by wear or cleaning.   The examination of the *bore* need only be carried out when loss of gas power has been experienced, and then only by an armourer or artificer, in comparison with a new *gas cylinder*.   It is not necessary for the face of the *gas cylinder* to abut on the *gas chamber,* and overturning is of negligible importance ; enlargement of the *bore*, however, may have serious consequences.   Other important causes of loss of gas power are friction in the *action*, escape at the junction of the *gas chamber* with the *barrel*, choking of the *gas hole* in the *gas chamber* and of the *gas regulator*.

A *cylinder* which is split at the end can be repaired by an armourer by brazing.

11. **Piston rod.**—See that the *fixing pin* joining the *piston rod* and the *rack* is not loose, that the teeth of the *rack* are not damaged, and that the *bent* is not worn or broken.

Examine the *striker post* to see that the working surfaces are not rough. Any roughness must be smoothed by the armourer with fine emery cloth. See that the *striker* is not damaged, and arrange occasionally with the armourer to test with the gauge for protrusion of the *striker point* through the *bolt*.

Examine the *cupped head* and *annular rings* for wear, and see that they form an effective gas check.

12. **Bolt.**—See that the edges of the *cam slot* are smooth. Any roughness must be removed by the armourer with fine emery cloth. The armourer should occasionally test the distance of the *boltface* from the end of the *chamber* with ·064-inch and ·074-inch gauges, removing the *extractors* before using the latter gauge. A *bolt* which closes over the ·074-inch gauge must be retested with a new *barrel*. If it still closes, it should be exchanged. If it passes this test, the worn *barrel* should be exchanged, but not the *bolt*.

13. **Pinion and casing.**—See that the teeth are not damaged or broken, that the *pawl* and its *spring* work correctly, and that the *axis pin* is secure.

14. **Return spring.**—See that it is not broken.

15. **Body.**—Examine this for excessive play in the *bayonet joint*, and at the joint with the *barrel* and *rear radiator casing*. In the latter case a *washer* or *washers* must be assembled, and the cartridge head space then re-tested. See also that the *body* is not fractured.

16. **Pinion casing hinge and pin.**—Examine these for wear.

17. **Safety catch.**—See that the *cocking handle* is securely held when the *safety catch* is raised. This should be tested on both sides of the gun.

18. **Feed arm.**—Examine the *latch* for weakness, the *axis hole* for play on the *magazine post*, the thin portion of the *arm* for bending or strain, the *stud* and *groove* for wear, the top of the *feed arm* for friction against the *ribs* on the *body cover*, the *pawl* for wear and the *spring* for weakness.

19. **Ejector.**—See that it is not broken or damaged.

20. **Body cover.**—See that the *pawls* and *spring* are undamaged, and that the *cartridge guide* is not weakened and is correctly assembled.

21. **Tangent sight.**—See that the *leaf* is not bent, that the *elevating screw* moves the *slide* correctly and is properly held by the *checking spring*, that the *aperture* is not damaged; and that the *fixing screw* of the *sight-bed* is not loose.

22. **Cocking handle.**—See that it is properly held in its slot in the *piston rod.*

23. **Trigger guard.**—See that the *nose of the sear* is not worn or broken. Wear of the *sear nose* or of the *bent on the rack* must be remedied by an armourer. See that the parts work correctly, and that there is no oil or dirt round the *plunger*, which would make the *sear* rise sluggishly.

24. **Butt cap.**—Examine this to see if it has been marked by the *piston rod* during recoil, and for security of fitting.

25. **Moving portions.**—See that they move freely, and that the *feed arm* is properly actuated by the *feed arm actuating stud*. Test the ejection with a few dummy cartridges. Place an empty *magazine* on the gun and, holding it in check by

pressing the left hand on its top, work the *cocking handle* to see that the feed works correctly.

26. **Mounts, Field Mark III.**—Examine the *legs* for wear at the corner. Any excessively worn should be removed and replaced by new ones; the unserviceable ones being returned to store for factory repair.

27. **Magazines.**—Examine thoroughly and test for distortion.

28. **Spare parts and accessories.**—Should be examined in the same manner.

NOTES FOR INSTRUCTORS.

The object of this lesson is to teach the man what to look for when he is examining the gun. He should be taught to examine the gun periodically and especially on taking over a fresh gun.

The gun should be stripped and each part dealt with thoroughly and put on one side before starting on the next part.

Kit required.—Gun complete with spare parts and accessories. Examples of damaged parts such as a bulged barrel, a cut barrel, &c., when these are available.

114. *Spare parts, diagrams and skeleton guns.*

1. The list of **spare parts** is set out in Appendix **II.** Vol. II. All trained Lewis gunners should know what *spare parts* are carried and be able to check for deficiencies without a written list.

2. A complete set of *spare parts* should be shown and packed in the *spare parts* bag by the class under instruction.

3. Lewis gun **diagrams** should be hung on the walls of drill halls and barrack room passages as far as the scale of issue permits.

4. Any points of the mechanism of the gun not fully understood by any of the class should be further demonstrated by means of **diagrams.** The best value is obtained from diagrams if they are so placed that men have access to them out of parade hours.

5. **Skeleton guns** are limited in number, but when obtainable they should be used to clear up any mechanical points which the class may be in doubt about.

115. *Packing of the limber.*

Details of packing limbers, &c., will be found in Appendix VIII.

ANTI AIRCRAFT ACCESSORIES—LEWIS GUN.

116. *Description of sights.*

1. **The backsight** (known as " Sight, back, A.A. Mark II ") is an aperture of $\frac{1}{2}$-inch diameter, fixed in position on the *leaf* of the ground *aperture backsight* of the gun.

2. **The foresight** (known as "Sight, fore, A.A. Mark II ") consists of two elliptical rings, one inside the other, with a bead in the centre, and is capable of being moved along the gun.

3. **The outer ring** gives the necessary "aiming off" for firing at aeroplanes flying at an altitude of 1,000 feet at a speed of 100 miles an hour, and at an angle of sight of 50°.

4. **The inner ring** gives the necessary "aiming off" for firing at aeroplanes flying at an altitude of 200 feet at a speed of 120 miles an hour, and at an angle of sight of 15°.

5. In view of the fact that these three factors are rarely if ever likely to coincide at any one moment, the following general rule is given for the use of the *foresight* :—

(a) For all machines flying at an altitude of between 500 feet and 3,000 feet, use the *outer ring*.

(b) For all machines flying below 500 feet, use the *inner ring*

6. If, in course of time, the average speed of aeroplanes increases beyond those for which the *sights* are calculated, the necessary adjustment can be made by moving the *foresight* along the gun towards the *backsight*, thus decreasing the sight radius.

7. This adjustment will only be made on the authority of an Army Council Instruction or an order by the Commander-in-Chief in the Field, which will lay down the distance that the *foresight* is to be moved.

117. *Method of fixing the sights.*

1. **The backsight** is fixed permanently to the top of the *tangent sight.*

2. It consists of two main portions. The larger portion, which contains the *sighting aperture*, is placed on the graduated side of the *tangent sight leaf*, with the *block* fitting

into the recess at the top of the *leaf.* The *sighting aperture* is kept uppermost. The smaller portion, together with a spring washer on the outside, is placed on the other side of the *leaf,* and the whole is then screwed together.

3. **The foresight** is fixed on to the *rear radiator casing* by a *spring steel ring,* secured by a *vice pin nut.* A *pointer* is attached for aligning with the *foresight* of the gun. *The spring steel ring* should fit closely against the rear edge of the *clamp ring,* and the *vice pin screw* should be on the right side of the gun.

4. **To affix the foresight to the gun.**—Slide the *foresight* over the *front radiator casing,* the *rings* towards the ground, and the *vice pin screw* to the **left** of the gun. Slide the *sight* along the *casing* until it is behind the *clamp ring.* Then twist it round until the *rings* are uppermost. Press it up tight to the *clamp ring* and screw until there is no chance of slipping. When screwed up the *pointer* on the *foresight* should be in exact alignment with the *foresight* on the gun.

5. Great care must be taken in putting on and removing the *foresight* that the *spring steel ring* is not strained in any way.

6. The *foresight* will be kept permanently on the gun. When not in use, it should be folded back flat on the *radiator casing.* When required for use, it should be raised.

118. *Method of using the sights.*

1. The first two rules for aiming with the rifle apply in this case also, namely :—

   i. *Sights* upright.

   ii Close the disengaged eye.

2. The third rule, however, is different, and is divided into three parts, as follows :—

iii. (*a*) The line of flight of the aeroplane, if prolonged, must pass through the *centre bead* of the *foresight.*

(*b*) The nose of the aeroplane must appear to touch the outer edge of whichever *ring* is being used. This junction is known as the " Point of contact."

(*c*) The " Point of contact " must be in the centre of the *A.A. aperture backsight.*

3. Fire should be continuous, and the gun should follow the movements of the aeroplane, the outer edge of the *ring* being kept on the aeroplane, and the *centre bead* on the line of flight.

4. In firing at an aeroplane which is diving directly at the gun, align the centre of the *A.A. aperture backsight* with the *centre bead* of the *foresight*, and aim at the centre of the upper plane of the machine. (*See* Plate 73.)

PLATE 73.

AIMING AT AIRCRAFT.

Plate 74.   [To face page 326.

PLATE 75 (a).

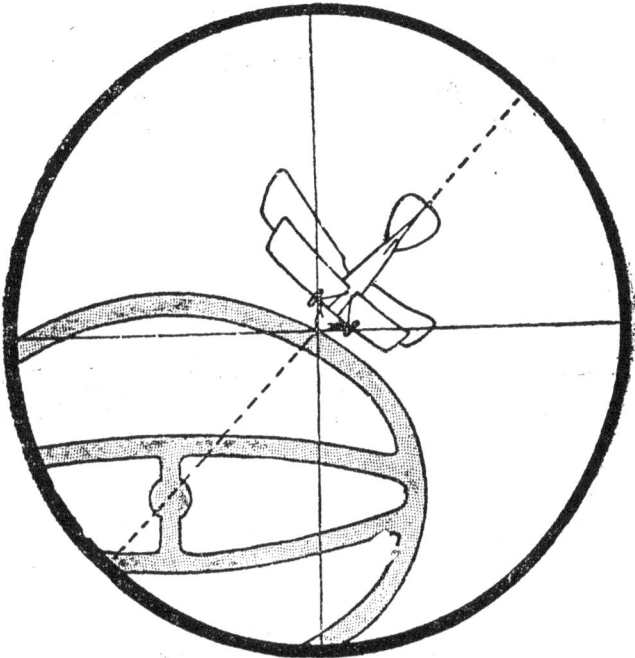

Outer Ring in Use, (Altitude: 500 to 3,000 feet.)

Correct.—The aeroplane is flying towards the centre bead, the nose of the aeroplane is touching the outer edge of the ring being used, and the point of contact between the nose of the aeroplane and the outer edge of the ring is in the centre of the backsight aperture.

PLATE 75 (b).

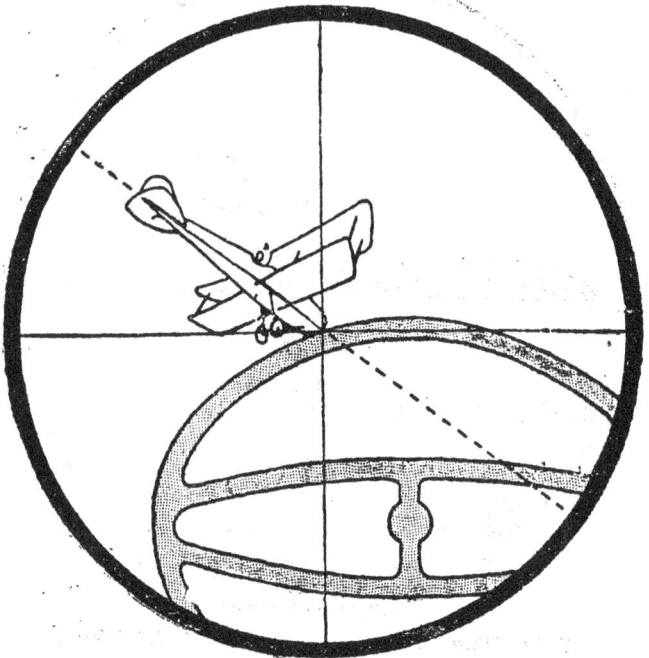

Outer Ring in Use.   (Altitude: 500 to 3,000 feet.)

Incorrect.--The aeroplane is *not* flying towards the centre bead.
The bullets will pass below the target.

Plate 75 (c).

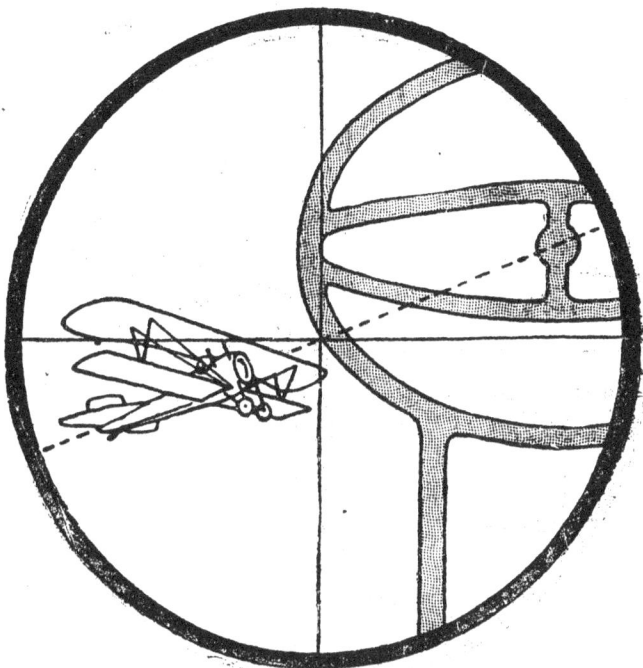

Outer Ring in Use. (Altitude: 500 to 3,000 feet.)

Incorrect.—The nose of the aeroplane is *not* touching the outer edge of the ring. Fire has been opened too soon and the bullets will pass in front of the target.

PLATE 75 (*d*).

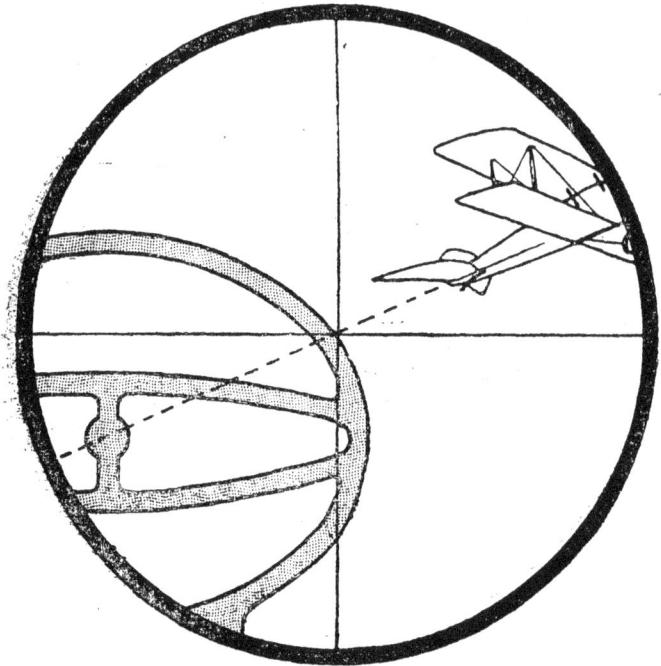

Outer Ring in Use.   (Altitude: 500 to 3,000 feet.)

Incorrect.—The aeroplane is flying *away from* instead of towards the centre bead.   The bullets will pass a long way behind it.

PLATE 75 (e).

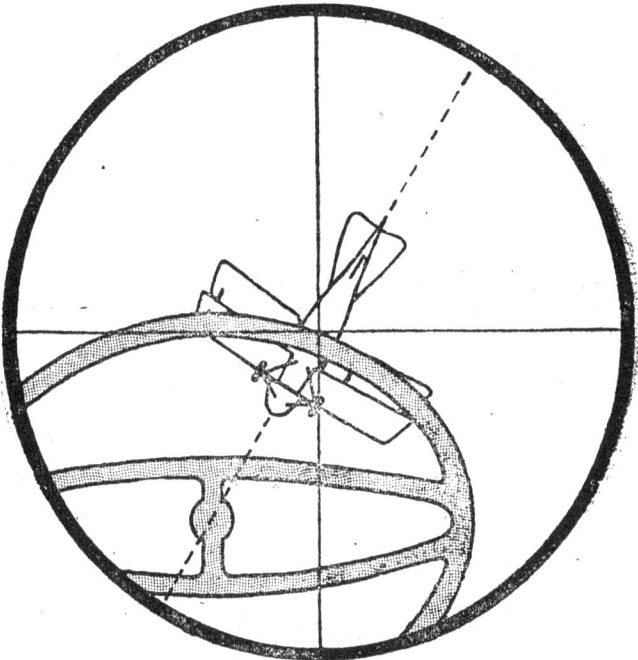

Outer Ring in Use.   (Altitude : 500 to 3,000 feet.)

Incorrect.—The nose of the aeroplane is not touching the outer edge of the ring.   Fire has been opened too late and the bullets will pass behind any vital portion of the aeroplane.

PLATE 75 (*f*).

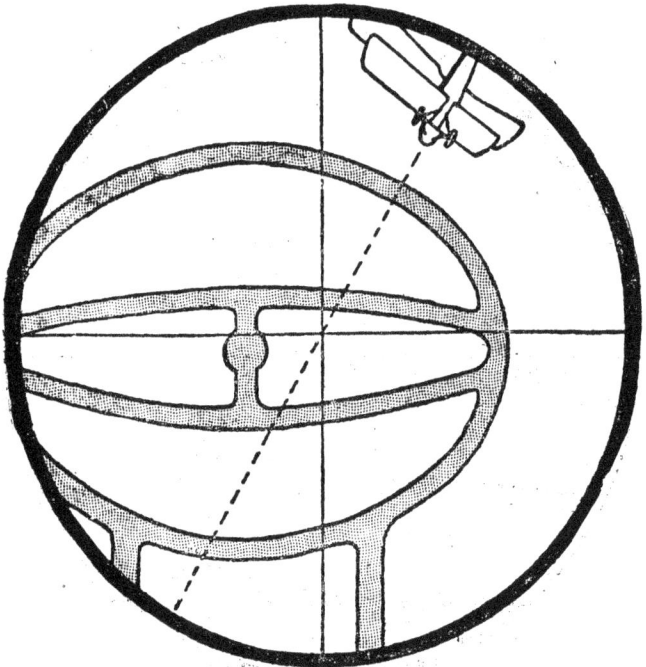

Either Ring in Use.

Incorrect.—The aeroplane is not flying towards the centre bead, the nose is not touching the outer edge of either ring, and the points where the nose of the aeroplane would touch either ring are not in the centre of the backsight. The bullets will pass in front and to the left.

PLATE 75 (g).

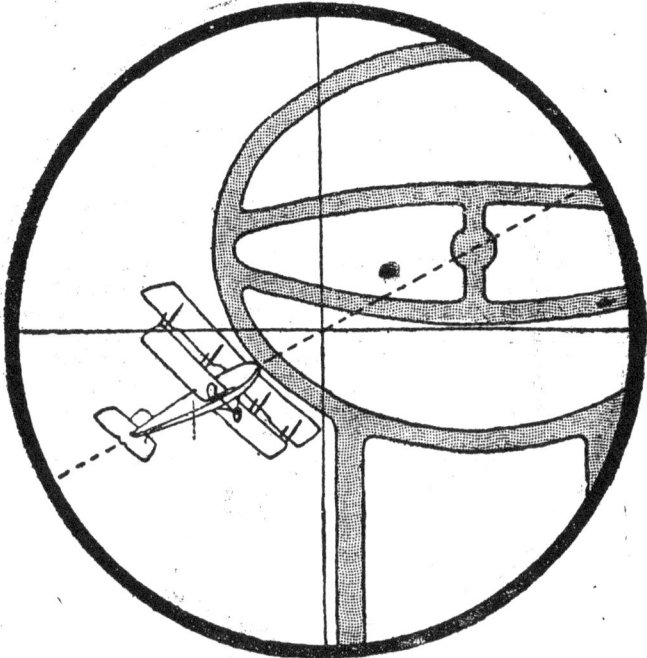

Outer Ring in Use.   (Altitude : 500 to 3,000 feet.)

Incorrect.—The point of contact between the nose of the aeroplane and the outer edge of the ring being used is *not* in the centre of the backsight aperture.   The bullets will pass in rear of the aeroplane.

PLATE 76.

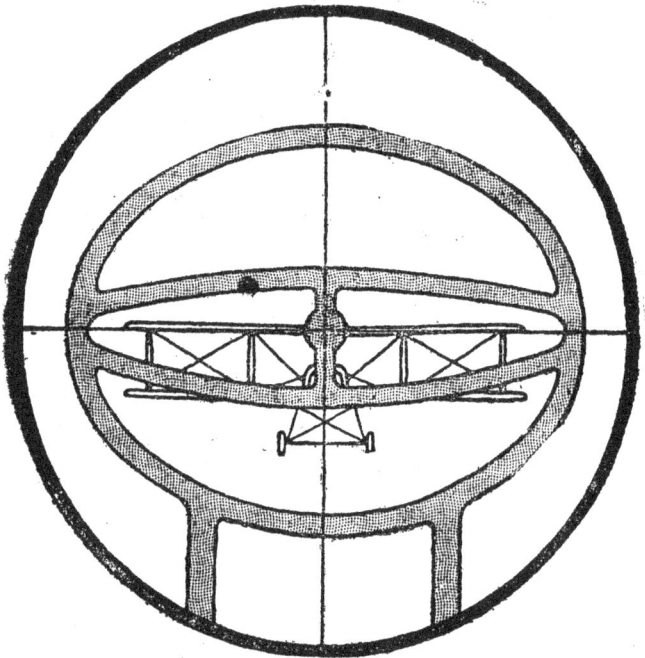

Centre Bead in Use.

Correct.—The aeroplane is diving at the position of the gun. Aim has been taken by aligning the bead with the centre of the backsight aperture upon the middle of the upper plane. The bullets will hit the vital parts of the aeroplane.

PLATE 77 (a).

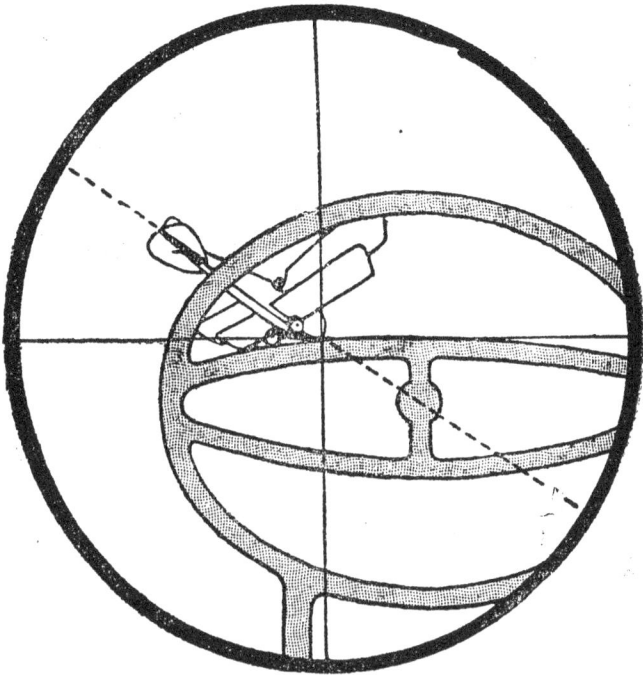

Inner Ring in Use. (Altitude: Up to 500 feet.)

Correct.—The aeroplane is flying towards the centre bead, the nose of the aeroplane is touching the outer edge of the ring being used, and the point of contact between the nose of the aeroplane and the outer edge of the ring is in the centre of the backsight aperture.

PLATE 77 (*b*).

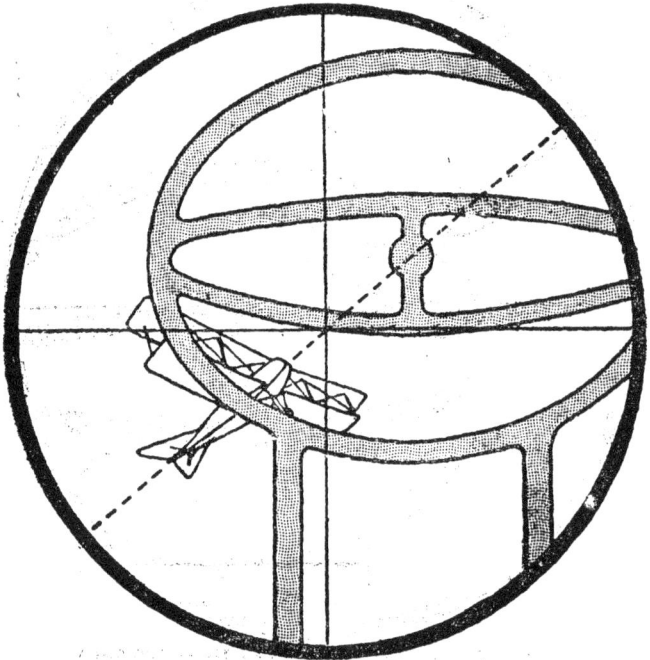

Inner Ring in Use.   (Altitude: Up to 500 feet.)

Incorrect.—The nose of the aeroplane is not touching the outer edge of the ring being used.   The bullets will pass in front of the target.

PLATE 77 (c).

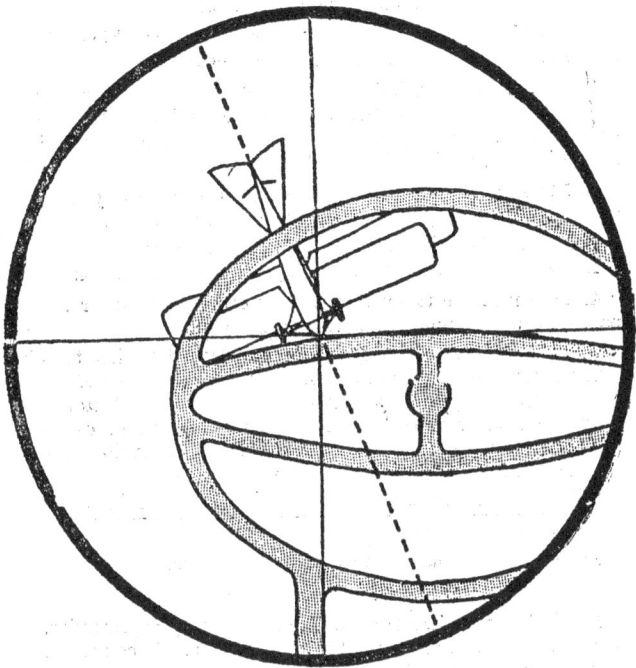

Inner Ring in Use.   (Altitude: Up to 500 feet.)

Incorrect.—The aeroplane is not flying towards the centre bead. The bullets will pass to the right.

119. *Stadia range indicator.*

1. This *indicator* is merely to show whether a machine is in range or not, and not to measure the exact range.

2. It consists of a flat piece of metal with four circular *apertures*—two for the two-seater type, and two for the single-seater. or scout type of aeroplane—and a string 24 inches in length, with a bead at the end.

3. **Method of use.**—Hold the *indicator* as far away from the eye as the string, held against the cheek, will allow.

If the aeroplane fills the *aperture*, it is within range.

If the aeroplane does not fill the *aperture,* it is out of range.

4. Care must be taken to use the correct *aperture* for the particular aeroplane which is to be ranged on.

5. The *indicator* was designed for use against typical two-seater aeroplanes and scouts ; if it is desired to make *apertures* for any special type of aeroplane for which the indicator is unsuitable, the required size of the *apertures* can be easily calculated by means of the following formula, having first ascertained the dimensions of the aeroplane :—

$$\frac{\text{Diameter of aperture}}{\text{Length of string}} = \frac{\text{Span or length of aeroplane}}{\text{Range}}$$

The equation should be worked out in inches.

120. *General remarks on training.*

1. " It is a principle of air defence that every commander, in addition to arranging for the protection of his command from surprise by hostile aircraft, is at all times responsible, whether on the move or at rest, for dealing with hostile aircraft flying over his command at an altitude not exceeding 3,000 feet."—(F.S.R., Vol. II,)

2. In the case of many commanders their only means of dealing with hostile aircraft is by small arms fire from the ground, for which purpose, the Lewis and Hotchkiss guns are the most suitable weapons.

3. The only appliances in addition to the *sights* and *mounting* needed for giving practical instruction in the correct use of the *sights* are a model aeroplane and an aim corrector.

4. Simple model aeroplanes can easily be made ; the following dimensions are advised, as models made in accordance with them will, when held at the correct distance from the gun, give the same appearance as an aeroplane flying at a height of 1,000 feet and an angle of sight of 50°.

		Width of span.	Length of body.
Two-seater type	...	12 inches	7 inches
Scout type ...	...	8 inches	6 inches

The model is held 10 yards from the gun.

5. An *aim corrector* is designed for use with the *A.A. Sights Mark II*. When fitted on the *tangent sight*, it enables the instructor to follow the aim of the firer and correct it if necessary.

6. Two hours should be sufficient for teaching men of average intelligence the use of the *A.A. sights*. Constant practice in aiming is necessary, however, in order that no time may be lost during actual fighting in engaging the target. Every opportunity should be taken of aiming at actual aeroplanes that happen to fly in the vicinity of the parade ground.

7. During the first hour of instruction a stationary model should be used, placed so as to represent any direction of flight, the aim being checked by the instructor with an aim corrector.

8. When the student is proficient in aiming at stationary models he should be practised in aiming at moving models. For this purpose one of the section should walk about, carrying the model aeroplane on the end of a pole. In every case the instructor should check the aim by means of the aim corrector.

9. Methods of training include :—
    (a) Aiming at models on poles, or painted on the ceilings of barrack rooms.
    (b) Firing the anti-aircraft practices of the annual courses.
    (c) The use of cinematograph films, which can be obtained from the Weapon Training Officers of Commands.

121. *Anti-aircraft elementary handling.*

1. The general instructions for ground elementary handling are equally applicable to anti-aircraft training.

2. The sequence is, however, slightly different, and a third "number" is introduced to carry the *mounting*.

3. Ammunition and *spare parts* will be placed on the left of the gun at two paces interval, and the *mounting* at another two paces. The target will be a model aeroplane.

4. On the command " **Take post** "—
    (a) No. 1 takes up his position and examines the gun as in ground elementary handling.
    (b) No. 2 at the same time examines his ammunition and *spare parts*, and hands No. 1 a *magazine*.

(c) No. 3 examines the *mounting* and *sling*, and places the *sling* over his left shoulder.

5. No. 3 reports "Correct (or otherwise)" to No. 2, who reports to No. 1 "Spare parts, &c., correct," who in turn reports to the commander "No. — gun, ready."

6. On the command "**Aircraft action**" being given (No. 1 repeats this and all subsequent orders) :—

    i. No. 3 runs to the firing point indicated, with the *mounting* and sets up the *mounting*, with one *leg* to the rear, at a suitable height for the firer.

    ii. No. 1 follows No. 3 to the firing point with the gun and, assisted by No. 3, mounts the gun. He then raises the *backsight* and fires without waiting for further orders.

        (*Note.*—The instructor should check this aim with an *aim corrector.*)

    iii. No. 2 follows No. 1 with the ammunition and *spare parts*. On arriving at the firing point he gets his ammunition ready for use.

7. No. 3 stands on the right side of No. 1, whilst No. 2 keeps his ammunition in readiness and stands on the left.

8. On the command "**Change**" :—

    (a) No. 3 presses back the *magazine catch*, No. 2 assists in the usual way, and places a new *magazine* on the gun.

    (b) When No. 2 has lifted the old *magazine* off the *magazine post*, No. 3 takes it, and hands it to No. 2 underneath the gun.

    (c) No. 1 reloads and carries on firing.

9. On the command " **Cease firing** " :—

   (*a*) Nos. 2 and 3 remove the *magazine* as in " Change."

   (*b*) No. 1 clears the gun, lowers the *backsight* and dismounts the gun.

   (*c*) No. 3 assists No. 1 and picks up the *mounting.*

   (*d*) Nos. 2 packs up the *ammunition.*

   (*e*) All move back when ready.

10. On reaching the original position :—

   (*a*) No. 1 lowers the *foresight.*

   (*b*) No. 3 folds up the *mounting.*

11. **Changing from air to ground target.**

   i. The command " **Stop** " will first be given.

   ii. On the command " **Range—Target—Action,**" No. 1 dismounts the gun, assisted by No. 3 as for " Cease firing."

   iii. When the gun is dismounted, No. 1 mounts it on the ground and continues as in elementary handling " Action," setting his *sights* to the range indicated **and firing without waiting for any further orders, as soon as his sights are aligned on the target.**

   iv. No. 3 gets under cover as quickly as possible, and lies down.

122. *Moral and material effect on aircraft of S.A. fire from the ground.*

1. Small arms fire from the ground has a considerable disturbing effect upon the occupants of an aeroplane. A pilot usually tries to avoid flying over an area in which a large volume of small arms fire is directed at him.

2. **Vulnerability of aeroplanes.**—The fact that an aeroplane does not at once crash to the ground when fired at is apt wrongly to discourage the firer. This need not be the case, for the ultimate effect of any shooting is often very considerable.

3. The vulnerable part of an aeroplane is very small, compared with its total surface. A machine flying at 500 feet at an angle of 5° to a flank presents a target approximately of 460 square feet.

4. Of this surface, 106 square feet is sufficiently vulnerable, if struck, to place the machine out of action for from 12 to 24 hours. The total surface, which, if struck, would render the aeroplane unserviceable for from 24 to 36 hours, is about 20 square feet, while the total surface, which, if struck would bring the machine down at once, is only about 2·5 square feet, or about 1/200th of the total target.

123. *Control of fire.*

1. If aeroplanes that are out of range are fired at, the only result will be a waste of ammunition.

2. **By day,** it may be taken as a general rule that a machine is within range so long as the struts or national markings are clearly visible to the naked eye.

3. At 3,000 feet, the side view of the struts and national markings are usually visible to the naked eye.

4. At 500 feet, such small objects as cross wires, machine guns, and identification marks, are visible, and the features of the pilot and observer may be distinguished.

5. **By night,** fire should only be opened (*a*) when the struts can be seen, owing to the aeroplane being in the beam

of a searchlight, (b) when it can be seen, without the aid of a searchlight, silhouetted against the sky.

6. An aeroplane travelling at a speed of 120 miles an hour, at an altitude of 500 feet, and directly over the gun, is only in range for 34 seconds. Speed in getting into action, and a sharp look-out are, therefore, essential.

7. **Ammunition.**—*Magazines* for use with anti-aircraft guns should be loaded with one round of tracer ammunition in every five rounds of Mark VII ordinary. If armour-piercing ammunition is being used, the *magazines* should be loaded with two rounds of armour-piercing and one of tracer ammunition to every five rounds of Mark VII ordinary.

8. All *magazines* specially loaded for anti-aircraft work should be so marked and kept apart from *magazines* loaded for ordinary work.

NOTES FOR INSTRUCTORS,

A.—Sequence of Instruction in the sights.

    I.—Describe briefly :—
        (a) *Mounting*,
        (b) *Connection*,
        (c) *Sling*.

    II.—Affix the *connection* to the gun.

    III.—Describe the *A.A. backsight.*

    IV.—Affix the *A.A. backsight* to the gun.

    V.—Describe the *A.A. foresight,*

    VI.—Affix the *A.A. foresight* to the gun

    VII.—Mount the gun.

VIII.—Tell the students which of the two *rings* to use, according to the height of the aeroplane.

IX.—Give rules for aiming, and show diagrams.

X.—Give the exception to the above rules, *i.e.,* diving aeroplane. Remember—an aeroplane must be actually nose-diving straight at the gun to be considered an exception.

XI.—Show the students correct aims—aim corrector. Draw diagrams.

XII.—Let the students lay aims—check by means of the aim corrector.

XIII.—Elementary aiming :—
         (*a*) Stationary with stick.
         (*b*) Moving with stick.

XIV.—Advanced aiming.
         (*a*) and (*b*).—As in No. XIII, but without stick.

B.—Sequence of instruction in A.A. elementary handling.

I.—Mounting and dismounting the *tripod.*

II.—No. I repeated with the addition of the gun.

III.—Points to note before going into action.

IV.—Positions of the gun " numbers."

V.—No. IV repeated with the addition of loading.

VI.—No. V repeated with the addition of aiming and firing.

VII.—No. VI repeated with the addition of " Change *magazines.*"

VIII.—No. VII repeated with the addition of "Stop."

IX.—" Aircraft action " complete.

X.—Unloading.

XI.—Moving the gun out of action.

XII.—" Cease firing " complete.

XIII.—Signals.

XIV.—Changing from air to ground target.

Note.—The No. 1, when he has aligned the gun on his ground target, fires without waiting for any further signal to fire.

Special Notes.

1. An aim corrector must be used on all instructional parades.

2. Practice must be given in using the inner as well as the outer *ring.*

3. During aiming instruction, the target aeroplane's direction of flight must be continually changed.

4. Make use of every opportunity when aircraft are flying overhead.

Tests of Elementary Training
(Lewis Gun).

124. *General instructions.*

1. Tests of elementary training suitable for testing a man's efficiency at three stages of his training are set out in the table below.

(a) Those of Standard " A " are suitable for the recruit
    to pass before firing the Lewis Gun part   of
    Table" A."

(b) Those of Standard " R " are suitable for the soldier
    to pass before firing the Lewis Gun part of Table
    " R " and Table " T."

(c) Those of Standard " L " are suitable for the soldier
    qualified to fire Table L.

2. Every soldier before firing the Range Practices of the
Annual Course should pass the Tests of the Standard applicable
to whichever table he is about to fire.

3. The passing of the Tests must on no account be judged
merely on the time limit, as accuracy of manipulation is the
important consideration. Consequently, even though a man
completes the test in the time limit but at the same time is
incorrect in some part of the handling, he should be judged as
having failed to pass the Test.

TESTS OF ELEMENTARY

In all Tests where No. 2 takes an active part, the test
is obviously due to faulty manipulation by

Method of

STAND

Name of Test.	Kit required.	Conditions before Test.
1. Loading.	Gun — *Spare parts* — *Magazines* — dummies.	Nos. 1 and 2 lying behind the gun. No. 2 to have a *magazine* ready but not on the gun. *Butt* on the ground. *Return spring* to be at the normal firing weight.
2. Adjustment of *sights*.	Gun.	No. 1 lying behind the gun. *Sights* to be at 400 yds. *Leaf* of *backsight* down.
3. Holding and aiming.	Gun — *Spare·parts* eye disc.	No. 1 lying behind the gun. *Butt* on the ground. **Gun** "**clear**" no *magazine* **on the gun.** *Cocking handle* back.

TRAINING—LEWIS GUN.

should be regarded as a test for both numbers and if failure one, the other should be given another trial.

conducting Tests.

ARD A.

Manipulation Tested.	Time.	Remarks.
1. On the command " Load " No. 2 places *magazine* on the *magazine post* correctly. No. 1 rotates the *magazine* and pulls back the *cocking handle.* Gun to be properly loaded.	3 secs. from the command " Load " until No. 1 has pulled back the *cocking handle.*	He will be tested 4 times and should pass in 3 of them.
2. On the range being given No. 1 sets the *sights.*	4 secs.	A maximum alteration in range of 400 yds. up or down will not be exceeded. Each man to be tested 4 times, 3 of which must be correct.
3. Correct holding and aiming.	5 secs. from command " Go " until No. 1 has pressed the *trigger.*	The man will be tested 4 times and must pass 3 out of 4 times. The *eye disc* should be held about 1 yd. from the end of the *front radiator casing.* The height of the *eye disc* should be varied for each aim taken.

STANDARD A—

Name of Test.	Kit required.	Conditions before Test.
4. Unloading without firing.	Gun — *Magazines* partially filled with *dummies.*	No. 1 in the correct firing position with the gun loaded. *Cocking handle* back.
5. Testing and adjusting the tension of the *return spring.*	Gun — *Combination tool* or *spring balance.*	No. 1 lying. Gun assembled but with the tension of the *return spring* between 4 and 10 lbs.
6. " Action."	Gun, with a *magazine* on the *post,* but not loaded. *Spare parts* — *Web equipment* — *magazine carrier,* with 2 *magazines.* No 2 to have his rifle slung over his back	No. 1 lying behind the gun, No. 2 two paces to the left of No. 1 and in the lying position. *Sights* at 600 yds. (a maximum alteration of 400 yds. can be given).

continued.

Manipulation Tested.	Time.	Remarks.
4. On the command "Unload without firing," No. 1 assisted by No. 2 removes *magazine* and the round in the *feed way.*	15 secs. from the word of command until both Nos. stand up.	—
5. Tension adjusted to the normal firing weight of the gun and tested with the *spring balance.* Stripping and reassembling performed correctly.	1 min. from the word "Go" until gun is reassembled.	To pass, the adjustment to be within ½ lb. of correct weight.
6. On the command "Range: indication: action" Nos. 1 and 2 will double forward 5 yds. independently. Gun to be mounted correctly on the spot indicated. Gun loaded, *sights* correctly adjusted and firer aiming at the target named. Positions of Nos. 1 and 2 to be correct.	20 secs. from the command "Action" until No. 1 says "Up."	"Gun mounted correctly" includes putting the *legs of the field mount* down gently and transferring the *butt* from the right to the left hand before No. 1 assumes the lying position.

STAND

Name of Test.	Kit required.	Conditions of Test.
7. Aiming.	Gun — *Spare parts* —*eye disc.*	No. 1 in the correct firing position but with head raised so that he is observing the target over the *back-sight slide*. **Gun clear.**
8. Adjustment of *sights.*	Gun.	Same as for Test 2 except that *sights* should be at 600 yds. before starting, and the maximum alteration of elevation allowed—600 yds.
9. Testing and adjusting the weight on *return spring.*	Same as for Test 5.	
10. Filling *magazines*.	Magazines — *loading handle* — ammunition.	Ammunition to be in a heap. The *magazine* with the *loading handle* may be rested on the loader's thigh but not on the ground.
11. Action.	Same as for Test 6	

ARD R.

Manipulation Tested.	Time.	Remarks.
7. Holding and aiming to be correct.	3 secs. from the word "Go" until No. 1 presses the *trigger*.	3 aims out of 4 to be correct. The height of the *eye disc* should be varied for each aim.
8. —	4 secs.	—
9. —	50 secs.	—
10. *Magazine* correctly filled with 47 rounds, no spaces missed.	1 min. 30 secs. from the command "Go" until loader says "Up."	Dummies or live ammunition may be used for this test but if live ammunition is used the test must be carried out on the range and precautions taken to prevent live ammunition becoming mixed with dummies.
11. —	17 secs.	—

STANDARD R—

Name of Test.	Kit required.	Conditions before Test.
12. " Immediate action."	Gun — *Spare parts magazines —dummies — landscape target.*	Four different I.A. stoppages to be set up. Nos. 1 and 2 in the correct firing position. The instructor will give the order " Fire," then " Gun stops — Position " and then either " gun does not fire," or " fires a few rounds and stops again " as necessary.
13. " Cease firing."	Gun — *Spare parts magazines — dummies — magazine carrier — landscape target.*	Nos. 1 and 2 in the correct firing position. Gun loaded with the *cocking handle* back.

STAND-

14. Action.	Same as Test 6.	—
15. Remedying broken *extractor* stoppage.	Gun — *Spare parts magazines —* dummies —empty *cartridge case — landscape target.* D.P. gun to be used.	Nos. 1 and 2 in the correct firing position. Gun " set up " for broken *extractor* stoppage. (The test starts after No. 1 has applied I.A. when the instructor gives the command " Gun does not fire ")

continued.

Manipulation Tested.	Time.	Remarks.
12. Immediate action performed correctly in all details.	5 secs. from the order indicating the cause of the stoppage, until No. 1 presses the *trigger* again, except damaged *magazine* 7 secs. Weak *cartridge guide* 15 secs.	In the case of the stoppage being due to a damaged *magazine* or a weak *cartridge guide* the time will be taken from the last word of the command "Gun does not fire" or "Gun fires a few rounds and stops again" respectively.
13. On the command "Cease firing," No. 1 unloads before he replaces a full *magazine* on the *magazine post.* Lower *sights.* Nos. 1 and 2 double back 5 yds. Gun to be carried and put down correctly.	12 secs. from the command "Out of action" until Nos. 1 and 2 are lying in the "Cease firing" position.	—

ARD L.

14. Same as Test 6.	14 secs	—
15. On the command "Gun does not fire," No. 1 clears the gun correctly, changes the bolt, reloads, relays his aim correctly and fires.	40 secs. from the command "Gun does not fire" until gun is again firing.	—

Name of Test.	Kit required.	Conditions before Test
16. A 2nd position stoppage. Friction.	Gun — *Spare parts magazines* — *dummies* — *landscape target*. D.P. gun to be used.	Nos. 1 and 2 in the correct position for firing. Gun to be set up for a 2nd position stoppage while No. 1 is firing. Instructor giving the command "Gun stops" No. 1 performs I.A. — Instructor, then again sets up the stoppage by adjusting the *cocking handle* and saying "Gun fires a few rounds and stops again."
17. Remedying a broken *striker* stoppage.	As for Test 16.	Nos. 1 and 2 in the correct position for firing. No. 1 fires the gun and performs the I.A. correctly until the cause of the stoppage is located to a broken *striker*, at which moment the test begins.
18. "Cease firing."	Same as for Test 13.	—
19. "Aircraft action."	Gun — *anti-aircraft sights* — *anti-aircraft mounting* fitted with *sling*— *aim corrector* — four *magazines* in a *carrier* — *Spare parts*—*model aeroplane target*.	Nos. 1, 2 and 3 perform the same duties as they do before reporting "Ready" in anti-aircraft elementary handling. No. 1 reports "Ready."

Manipulation Tested.	Time.	Remarks.
16. On the command " Gun fires a few rounds and stops again," No. 1 clears the gun : takes 3 lbs. weight off the *return spring* : reloads, relays his aim and fires.	18 secs. from the command " Gun fires a few rounds and stops again " until gun is again firing.	The instructor will test the weight of the *return spring* before and after this test, to see that the tension has been reduced by between 2½ and 3½ lbs.
17. On the command " Gun still won't fire," No. 1 clears the gun and changes the *piston rod* correctly : reloads, relays his aim and fires.	35 secs. from the command " Gun still won't fire " until the gun is firing again.	The instructor gives the command " Gun stops " and " Gun won't fire," and No. 1 performs the necessary immediate action, before he gives the command " Gun still won't fire."
18. Same as for Test 13.	9 secs.	—
19. On the command " Aircraft Action," the gun numbers perform the necessary duties as laid down in A.A. elementary handling. No. 1 fires as soon as he gets a correct aim on his target. *Mounting* to be correctly adjusted to the height required by No. 1 ; Nos. 1, 2 and 3 in their correct positions ; gun loaded and a correct aim taken.	14 secs. from the command " Action " until No. 1 has pressed the trigger.	The instructor will check the aim by means of the *aim corrector.*

CHAPTER IV.

·303-INCH HOTCHKISS GUN TRAINING.*

Hotchkiss Gun Handling.

125. *General instructions.*

1. The general instructions on training contained in Secs. **94-96** for the Lewis gun apply similarly to the Hotchkiss gun.

2. As the duties in connection with the handling of the gun are distributed amongst all the members of the Hotchkiss gun detachment, differentiated according to their " numbers," and furthermore as every man in the detachment must be able to carry out the duties assigned to any particular " number," instruction must be carried out in such a manner that the duties of each " number " of the detachment are learnt by all.

---

* *Note.*—Reference to the use of the Hotchkiss gun in tanks is excluded from this manual as it is dealt with in Tank Training, Vol II, 1920 (Provisional).

3. For the purposes of instruction, therefore, the subject can be divided into the following distinct and progressive stages :—

    i. *Elementary handling.*—This deals with the actions required of Nos. 1 and 2 in accordance with certain orders or signals.

    ii. *Advanced handling.*—This is a further stage in which the main consideration is the adaption of the actions of elementary handling to varying conditions of ground.

    iii. *Duties of Nos,* 1, 2 *and* 3, *and handling from the pack.*— This comprises such detailed individual training as is necessary to enable the men to perform the duties allotted to these numbers.

        (*See* Cavalry Training, Volume 1 (1924), Sec. **202** *et seq.*)

    iv. *Mounted drill.*—(*See* Cavalry Training, Volume I.)

126. *Elementary handling.*

1. Training under this heading is designed to teach men to bring the gun into action quickly, correctly mounted in a position suitable for firing.

2. The gun, etc., having been placed in a position suitable for carrying out the exercises, the class falls in. The men form in line in rear of the gun and number from right to left.

3. On the order to "**Take post**" being given, No. 2 slings the *spare parts bag* over his left shoulder and lies down behind the gun. He at once examines the gun to see that it is ready for action, looking especially to—*foresight, gas regulator, barrel locking nut, tripod adjustments, feed mechanism, moving portions* and *trigger mechanism.*

4. No. 2 reports to No. 1 "correct" or otherwise on completion of his examination.

5. No. 1 simultaneously lies down about two paces to the right of No. 2. He examines all the *strips* in the *carrier* to ensure that they are correctly filled and undamaged. He will also examine the spare *barrel.*

6. No. 2 then reports "No. ... gun ready" to the instructor. (Henceforth No. 2 will repeat all orders given by the instructor.)

7. The instructor will then indicate certain aiming marks on the landscape target and give them brief titles.

8. On the command "**Range — Aiming mark — Action,**" No. 2 will rise and carry the gun forward, holding the *tripod* with his left hand and the *small of the butt* with his right hand.

9. On reaching the position indicated by the instructor he will mount the gun, placing the *tripod* on the ground with one of its *legs* towards himself. He transfers his left hand to the *small of the butt*, releasing his right hand, which he places on the ground palm downwards. Using his right hand as a support, he drops down straight behind the gun.

10. He then loads, assisted by No. 1, adjusts the *sights,* holds the gun in the firing position, and aims at the mark indicated.

11. No. 1, carrying the *ammunition carrier* and spare *barrel,* will advance with No. 2 and drop down on the latter's right. He must lie in such a position that he can readily assist in loading or supplying *spare parts* when wanted, whilst at the same time he offers the minimum possible target surface to the front.

12. When in position, No. 1 will take a second *strip* from the *carrier* and hold it in readiness for use. He will also see that the *spare parts bag* on No. 2 is in a position of readiness.

13. When No. 2 is ready to open fire he calls out " On " to No. 1, who will raise his left hand over the shoulders of No. 2, and at the same time watch the troop leader for signals.

14. On the command " **Fire,**" No. 1 will shout " Fire," whereupon No. 2 will press the *trigger* and fire in short bursts of about one second's duration, pausing to observe fire and to relay his aim between bursts.

15. On the command " **Change** " (strips), No. 2 (keeping the *butt* in his shoulder) will press up the *feed piece* with his right hand, whilst No. 1 withdraws the *strip* from the gun (unless it has already been thrown out by the action of the gun) and inserts a fresh *strip* into it. As soon as No. 2 sees that the gun is again loaded he will continue firing.

16. On the command " **Stop,**" No. 2 will cock the gun (if moving parts are forward) and, assisted by No. 1, change *strips.* He will then place the *butt* on the ground, and await further orders.

17. On the command "**Unload**," No. 2 will lift up the *feed piece* while No. 1 removes the *strip*, press the *trigger*, cock the gun, press the *trigger* again, set the *cocking handle* at "S," then lower the *slide* of the *backsight*. No. 1 replaces all *strips* in the *carrier*.

18. Both No. 1 and No. 2 will then rise from the gun, and No. 1 reports "No. — gun clear."

19. On the command "**Cease firing**," No. 2, assisted by No. 1, will unload the gun, press the *trigger*, set the *cocking handle* at "S" and lower the *backsight*. He will then carry the gun to the "Cease firing" position. No. 1 replaces the *strips* in the *carrier* and moves to the "Cease firing" position.

20. **Signals.**—The following signals will be used :—

"**Action.**"—Both arms raised and lowered in line with the shoulders.

"**Ready to open Fire.**"—No. 1 raises his hand over the shoulders of No. 2.

"**Stand by, ready to Fire.**"—Hand raised.

"**Fire.**"—Hand lowered to side.

"**Stop.**"—Hand waved horizontally.

"**Cease Firing.**"—Arm circled from shoulder.

NOTES FOR INSTRUCTORS.

Preliminary.—In teaching elementary handling the subject should be divided progressively into stages which gradually work up to the stage at which the handling actions are carried out by word of command and signals.

Subjects.—The progressive stages should be :—

Working up to—	Progressive Stages.
I.—Take Post ...	i. Class arrangements (falling in and numbering off, &c.). ii. Action of No. 1. iii. Action of No. 2. iv. Carry out by word of command.
II.—Action	i. No. 2 carrying forward, and placing the gun in position. ii. Position of No. 1. iii. Repeating i. and ii., adding loading. iv. Repeating iii., adding adjustment of *sights* and aiming. v. Repeating iv., adding firing. vi. Carry out by word of command.
III.—Change *Strip* ...	i. Each action of Nos. 1 and 2. ii. Carry out by word of command.
IV.—Stop	i. Each action of Nos. 1 and 2. ii. Carry out by word of command.
V.—Unload	i. Each action of Nos. 1 and 2. ii. Carry out by word of command.
VI.—Cease firing ...	i. Each action of Nos. 1 and 2, in preparing the gun for movement. ii. Each action of Nos. 1 and 2 in moving to the " cease firing " position. iii. Carry out by word of command.
VII.—Signals	i. Teach the signals and test recognition. ii. Carry out Elementary Handling, substituting signals for words of command.

SPECIAL NOTES.

1. Training in this subject should be carried out on level ground, and the distance between the " Action " and the " Cease firing " positions should be about 5 yards.

2. From the time the recruit has learnt how to carry out the actions required for elementary handling he should receive constant practice, so as to ensure that he instinctively carries out the correct action on any given word of command. This practice comes under the heading of " Handling exercises." As the man's training progresses the exercises should include any further stages of manipulation which have been learnt, such as " Immediate action " and stoppage remedying.

3. In timing the pace of these exercises the instructor should gradually shorten the interval between his words of command to conform to the increased efficiency of the detachment. At the same time he should be careful to balance the claims of speed with those of accuracy of manipulation.

127. *Advanced handling.*

1. Advanced handling consists of exercises for the purpose of teaching the Nos. 1 and 2 to make the best use of ground features when occupying fire positions, in order to secure the maximum cover consistent with the full use of the gun for fire action.

2. The use of both natural and artificial cover will be practised in mounting the gun for action.

3. The way in which the gun should be mounted will be determined in every case by the shape of the ground.

4. Suitable exercises include :—

(a) *Mounting the gun for firing over or round cover of varying heights,* such as breastworks, trench parapets, banks, shell-holes, minor undulations, hedges or undergrowth giving cover from view. The types of position selected should be such that sometimes the tripod is used and at other times not used.

(b) *Firing from behind the crest of a gentle slope.*

(c) *Methods of crawling with the gun.*—As crawling is fatiguing and slow, it should be limited normally to movement over the last 2 or 3 yards on to a fire position, or for crossing short exposed stretches in an otherwise concealed line of approach.

Crawling should only be employed when other forms of movement would spoil the chance of surprise by disclosing the movement.

(d) *Nos. 1 and 2 carrying the gun together, moving behind cover,* which only affords concealment to a man in a crouching attitude.

5. The actions of Nos. 1 and 2 are legislated for in the foregoing sections, elementary and advanced handling.

6. No. 3 is the pack leader, and when the gun is in action he becomes the horse-holder. In addition to the normal duties of a horse-holder No. 3 must, as soon as he has got his horses under cover, be prepared to off load the ammunition in case the troop leader requires more strips for the gun.

PRELIMINARY TRAINING.

(WITH NOTES FOR INSTRUCTORS.)

128. *Loading and unloading.*

1. **To fill the strip.**—Force the cartridges between the *clips* until the rear face of the base of each cartridge rests against the front face of the *small raised nib* or the *continuous rib* on the rear edge of the *strip*.

(For description of the machine for filling *strips* and *belts, see* Appendix III, Section 3 (1).)

2. **To remove the cartridges from the strip.**—Hook the forefinger under the bullet, and, pressing the thumb on the *strip*, force the cartridge out of the *clips*.

3. **To load the gun.**—

    i. Pull back the *cocking handle* sharply to the full extent.

    ii. Raise the *feed piece* by pressing up the base of the *feed piece stem*.

    iii. Insert the *strip* into the *strip guides* with a slight upward as well as a lateral movement and push home the *strip* until the *cartridge stop plunger* protrudes about $\frac{1}{8}$ inch from its housing, or about twice as much as in the " rest " position. This protrusion indicates that the *strip* is fully home, the cartridge then being opposite the *chamber* and the gun ready to fire.

4. To unload the gun.—When fire ceases, the *moving parts* are normally in the backward position. If a partially expended *strip* is in the gun it must be removed by pressing the *stem* of the *feed piece* up as far as possible and withdrawing the *strip* to the right. The *trigger* must then be pressed to release the *recoil spring* and close the *breech*. If, however, the *moving parts* are in the forward position when fire ceases, as will be the case when using dummies, or when there is a stoppage, the *cocking handle* must first be pulled sharply back. Finally, the *trigger* must be pressed to release the *recoil spring* and close the *breech*.

5. If it is required to close the *breech* before a *strip* has been inserted, it is necessary first to raise the *stem* of the *feed piece* so that the lower *arm* is disengaged from the *shoulder* on the *piston rod*. The latter then moves forward until it is held by the *sear*, and when the *trigger* is pressed the *piston rod* will fly forward.

NOTES FOR INSTRUCTORS.

Subjects—

I.—Filling the *strip*.

II.—Unloading the *strip*.

III.—Introducing the *strip* into the gun.

IV.—Unloading the gun.

Note.—Each of these lessons should be learnt and practised by each member of the class before proceeding to teach the next lesson.

SPECIAL NOTES.

In the course of the instruction the instructor should impress on the recruit :—

1. The consequences if the rim of any one cartridge is not against the *nib* on the *strip*.

2. To avoid leaving spaces in the *strip* and to begin filling at the right end.

3. The necessity of lifting the *feed piece* when loading and unloading the gun.

4. The object of the *cartridge stop*.

5. That the position of the cartridge when the gun is loaded differs from that of a rifle in that in the latter case the cartridge is in the *chamber*, whereas in the former it is still in the *strip* and the *breech* is open.

Kit required.—Gun, strips, drill cartridges Mark VI, ground sheets.

129. *Holding, aiming and firing.*

A.—Holding.

1. To hold the gun in the firing position, the firer lies in a straight line behind the gun with both elbows on the ground.

2. He holds the *pistol grip* with his right hand, the forefinger reaching round the *trigger*, whilst the remaining three fingers clasp the *pistol grip* (the second finger being close up against the *trigger guard*). He uses his thumb to secure the grasp by pressure on the *disc* of the *cocking handle*, but clear of the *tongue* of the *trigger*.

PLATE 78.

Fig. A.

HOTCHKISS—HOLDING.

Fig. B.

HOTCHKISS—HOLDING.

3. By a steady pressure with his right hand the *butt* is held tight against his shoulder, and the hold locked by a steady downward and backward pressure of the left hand which grips the *small of the butt*, with the fingers passing over the top and the thumb passing underneath.

4. The " *hinged strap* " rests on the top of the shoulder.

5. The *tripod legs* should be firmly fixed in the ground with one *leg* towards the firer, and the *yoke* should be maintained in a vertical position.

B.—Aiming.

6. The principles of aiming with the rifle *sights* apply equally with the Hotchkiss gun *sights*, except that the Hotchkiss gun is fitted with a *barleycorn foresight* and a *V backsight*.

PLATE 79.

HOTCHKISS GUN—CORRECT AIM.

C.—Firing.

7. In order not to disturb the aim the gun must be fired by a steady pressure of the forefinger on the *trigger*, whilst maintaining a firm hold of the gun.

8. When employing automatic fire, the *trigger* should be held back for about one second and then released, as by this

means the rate of fire is regulated in short bursts of 4 or 5 rounds at a time. Simultaneously with releasing the trigger, the firer should observe the result of his fire by looking over or round the *sights* at the target.

9. The firer must always relay his aim between the time of releasing the *trigger* and pressing it again.

NOTES FOR INSTRUCTORS.

Subjects—
Instruction in holding, aiming and firing can normally be combined in the same lesson period, and must be taught in that sequence.

SPECIAL NOTES.

Holding.

1. Although there is no appreciable shock of recoil to " hold " against, the vibrations set up when the automatic action of the gun is in play are such that unless countered they will throw the gun completely off its alignment. A firm hold is, therefore, the foundation of accurate shooting—any tendency to loose holding, even during some part of instructional training when live ammunition is not being used, is sowing the seeds of failure in marksmanship.

Aiming.

2. Men should be taught to adjust the *backsight* elevation before they are taught to aim.

3. Aiming is best taught as follows :—
First, by explanation of correct and incorrect aims by diagrams.
Second, the instructor lays the gun (rested in any convenient way) with a correct aim and lets each recruit see

that aim. Then the recruit lays an aim and the instructor checks.

Third, the recruit aims at the *eye disc* which is held by the instructor about one yard from the *muzzle* of the gun.

(*Note.*—Before doing this the instructor **must** satisfy himself by personal inspection that the gun is unloaded.)

4. Although some form of bullseye aiming mark can be used in the first stages of aiming instruction, the subject cannot be considered to be learnt until the instructor has satisfied himself that the recruits can aim correctly at " landscape " aiming marks. Thereafter the landscape aiming marks should be used in all subsequent training.

Firing.

5. The recruit should be taught to observe his fire by developing the habit of looking at the target over or round the *sights* every time he releases the *trigger*. The sequence of acts being—Aim—press *trigger*—release *trigger*—look—relay aim—press *trigger*—and so on.

6. Instruction in aiming and firing should include changing the point of aim along a linear target by, approximately, a width of the *foresight*.

Kit required.—Gun, aiming diagrams, an aiming mark, an *eye disc*, a landscape target, *ammunition carriers* or some other form of rest for the gun when laying an aim.

130. *Stripping and assembling.*

1. **To strip the gun.**—The gun is stripped in the order set forth in the succeeding paragraphs.

2. 1st, **Cocking handle.**—See that the *breech* is closed. Turn the *lever* of the *cocking handle* upwards until it will go no

further. It is then slightly to the left of the vertical, and the *tenons* correspond with the *tenon recesses* in the rear opening of the *guard*. Draw back the *cocking handle* until the *tenons* are clear, then turn it to the right so that it is at an angle of 45° with the vertical. This brings the open *grooves* on the *stem* opposite the *nibs* of the *collar* in the *guard*, and the *lugs* on the *stem* in line with the *recesses* in the *collar* in the *piston rod*. The *cocking handle* can then be withdrawn.

3. 2nd, **Butt and Guard.**—Unscrew the *guard locking screw* three turns and, pressing the *butt* forward and then downwards, disengage the *projections* on the sides of the *guard* from their *recesses* in the *body* and the *trunnions* from their *hooks*. Remove the *butt* and *guard*.

4. 3rd, Take out the **recoil spring**.

5. 4th, **Piston rod.**—Insert the *cocking handle* in the *piston*, with its *handle* at an angle of 45° to the right of the vertical, so that the *lugs* enter the *recesses* in the *collar* in the *piston rod*. Turn the *lever* vertical and draw the *piston rod* with the *breech block* out of the *body*. **No force must be used in removing these parts.**

6. 5th, **Breech block.**—Lift the *breech block* off the *piston rod*.

7. 6th, **Firing pin.**—Turn the *upper boss* of the *firing pin* out of the *recess*, and draw the *firing pin* backwards out of the *breech block*, raising its rear end while so doing.

8. 7th, **Tripod.**—Press in the *clips* of the *yoke* and remove the *tripod*.

9. 8th, **Barrel.**—Turn the *locking nut* to the right as far as the *stop* will permit, by means of the *wrench*. Draw the *barrel* out to the front. Unscrew the *regulator* and remove it.

10. 9th, **Handguard.**—Turn the *locking nut* slightly to the left to disengage its *stud* from the *handguard* and remove the latter.

11. 10th, Unscrew the **Barrel locking nut** and remove it.

12. 11th, Take out the **Fermeture nut** from the *body*.

13. **To assemble the gun.**— *Reverse the operations.*

14. Before replacing the *piston rod* and *breech block*, the *fermeture nut* must, if necessary, be rotated by hand to the unlocked position, when its *slot* corresponds with the *ejection opening* in the *body*. The *upper boss* of the *firing pin* must be placed in the *recess* in the *breech block* in order to allow it to lead in to the *body*.

15. After inserting the *piston rod* and pushing it partly forward, it will be checked by the *shoulder* on its right coming against the *lower arm* of the *feed piece*. The *stem* of the latter must be pushed upwards to allow the *piston rod* to pass and go fully forward. **No force must be used in replacing the piston.**

16. When replacing the *guard,* an inch or so of the *stem* of the *cocking handle* should be inserted through the hole in the rear face of the *guard* in such a manner as to secure the rear end of the *spring*. The *cocking handle* should lie diagonally downwards on the left of the *butt stock* and be grasped, as well as the *butt stock,* with the right hand.

131. *Stripping component parts.*

1. **The extractor.**
   (*a*) Insert the *hook* of the *hand extractor* or a small *drift* or *screwdriver* between the two rear *coils* of the *extractor spring* and compress the *spring*. When

the base of the *spring* is clear of its *recess,* the *extractor* and *spring* may be drawn outwards and removed from the *breech block.*

(*b*) To remove the *extractor* without stripping the gun.— Remove the *strip* from the gun. Take an empty case and place it in the front end of the *ejection opening.* Pressing the *trigger* and controlling the *moving parts* by means of the *cocking handle,* allow them to go forward slowly till they are stopped by the case. The *extractor* and *spring* will then be accessible through the *ejection opening,* and can be removed in the ordinary way.

2. **The trigger mechanism.**—Lift the *T-headed arm* of the *trigger mechanism* until it is clear of the *sear arm,* then revolve the *milled head* until the *sear axis* can be lifted out. Pushing the *trigger bar* backwards to its full extent, lift the front end to get the *trigger* clear of its *slot,* and remove the *trigger* mechanism. Separate the two portions by removing the *spiral spring.*

3. **The feed piece spring.**—See that the *feed piece* is in such a position that the undercut *stud* can be disengaged. Push the *feed piece spring* slightly forward to disengage it from the undercut *stud* on the stem. Then lift the *finger piece of the spring* and draw it backwards until the *tongue* is clear of the undercut *recess* on the front *feed guide.* **Care must be taken not to lift the spring more than is necessary, to avoid straining or breaking it.**

4. **The feed piece.**—Open the *feed piece cover* and raise the *backsight* to a vertical position. Lift the *stem* and revolve it to the rear until the *flat* is opposite the opening in the upper *bearing.* Remove the *stem.*

(B 27/7)Q   N

5. **The ejector.**—Using the *ejector key*, unscrew the *ejector cap* and remove the *ejector*.

6. **The cartridge stop.**—Unscrew the *cartridge stop holder*, and remove the *plunger* and *spring*.

7. **To change the barrel.**—With the *dismounting wrench* turn the *locking nut* as far as it will go, and draw the *barrel* out of the *body*. If the *barrel* is too hot to handle, one man should firmly hold the *barrel* with the *dismounting wrench*, while the other draws the *body* and *guard* to the rear. The spare *barrel* is then inserted and the *locking nut* turned back into the locked position. A hot *barrel* after removal from the gun can be handled by passing the *slot* in the centre of the *dismounting wrench* over the *stud* underneath the *muzzle* for the *barrel rest*.

8. **The foresight** can be driven out of its bed with a *punch*.

9. To remove the **backsight.**—Unscrew the *fixing screw* in the front end of the *backsight bed* and remove the *spring washers;* press the *sight* backwards and lift off.

NOTES FOR INSTRUCTORS.

Preliminary.

1. This subject should be dealt with under two distinct headings :—

    i. *Stripping* necessary in order to clean the gun and to keep it in good order.

    ii. *Stripping component parts* which might break when firing, so that they can be exchanged for spare parts quickly. Only those parts which it is absolutely necessary to move should be stripped when changing a damaged part.

2. Sequence of lesson :—

    i. Stripping and replacing each part.
    ii. Practice.
    iii. Stripping component parts.

Subjects.—Sequence is necessary during the early lessons in stripping for cleaning, so that the reasons for certain precautions may be impressed on the men. When they are proficient it does not greatly matter in what order the various parts are removed, provided there is no chance of the gun being damaged.

Sequence of stripping.

  I. **Body Group.**—*Cocking handle, butt stock and guard, recoil spring, moving parts (i.e., piston* and *breech block), firing pin.*

  II.—**Barrel Group.**—*Tripod, barrel, handguard, barrel locking nut, fermeture nut* and *gas regulator.*

  III.—**Stripping component parts.**—These include the *trigger mechanism, feed piece* and *spring, extractor, ejector* and *cartridge stop.*

SPECIAL NOTES.

1. The greatest value will be obtained from the instruction by allowing the man to try to remove certain parts without any assistance ; the instructor should not interfere except to prevent damage to the gun, or to offer suggestions if the man finds his task difficult or impossible.

2. Each part of the gun should be removed and replaced by the whole section before going on to the next. For each part a different man should be selected as the first to attempt it.

132. *Cleaning the gun.*

1. **When a screw thread is found to have seized, no attempt should be made to unscrew the part by force. The joint should be thoroughly soaked in mineral burning oil (paraffin), which will loosen it.**

2. **When to clean the barrel, gas cylinder, and gas regulator.**

When ball ammunition has been fired, daily cleaning of the *barrel, gas cylinder, gas regulator* and *cup* of the *piston* is necessary for at least 10 days afterwards.

3. Subsequent cleaning must depend on the discretion of the officer in charge of the gun ; in a dry climate once a week .should be sufficient, but in situations where the gun is exposed to a moist atmosphere, daily cleaning may be necessary.

After cleaning, all parts must be left lightly coated with G.S. lubricating oil.

4. Mineral burning oil (paraffin) is a convenient means of loosening and removing rust, but if left in contact with steel it assists the formation of rust. After use, therefore, it must be carefully removed and the part oiled with G.S. lubricating oil, which, in addition to being a lubricant, is also a preserva-tive.* The use of emery or other cutting or gritty sub-stance is strictly forbidden.

5. **How to clean the barrel.**—Normally, the gun should be stripped in order to clean the *barrel*. If it is impracticable to strip the gun, the *cleaning rod* must be used, with successive pieces of flannelette, about 4 in. by 1½ in. in size, the first

---

* When a mixture of mineral burning oil and G.S. oil has been used for cleaning any part of the gun, that part must be carefully dried and then oiled with G S. oil.

one oily and the remainder dry, until the *bore* is rag-clean. Finally, pass a slightly smaller oily piece of flannelette through the *bore* unless the gun is to be fired immediately.

6. Great care must be exercised in using the *cleaning rod* to avoid breaking it at the *joints*. When inserting, it must be supported by one hand close to the point of entry to the *barrel*; flannelette which is too large to enter the *bore* with reasonable ease must not be used, and the push and pull of the *rod* must be in a line with the axis of the *bore*.

7. A damaged *cleaning rod* must not be used, on account of its liability to scratch and cut the *bore*.

8. The normal method of cleaning will be by use of the *double pull-through* and flannelette. For this, the *barrel* will always be removed from the gun.

9. One of the *double pull-throughs* provided should have a piece of wire *gauze* attached as laid down in Sect. **38**, 4, while the other should be used for dry flannelette only.

10. Having carefully oiled the *gauze*, drop the *weight* of the *pull-through* through the *bore*.

11. The *barrel* should then be fixed in a vice, or held by a man, while one man works either end of the *pull-through*.

12. Unless rust or metallic fouling are present in the *bore*, the *gauze* should not be pulled backwards and forwards more than three times, in order to avoid wearing out the *barrel*.

13. The gauzed *pull-through* should then be laid aside, and the other one used with dry flannelette until the *bore* is rag-clean. In doing this, the flannelette must be pulled out of the *bore* each time. To reverse the direction of the pull while the flannelette is in the *bore* will lead to its becoming jammed.

14. Finally, a slightly smaller oily piece of flannelette should be placed in the loop of the *pull-through* and passed once through the *bore* in order to leave it slightly oiled. If the gun is to be fired immediately, this operation should be omitted and the *bore* should be left dry.

15. The utmost care must be taken to avoid the cord rubbing against either the *muzzle* or the *breech*. If this precaution is not insisted upon, a groove will be worn by the cord, which, if at the *chamber end*, will tend to cause burst cartridge cases, and, if at the *muzzle end,* will destroy the accuracy of the *barrel*.

16. Whatever method of cleaning is adopted, the greatest care must be taken to see that the *chamber* is thoroughly cleaned, all dried oil and dirt being removed from it.

17. Fouling can most easily be removed before it has had time to set and become hard. The *barrel* should, therefore, be cleaned as soon as possible after firing.

18. **To clean the gas cylinder and regulator.**—After removing the *gas regulator* (which if very tight should be saturated with mineral burning oil (paraffin) for a time before attempts are made to remove it), clean the *stem* and *head* with a piece of flannelette and wipe out the *gas cylinder*.

19. If hard fouling is present in the *gas cylinder*, remove it carefully by means of the *gas cylinder cleaner*, then wipe out the *gas cylinder* again with oily flannelette, seeing that all chippings are removed.

20. Reassemble the *gas regulator* right home to see that all is clear, and again remove it and wipe both *regulator* and *cylinder* dry; then with a piece of clean flannelette oil both

very lightly with G.S. lubricating oil and reassemble the *gas regulator* into the position before the first removal.

21. **To clean the cup of the piston.**—Remove fouling with an oily piece of flannelette, leaving the *cup* slightly oiled unless the gun is to be fired immediately.

22. **To clean the mechanism.**—The *moving parts* must be removed, but it will not always be necessary to strip the *trigger mechanism, extractor, ejector* or *cartridge stop.*

23. All parts must be thoroughly cleaned with a mixture of equal parts of G.S. lubricating oil and mineral burning oil. They must afterwards be dried and lightly oiled with G.S. lubricating oil before they are replaced.

24. Dirt must be carefully removed from all parts of the *stationary portion*, particular attention being paid to *recesses* which are likely to harbour dirt.

Dried oil can be removed by the use of mineral burning oil (paraffin).

After the *parts* have been replaced, the exterior of all metal portions should be rubbed over with a piece of flannelette and lightly oiled with G.S. lubricating oil.

25. **To clean the strip.**—Rust should be removed and the *strip* lightly coated with G.S. lubricating oil as a preservative (the armourer's *hard brush*, lightly oiled, is convenient for this purpose). No more oil than is absolutely necessary must be used, as any excess will be carried into the *chamber* by the cartridges, where it will dry and obstruct the entry of the cartridge.

26. **Sandy and dusty countries.**—When working in sandy and dusty countries, great care must be taken to avoid

grit getting into the *moving parts* and on the *strips*. This applies more when the gun is being fired than when resting, as in the latter case it is easy to cover the gun. When firing. arrangements should be made to avoid the disturbance of dust, caused by the action of the *moving portions* and gases escaping from the *handguard*.

The following notes will assist in overcoming this difficulty :—

    i. Guns not in use should be kept covered.

    ii. When cleaning, use a lightly oiled rag, if the gun is not actually in use. The *oil-can* will always be at hand if required.

    iii. Damp the ground, or lay a ground sheet or greatcoat under and around the gun position.

    iv. Clear the gun of grit at every available opportunity.

    v. *Strips* will be kept in *carriers* or *boxes* until required. Should a strip become fouled with grit, put it aside until unloaded and cleaned.

    vi. Keep the *breech* closed until it is necessary to load.

    133. *Protection of the gun from the effect of gas attacks.*

1. Measures should be taken by means of blankets soaked in anti-gas solution to protect ammunition and gun recesses.

2. The gun must be kept carefully cleaned and well oiled with G.S. oil.

3. The effect of corrosion on ammunition is even more serious than the direct effect of gas upon the guns. *Strips* of ammunition should, therefore, be kept in their *carriers* with the *joints* made gas-tight by inserting strips of flannelette,

4. Occasional short bursts of fire will lessen the chance of guns jamming from the action of gas during a gas attack.

5. After a gas attack the gun should be cleaned and re-oiled at once. Oil cleaning will only prevent corrosion for about 12 hours or more. At the first available opportunity the gun must be stripped and the working parts cleaned with boiling water containing a little soda.

Ammunition and *strips* will be carefully examined; any rounds affected by gas will be replaced, then cleaned and used as soon as possible.

NOTES FOR INSTRUCTORS.

Subjects—
  I.—Daily cleaning of the *barrel* and *mechanism* when
        necessary.
 II.—Cleaning after firing.
III.—Use of the *double pull-through* to remove fouling.
 IV.—Cleaning *strips*.
  V.—Protection of the gun from the effects of gas.

  Kit required—Gun, spare parts, cleaning accessories.

134. *Points to be attended to before firing.*

1. Examine the gun to see that no part is deficient and that the *mechanism* works freely.

2. Remove the oil and examine the *bore* to see that there is no obstruction in it.

3. Remove the oil from the *gas cylinder* and *gas regulator,* and set the *gas regulator* to the proper graduation.

4. In order to avoid smoke, which would disclose the gun position, remove the oil from the exterior of the *barrel*.

5. These precautions should be taken with the spare *barrel* as well as that in the gun.

6. Thoroughly oil with G.S. lubricating oil all *working parts* and surfaces of the *mechanism*.

7. Test the action of the *ejector* and the *cartridge stop*. They should work freely and without stiffness.

8. The *tripod* should be attached to the *trunnions* by means of the *spring catches* provided in the *yoke* for that purpose, with the *vice pin* to the **rear**; this allows the *legs* to fold up into their correct position and ensures the *clamping screws* being on the right hand, or *feed* side of the gun.

9. The *vice pin* should be left **loose** to allow the aluminium *yoke* to be pivoted to either side, thus enabling the *sights* to be kept upright.

10. The *clamping screw*, which fixes the underside of the *saddle* to the *traversing pivot*, should be kept loose; this allows the gun to move backwards or forwards, the *legs* of the *tripod* remaining steady.

Note.—If this *screw* is tight, every movement of the gun will act directly on the *legs*, causing them to jump about, and the shooting will be affected.

11. In the vertical *pillar*, ¾-inch below the *collar* of the pivot, a small hole will be found which corresponds with a similar hole in the base of the *pivot*. By inserting a *pin* into these holes the traverse is completely stopped, and the gun can be set for night firing.

12. Before filling, examine each *strip* to see that the *clips* are not distorted or cracked. If weak, re-size with *re-sizing tool*.

13. See that the *strips* are carefully filled, the cartridges being pushed home until their rims lie in front of the *nibs* or *rib* on the *strip*.

14. See that all *spare parts* and *tools* are in the *spare parts bag* or *box*.

15. See that the *oil-can* and, if provided, the *oil-bottle* in the *butt* are full of oil.

16. See that all *cases* and *bags* are properly secured, to avoid loss or damage in transit.

135. *Points to be attended to during firing.*

1. Keep the *strips* in their *boxes* until they are required, and replace empty *strips* in the *box* as soon as possible. Take care to avoid damaging them and to prevent the risk that they might carry dirt into the *mechanism* or *chamber*.

2. Manipulate the *gas regulator* as may be required to maintain the desired rate of fire. It can, as a rule, be opened out as the gun gets hot.

3. During a temporary cessation of fire, if time permits, the gun should be unloaded and the *moving parts* oiled.

A partially empty *strip* should be replaced by a full one when fire ceases temporarily. Empty or partially empty *strips* must be filled without delay provided ammunition is available.

4. In cold weather, the amount of oil used for lubrication should be reduced to a minimum, as it is likely to congeal and affect the working of the *mechanism*.

5. The *barrel* may be cooled by cold water. The water may be applied externally by means of a sponge or cloth, or the *barrel* may be dipped in it. In the latter case, the water must be removed from the *barrel* and *gas cylinder* before firing is resumed.

6. When the gun ceases firing and on opening the *breech* it is found that a cartridge case has been withdrawn from the *chamber,* the case must be carefully examined to see if the propellant has been ignited. If the propellant has not been ignited, the bullet will most likely be found in the *bore* near the *breech* and should be removed by means of the *cleaning rod* inserted from the *muzzle*. In all cases the *reflector mirror* should be used to see that the *bore* is clear before firing is resumed.

136. *Points to be attended to after firing.*

Immediately after firing :—

1. See that the gun is unloaded.

2. See that the *bore and chamber,* and also the *cup* of the *piston rod* and the *nozzle* of the *gas cylinder,* are well oiled directly firing has finished.

3. See that the *recoil spring* is eased.

4. See that any live cartridges which may be among the fired cases are collected.

5. See that the gun is thoroughly cleaned without delay. All parts of the *mechanism,* as well as the *strips,* must be examined at the same time to see that they are in good order.

On return to quarters :—

6. See that any repairs to the gun which may be necessary are carried out by the armourer, and that the unserviceable parts which have been replaced from the *spares* are exchanged for serviceable parts from store to complete the spare equipment

MECHANISM AND STOPPAGES.

137. *Mechanism, gas and spring.*

A.—Action of the gas.

1. The gases generated by the explosion of the charge force the bullet up the *barrel* ; when the bullet has passed the *gas vent*, a portion of the gases rush with great force into the *gas cylinder*, and find their way out by the passage in the rear end of the *cylinder*.

2. The *cupped head* of the *piston* being over this end, the *piston* is given a sharp blow and forced backwards.

3. The under *boss* of the *firing pin*, being engaged between the two *blocks* on the *piston rod*, is taken back with the *piston*.

4. The early part of the *piston's* backward movement causes the *fermeture nut* to revolve, as the forward sloping *surface* of its *boss* is engaged with the forward *edge* of the *cam groove* on the *piston*, thus unlocking the *breech block*,

5. When the *firing pin* is fully withdrawn, the large *block* on the *piston rod* carries back the *breech block*, and during this

motion the *cam groove* inside the *body* turns the *firing pin* over to the left, so that its upper *boss* lies in the *recess* in the *breech block*.

6. The empty case, being gripped by the *extractor*, is extracted until its base strikes the *ejector*, when it is ejected.

7. The lower *cam* on the right of the piston rod, working against the forward lower *arm* of the *feed piece*, causes the *lever* of the *feed piece* to move to the left. The *claw* on the *lever*, being kept in one of the centre *clips* of the *strip* by the *spring*, pushes the *strip* over to the left, thus placing a fresh cartridge into position. The *tooth* of the *feed piece spring* rides over the *strip* into the next rear *clip* of the *strip*.

8. As the end of the backward travel of the *piston* is neared, the *bent* on the *piston* rides over the *sear*, depressing it.

9. When the *bent* has passed, the *sear* rises by the influence of the *sear spring*.

10. The *piston* now comes up against the *standard* of the *trigger guard* and can go no further back.

During the backward movement the *recoil spring* has been gradually compressed between its seating in the *collar* in the *piston*, and the *collar* in the *guard*.

B.—Action of the recoil spring.

11. The actions caused by the force of the gas cease when the *piston rod* is arrested in its backward travel. The *spring* then comes into play and moves the *piston rod* forward until the *bent* is caught and held up by the *sear*.

12. If the *trigger* is now pressed the *block* of the *sear* is lowered and released from contact with the *bent* of the *piston rod*. The *recoil spring* coming into play forces the *piston rod* forward.

13. The *firing pin* is taken forward with it, and the upper *boss* of the *firing pin*, being in the *recess* of the *breech block*, takes the *breech block* forward too.

14. The next cartridge, partly forced out of the *strip* by the wedge-shaped *tongue*, is opposite the *chamber*, and the *strip* is held so that it cannot move by the *tooth* on the *feed-piece spring ;* when the *breech block* is taken forward the top edge of its face strikes the bottom of the base of the cartridge, and forces it clear of the *strip* into the *chamber*.

15. The upper *cam* of the *piston* working against the rear *lower arm* of the *feed-piece* causes the *feed-piece* to rotate to the right. This causes the *lever* to ride over the *strip*, until the *claw* is forced into the next centre *clip* of the *strip*, by the *eed-piece spring*.

16. By this time the *breech block* has been sent completely forward, and the *extractor* rides over the rim of the cartridge and grips it.

17. The *groove* in the top of the *body* now rotates the *firing pin* so that its upper *boss* is clear of the *recess*, and opposite the long slot in the *breech block*.

18. As this movement finishes, the *cam groove* on the top of the *piston*, working against the *boss* on the *fermeture nut*, rotates the latter, until it locks the *breech block* securely to the *barrel*.

19. While this rotation is going on, the *firing pin* is still being carried forward, and at the moment after the locking rotation has been completed is carried against the cap and ignites the cartridge.

C.—Mechanism of the trigger.

20. The behaviour of the *trigger mechanism* is controlled by the position of the *disc* on the *cocking handle*.

21. When the *disc* is set to " S " it prevents the backward movement of the *trigger bar*, and the gun cannot be fired.

22. When set to " R " the smaller of the two *recesses* in the *disc* is opposite the *tail* of the *trigger bar*. As the latter is pulled back by pressure on the *trigger*, the *hook* on the front of the *T-headed arm* draws with it the *arm* of the *sear*. This causes rotation of the *sear axis*, and a consequent depression of the *block* of the *sear* which releases the *piston rod*.

23. During this motion, the *sear spring* is put in tension, both by the pulling back of the *trigger bar* and by the rotation of the *sear axis*.

24. As soon as the *trigger bar* has come back far enough to cause the release of the *piston rod*, the *ramp* on its *tail* causes the *disc* to depress it, with the result that the *hook* of the *T-head* is lifted and released from the *arm* of the *sear*. The latter flies forward under the influence of the *spring*, and the *block* of the *sear* therefore rises ready to intercept the *piston rod* when it returns after firing the cartridge.

25. The gun cannot again be fired until the *trigger* is released and the *T-head* allowed to go forward into engagement with the *arm* of the *sear*.

26. In this position of the *disc*, therefore, it is impossible, provided the *mechanism* is in working order, to fire more thar. one shot for each pressure of the *trigger*.

27. When the *disc* is set to " A " its larger *recess* lies opposite the *trigger bar*. The latter, therefore, is not depressed as it passes the *disc*, the *T-head* is not disconnected from the *sear arm*, the *block* of the *sear* is held permanently depressed, and the *piston rod* is not retained at the end of its backward travel. It therefore flies forward again, and continuous fire is obtained so long as pressure is kept on the *trigger*.

28. The *disc* of the *cocking handle* is prevented from turning during firing by the pressure of the *recoil spring* against the *collar* in the *guard* keeping the *nibs* on the front of the *tenons* engaged in the corresponding *recesses* in the *collar*.

D.—Action of the feed-piece after the last round of each strip has been fired.

29. When the last round of a *strip* has been fired, the motion of the *feed-piece lever* to the left generally ejects the empty *strip*, the *head* of the *lever* acting on the extension at the right-hand end of it.

30. The *stem* of the *feed-piece* is forced down by the *feed-piece spring*, as there is no *strip* in the gun to hold it up; consequently the forward *lower arm* of the *feed-piece* becomes engaged with the *shoulder* on the front of the extension on the lower right side of the *piston rod*, thus holding the *piston rod* back.

31. To continue firing, the *stem* of the *feed-piece* must be raised. This action releases the *piston rod* until it is again held up by the *sear*. A fresh *strip* will be inserted.

E.—Cocking the gun by hand.

32. When cocking by hand, the *lugs* on the end of the *cocking handle* engage against the *collar* in the *piston rod*, thus enabling the *piston rod* to be drawn back. The movement is identical to that caused by the gases.

33. The *stops* at the end of the *grooves*, coming against the *nibs* on the *collar* in the *guard*, prevent the *cocking handle* from being pulled out of the gun.

NOTES FOR INSTRUCTORS.

Preliminary—

1. Knowledge of the mechanical actions caused by the two forces " gas " and " spring " is the foundation of a man's line of thought in detecting the cause of any stoppage, and so grasping the action necessary to remedy it.

2. He must, therefore, have a clear mental picture of the mechanical actions caused by each of these forces.

Although aids to establish this picture in the man's mind—such as models, cut guns, diagrams and cinema pictures—are a great help, a good instructor can show it quite clearly by using a gun with certain removable parts detached.

Subjects—

   I.—How a portion of the gases operate the *piston.*

   II.—That the *piston* rotates and unlocks the *fermeture nut.*

   III.—That the *piston* takes back the *firing pin* and *breech block.*

IV.—The rotation of the *firing pin*.

V.—The movement of the *feed-piece* and *strip*.

VI.—The compression of the *recoil spring*.

VII.—How the *recoil spring* actuates the *piston*.

VIII.—The *firing pin* takes the *breech block* forward and is rotated.

IX.—The *upper arm* of the *feed-piece* is moved to the right.

X.—The rotation of the *fermeture nut* and locking of the breech.

XI.—How the *bent* of the *piston* is caught by the *block* of the *sear*.

XII.—On pressing the *trigger*, how the *block* of the *sear* is released from the *bent* of the *piston*.

Kit required.—Gun, spare barrel, ammunition carrier.

NOTES FOR INSTRUCTORS.

Additional mechanism.

Preliminary.

1. There are a few parts of the mechanical functions of the gun which do not lend themselves readily to explanation during the reasoning of the causes of stoppages, and these portions must be taken separately, at a later date.

2. As these parts of the *mechanism* do not come under the heading of the explanation of stoppages, it follows that, as a rule, they do not fail. The same exact knowledge of them is

therefore not required by the man, but the instructor must have complete knowledge, so that he may have confidence in teaching.

3. The best time for the lessons on additional mechanism is after the causes of stoppages not cured by immediate action have been reasoned out.

Subjects—

I.—The *trigger mechanism*.

II.—The action of the *feed-piece* on the last round of the *strip* being fired.

III.—How the gun is cooled.

138. *Stoppages.*

1. It is essential to train men to remedy stoppages in the automatic action of the gun when firing. The aim must be to teach the men to detect the cause of the stoppage quickly and to rectify it without delay.

2. Some causes of stoppages will occur with marked frequency whilst others may never occur within the experience of numerous individuals. For training purposes, therefore, the causes of stoppages can be considered in two categories : (a) **Probable ;** (b) **Possible**.

3. The greater part of the instruction in stoppage remedying must be devoted to ensure speedy and correct action in dealing

with probable causes, whilst only a limited proportion of the available time should be spent on possible causes.

4. A large proportion of stoppages are remedied by certain actions on the part of the firer which can be learnt as a drill and carried out instinctively whenever the gun stops firing. These actions are termed " Immediate Action," and the stoppages cured by their employment are classified as " Immediate Action Stoppages," whilst those which require a further action for their remedy are classified as " Additional Stoppages."

Whenever a stoppage occurs the first action on the part of the firer must always be to perform " Immediate Action."

5. For the purpose of grouping stoppages, three distinct categories are obtained from the position of the *breech block* when the gun stops, viz. :—

(a) When the *breech block* is right forward.

(b) When the *breech block* is *not* right forward.

(c) When the *breech block* is sometimes forward and sometimes back, and the gun fires only a few rounds after applying " Immediate action."

Stoppages.

The position of the *breech block* will be sufficiently indicated by the feel of the gun in the firer's shoulder and the resultant noise after applying " Immediate Action " to eliminate any necessity for actually looking for its position.

The Table should be read from left to right in each horizontal
stoppage the remedy shown in the horizontal column nex
down the pag

1. If the gun stops with the *breech block* forward :—		
A. **COCK THE GUN, RAISE THE FEED PIECE, SHOUT "FEED" TO No. 1, WHO PUSHES THE STRIP HOME, RELAY AND FIRE.**	—	—
B.	If on pressing the *trigger*, the gun does not fire.	UNLOAD AND STRIP GUN AS FAR AS, AND EXAMINE—(i) RECOIL SPRING ; (ii) FIRING PIN. If either is defective :—
C.	—	If neither is defective :—

column (A., B., &c.). If the remedy given does not cure the
below will be tried. Thus the Table will be read across and
diagonally.

A. —	—	**Cause :**—(i) Bad introduction (only occurs on loading); or (ii) Missfire; or (iii) Space in *strip*; or (iv) Hard extraction.
B. CHANGE IT, RELOAD, RELAY, AND FIRE.	—	**Cause :**—(i) Weak or broken *recoil spring* ; or (ii) Worn or broken *firing pin.*
C EXAMINE THE FEEDWAY AND FERMETURE NUT FOR—(i) LOOSE CARTRIDGE CAP;	(i) REMOVE CAP, REASSEMBLE, RELOAD, RELAY AND FIRE.	**Cause :**—Loose cap preventing the *breech block* from closing properly.
(ii) FILINGS OR DIRT.	(ii) STRIP DOWN TO THE FERMETURE NUT, CLEAN MOVING PARTS, REASSEMBLE, RELOAD, RELAY AND FIRE.	**Cause :**—Filings or dirt preventing the *breech block* from closing properly.

2. *Breech block no! forwar* d : —

D. **AS FOR " A."** ...	—	—
E.	If on pressing the *trigger*, the gun does not fire.	EXAMINE THE BAR-REL LOCKING NUT. If *barrel* is out of position.
F.	—	If correct, EXAMINE THE EJECTION OPENING AND CHAMBER.
G.	—	—
H.	—	—

3. Gun fires a few rounds and stops again, or while firing repetition fire, fires 2

I.	—	SCREW UP THE GAS REGULATOR 3 TO 5 TURNS, RELOAD, RE-LAY AND FIRE

Note.—With this stoppage the position of the *breech block* may be either forward stoppage, the position of the

D.		
—	—	**Cause :**—(i) Bad introduction ; or (ii) Hard extraction.
E. RECTIFY, RELOAD, RELAY AND FIRE.	—	**Cause :**—Loose barrel.
F. If an empty case is found jammed in the *ejection opening* at right angles to the *body.*	CLEAR GUN, SCREW UP THE GAS REGULATOR 3 TO 5 TURNS, RELOAD, RELAY AND FIRE.	**Cause :**—Lack of gas pressure.
G. If an empty case is found in the *chamber* with a live round being fed in.	CLEAR GUN, CHANGE THE EXTRACTOR AND SPRING.	**Cause :**—Broken *extractor* or *spring.*
H. If (i) the *breech block* is jammed under a live round with nothing in the *chamber*; or (ii) there is a live round in the *feedway* and another being fed into the *chamber.*	CLEAR GUN AND CHANGE THE STRIP, RELAY AND FIRE.	**Cause :**—Loose round in *strip.*
rounds at one pressure of	the *trigger.*	
I.	—	**Cause :**—Lack of gas pressure.

or back, but as the knowledge of this fact does not assist the firer to remedy this *breech block* is immaterial.

Possible stoppages.

Breech block not forward.	Examine ejection opening and chamber.	
If an empty case is found on the face of the *breech block* or loose in the *feed-way* jammed against another round being fed into the *chamber*.	Change the ejector and spring.	**Cause.** — Broken *ejector* or *spring*.
If a live round is found half-fed into the chamber.	Change the barrel, reload, relay and fire.	**Cause.**— Separated case.

Note.--Generally a cloud of smoke issues from the *ejection opening* as well.

NOTES FOR INSTRUCTORS.

1. For instructional purposes this subject should be divided into the two distinct parts, *i.e.*, " Immediate Action " and " Additional Stoppages."

2. The instinctive procedure termed " Immediate Action " should be taught first. When the recruit is proficient in performing " Immediate Action," he can be taught the causes of those stoppages which are cured by this " Immediate Action." (These are printed in thick type in the foregoing table.) Then, later, the recruit comes to the Additional Stoppages, reasoning from the point where the " Immediate Action " failed.

3. It is unnecessary for men to know every detail of the mechanism of the gun, but they require to know the action of certain parts in order to be able to locate the cause of stoppages. Consequently, teaching of mechanism should be

confined to that which is concerned with each stoppage taught.

4. The following table gives the mechanism that should be taught with each particular stoppage. (The letters refer to the stoppage given in the preceding table.)

Stoppage.	Mechanism.
A	Feeding of the round from the *strip* into the *chamber*.
C	Locking of the *breech*.
G	Extraction.
I	Feeding complete, and the action of the *gas regulator*.

5. As the sights are thrown off the target when a stoppage is remedied, the instructor should insist on the importance of relaying the gun after every stoppage. To inculcate this procedure, he should always give an aiming mark when teaching stoppages and their remedy.

6. Possible stoppages should only be dealt with when the soldier can remedy the probable stoppages efficiently. Moreover, the object of such instruction will rather be to make him thoroughly conversant with the working of the gun under all circumstances than to teach him definite remedies.

7. In quarters, when teaching stoppages, the gun must be set up to simulate what would be the condition of the gun when the stoppage actually occurs. (*See* Section **139** Setting up stoppages.)

Kit required.—Gun and spare parts complete, dummies, empty cases, portion of separated case, instructional landscape target.

139. *Setting up stoppages.*

1. This subject need only be taught to instructors.

2. It is important that the gun should be made to stop under as nearly as possible the same conditions as would occur if firing live ammunition. When the instructor wishes to convey to the firer that " Immediate Action " has failed, he should say " Gun does not fire," or " Gun fires a few rounds and stops again."

3. Some stoppages cannot be set up, but most of the probable ones are easily arranged. The following table is a guide :—

Cause.	In barracks.	On the range.
Breech block forward		
A.—(i) Bad introduction.	Load and then move the *strip* a little to the right.	As for in barracks.
(ii) Misfire.	Allow the firer to begin firing, and then say " Gun stops."	Place a dummy round in the *strip.*
(iii) Space in *strip.*	Cock the gun, move the *strip* back a space and press the *trigger.*	Remove a round from the *strip.*
(iv) Hard extraction.	As for space in *strip,* but place an empty case in the *chamber* before pressing the *trigger.*	As for (ii) or (iii).
B.—(i) Weak or broken recoil *spring.*	As for misfire and when " I.A." has been performed, instructor says " Gun does not fire."	Place 2 dummy rounds in the *strip.*
(ii) Broken *firing pin.*	As for B (i), instructor indicating that the *recoil spring* is correct.	As for B (i).
C. Loose cap or filings.	As for B (i).	As for B (i).

Cause.	In barracks.	On the range.
Breech block not forward.—		
E. Loose *barrel*.	Loosen the *barrel*.	Do not attempt to set up this stoppage.
G. Broken *extractor*.	Load and place an empty case in the *chamber*.	As in barracks.
F. Lack of gas pressure.	Load and place an empty case in the *ejection opening*, at right angles to the gun.	As in barracks.
H. Loose round in *strip*.	Load and lever the nose of the bullet down, so that the *breech block* will miss the base of the round when it goes forward.	As in barracks.
I. Lack of gas pressure.	As for "hard extraction," the instructor saying "Gun fires a few rounds and stops again," after "I.A." has been applied.	Open out *gas regulator* or place 2 dummy rounds in the *strip* 3 or 4 rounds apart.

NOTES FOR IUSTRUCTORS.

Preliminary.—In setting up stoppages the gun should first of all be firing normally, *i.e.*, the firer should be made to load and fire.

1. The stoppages should be set up while the class, including the firer, have their heads turned away from the gun. Thus, in " G," the firer loads, fires and, after pressing the *trigger* to represent a number of bursts, he should be told to pull back

the *cocking handle*, and turn his head away ; the instructor then inserts the empty case, and orders the firer to continue firing, saying " Gun stops " when the *trigger* has been pressed, and " Gun does not fire " when the '' I.A." has been performed.

140. *Examination of the gun.*

1. The following are the principal points to which attention must be paid in examining the gun. Except for the replacement of damaged parts from the parts provided as spare, repairs cannot as a rule, be carried out by the section. The repairs detailed below, as well as the tests to be made by means of gauges, will be undertaken only by a qualified armourer.

2. **Barrel.**—Examine the condition of the *bore, rifling, lead* and *chamber ;* see that the *foresight* is not damaged or displaced ; that the *stud* for the *barrel rest,* the *stop* for the *locking nut,* the interrupted *flanges,* the *key* and *projections* on the rear face of the *barrel* are not damaged ; that the *gas cylinder nozzle* is clear ; and that the *gas regulator* works sufficiently freely to be moved by hand, though not so freely that it will jar round during transport.

3. **Body.**—See that it is not deformed in any part ; that the *thread* for the *locking nut* is not damaged ; that there is no obstruction in the *grooves* of the *feed guides ;* that the *feed mechanism,* the *cartridge stop* and the *ejector* function correctly ; that the *guide groove* for the *firing pin,* in the rear portion, is clear and in good condition ; that the *locking screw* is in good order ; that the *backsight* and *slide* are not damaged; and that the *handguard* fits correctly.

4. **Locking nut.**—See that it functions correctly and is properly held by the *serrations* on the *spring arm.*

5. **Formetura nut.**—See that it is not burred or cracked, and that its *threads* and *boss* are not damaged.

6. **Piston rod.**—See that the working surfaces and the *cam slot* are smooth and not burred ; that the *piston head* is not cracked ; and that the face of the *recess* on the underside with which the *sear* engages has not been tampered with.

Note.—No attempt must be made to lighten the pull-off by altering the shape of the rear *face* of the *recess* or of the *sear*. If this is done, the *sear* will fail to retain the *moving parts* when the *stem* of the *feed piece* is pressed up to release them and so prevent the gun from being loaded ; also if the retention of the *piston* is insecure it will render the gun unsafe. As a test for this the gun, unloaded, should be cocked, set at " safe," and then jarred by grounding the butt.

7. **Breech block.**—See that all the surfaces are smooth and not burred ; that the *interrupted thread* is in good condition ; that the front *shoulder* of the *recess* on the left for the *firing pin* is not cracked or broken ; that the hole in the face for the point of the *firing pin* is clear ; and that the *extractor* is in good order.

8. The armourer should occasionally test the distance of the face from the end of the *chamber* with ·064 in. and ·074 in. gauges. In order to do this, the *cocking handle, guard* with *butt stock, recoil spring, firing pin, extractor, feed piece* and *hand guard* must be removed. The removal of the *firing pin* and *extractor* necessitates the removal of the *piston* and *breech block*, both of which must subsequently be replaced. The removal of the *hand guard* also necessitates the removal of the *barrel.* The forward end of the *piston* can now be controlled with one hand whilst the thumb of the other hand is applied to the rear end of the *breech block* to push it forward,.

thereby ensuring a ight control on to the gauge. The *breech block* should clo e over the ·064-in. gauge, but ot over the ·074-in. gauge. In the latter ca e, the *fermeture nut* should not turn into its complete locking position ; if it does, either the *breech block* or the *fermeture nut* is defective.

9. **Firing pin.**—See that the *point* is not damaged and that the upper and lower *bosses* are in good condition, and their surfaces smooth.

10. **Recoil spring.**—See that it is not cracked or broken.

11. **Guard.**—Examine the *trigger mechanism,* and see that it works correctly ; that the rear face of the *sear* has not been tampered with ; that the *collar* against which the *recoil spring* bears is correct ; that the *butt* is not split or broken ; and that the *hinged strap* is in good condition. If the *oil bottle* is fitted it should be seen that it is firmly fixed in the *butt.* If it cannot be tightened up by means of the *screw collar* a *washer* of leather or other suitable material should be inserted under th flange at the bottom.

Note.—Where burrs or roughness on working surfaces are found during examination, the parts should be taken to the armourer who will smooth them down with fine emery cloth.

12. **Tripod.**—Examine the *yoke* and *spring catches* and see that they fit the *trunnions* of the *barrel* correctly ; see that the *vice pins* and *clamps* function properly ; that the *legs* are in good condition and not over splayed.

13. **Strip.**—See that the *clips* are not cracked or broken, and, if necessary, use the *resizing tool* to restore their shape.

14. **Spare parts.**—See that they are complete and in good order.

NOTES FOR INSTRUCTORS.

The object of this lesson is to teach the men of the Section, especially No. 1, what to look for when examining the gun. This examination should be done periodically, and whenever a fresh gun is taken over.

Kit required.—Gun and spare parts complete. Any examples of defective parts, such as a bulged barrel, cut barrel, &c., as may be available.

141. *Spare parts, diagrams and cut guns.*

1. The list of **spare parts** is set out in Appendix III to this manual. All trained Hotchkiss gunners should know what *spare parts* are carried, and be able to check for deficiencies without a written list.

2. A complete set of *spare parts* should be shown and packed in the *spare parts bag* by the class under instruction.

3. Hotchkiss gun **diagrams** should be hung on the walls of drill halls and barrack-room passages as far as the scale of issue permits.

4. Any points of the mechanism of the gun not fully understood by any of the class should be further demonstrated by means of diagrams. The best value is obtained from diagrams if they are so placed that men have access to them out of parade hours.

5. **Skeleton guns** are limited in number, but when obtainable they should be used to clear up any mechanical points which the class may be in doubt about.

ANTI-AIRCRAFT—HOTCHKISS GUN.

The system of anti-aircraft training with the Hotchkiss gun is the same as for the Lewis gun, except that the *sights* are attached to the gun in a different manner (see Secs. **116** to **123**).

142. *Fixing the sights to the gun.*

1. The *foresight* is clamped on to the *foresight stool* of the gun by means of the *clamping screw*, and the *tension screw* tightened to prevent the *clamping screw* becoming loose during firing. The *body* of the *foresight* should be flush with the *gun foresight stool* and with the *screw* to the left.

2 The *backsight* is assembled to the *leaf* of the *gun backsight*, the *slide* of the latter being moved forward sufficiently to enable the *body* of the *A.A. backsight* to be assembled from underneath. A *clamping plate*, pivoted to a *thumb screw* on top of the *body* on the right is then swung inwards over the upper surface of the *gun sight leaf*, its free end engaging a *retaining groove* in the left wall of the *leaf groove* in the *body*, which is finally secured by tightening up the *thumb screw*. The *slide* of the *gun backsight* should be set at 400.

3. The *sights* should be hinged down when not in use, in order to avoid damage.

143. *Anti-aircraft elementary handling— Hotchkiss gun.*

1. The ammunition will be placed on the right of the gun at two paces interval, with the *A.A mounting* at another two paces.

2. A model aeroplane will be used as a target.

3. On the command " **Fall In** " :—

   (a) No. 1 takes up a position on the left of the *ammunition carrier*, and examines the ammunition.

   (b) No. 2 takes up a position on the left of the gun, examines the gun, raises the *foresight*, and reports " Ready."

   (c) No. 3 takes up a position, examines the *mounting*, and slings it on his shoulder.

4. On the command " **Aircraft Action** " :—

   (a) No. 3 runs to the firing-point with the *mounting*.

   (b) No. 2 runs to the firing-point with the gun as soon as No. 3 has reached the firing-point.

   (c) No. 1 follows No. 2 with the ammunition.

5. On arriving at the firing-point :—

   (a) No. 3 sets up the *mounting* at a suitable height for the firer.

   (b) No. 1 gets a *strip* ready to load.

   (c) No. 2 mounts the gun with No. 3's help, raises the *backsight*, loads, and fires without further orders.

   (d) No. 3 stands on the left of No. 2.

   (e) No. 1 keeps the ammunition ready on the right of No. 2.

6. On the command " **Cease Firing** " :—

   (a) No. 2, assisted by No. 1, unloads and shouts " Gun Clear," lowers the *backsight,* and dismounts the gun.

   (b) No. 3 assists No. 2, and picks up the *mounting.*

   (c) No. 1 packs up the ammunition.

7. All move to the " **Cease firing** " position when they are ready.

8. On reaching this position :—

   (a) No. 2 lowers the *foresight.*

   (b) No. 3 folds up the *mounting.*

Tests of Elementary Training— Hotchkiss Gun.

144. *General instructions.*

1. Tests of elementary training suitable for testing a man's efficiency at three stages of his training are set out in the Table below :—

   (a) Those of Standard " A " are suitable for the recruit to pass before firing the Hotchkiss Gun part of Table " A."

   (b) Those of Standard " R " are suitable for the soldier to pass before firing the Hotchkiss Gun part of Table " R " and Table " T."

(c) Those of Standard " L " are suitable for the soldier
    qualified to fire Table L.

2. Every soldier before firing the Range Practices of the
Annual Course should pass the Tests of the Standard applicable to whichever Table he is about to fire.

3. The passing of the Tests must on no account be judged
merely on the time limit, as accuracy of manipulation is the
important consideration.   Consequently, even though a man
completes the test in the time limit but at the same time is
incorrect in some part of the handling, he should be judged
as having failed to pass the Test.

TESTS OF ELEMENTARY

In all tests where number 3 takes an active part, the test
       is obviously due to faulty manipulation by

Method of

STANDARD

Test.	Kit required.	Conditions before Test.
1. Loading.	Gun — *Spare parts* —*Strips* — *Drill ammunition.*	Nos. 1 and 2 lying behind the gun. No. 1 to have a full *strip* ready. *Breech block* to be forward. *Butt* on the ground. *Hinged strap* down and *Cocking handle* at " S."
2. Unloading.	Ditto.	Nos. 1 and 2 in the correct firing position. *Breech block* to be back. *Sights* set at 300 yds
3. Adjustment of *Sights.*	Ditto.	No. 2 lying behind the gun. Gun loaded and *sights* at zero.
4. Aiming.	Gun — *Spare parts* eye disc.	No. 2 in the correct firing position, but with head raised so that he is observing the target over the *backsight*. *Breech block* back. *Feed piece* raised. Instructor must see that the **Gun is " clear."**

TRAINING.—HOTCHKISS GUN.

should be regarded as a test of both numbers, and if failure one the other should be given another trial.

conducting Test.

" A."

Manipulation Tested.	Standard Time.	Remarks.
1. On the command " Load," No. 2 cocks the gun, and assisted by No. 1, loads correctly, leaving the *cocking handle* at " A."	4 secs. from the command " Load " until No. 2 says " Up."	The man will be tested 4 times and must pass 3 times.
2. On the command " Unload," No. 2 unloads correctly, assisted by No. 1, No. 1 puts the *strips* back in the *carrier.*	6 secs. from the command " Unload " until both numbers are standing up.	—
3. On the range being given, No. 2 sets the *sights.*	5 secs.	A maximum range of 400 yds. may be given. Each man to pass 3 out of 4 times.
4. Correct holding and aiming.	5 secs. from the command " Go " until No. 2 presses the trigger.	3 out of 4 aims to be correct. The height of the eye *disc* will be varied for each aim.

Test.	Kit required.	Conditions before Test.
5. "Action" (Dis-mounted).	Gun — *Spare parts* — Spare *barrel* — *Ammunition carrier* — *Landscape target.*	No. 2 lying behind the gun. No. 1 two paces to the right of No. 2, in the lying position. *Sights* at zero.

" A "—*continued.*

Manipulation Tested.	Standard Time.	Remarks.
5. On the command " Range — Indication — Action " Nos. 1 and 2 double forward 5 yds. independently, No. 2 mounts the gun correctly on the spot indicated, and, assisted by No. 1, loads, sets the *sights* to the range given and aims correctly.	20 secs. from the command " Action " until No. 1 puts his hand up.	A maximum range of 400 yds. may be given.

Test.	Kit required.	Conditions before Test.
6. Adjustment of *sights*.	Same as Test 3.	Same as Test 3.
7. Aiming.	Same as Test 4.	No. 2 lying behind the gun. *Butt* on the ground, *breech block back*, with *feed-piece* raised. *Sights* at 300 yds **Gun to be " clear."**
8. Filling *strips*.	*Strips* — Ammunition.	Ammunition to be in a heap. Loader to be sitting. The *strip* to be on the loader's thigh, not on the ground. He may be ready to put the first round into the *strip*
9. " Action."	Same as Test 5.	Same as Test 5.
10. Immediate action.	Same as Test 5.	Nos. 1 and 2 in the correct firing position. The instructor gives the command " Fire "—" Gun Stops."
11. " Cease firing."	Same as Test 5.	Nos. 1 and 2 in the correct firing positions. Gun loaded with the *breech block* back.

Manipulation Tested.	Standard Time	Remarks.
6. Same as Test 3.	4 secs.	—
7. Instructor gives the command " Go." No. 2 aims and presses the *trigger.*	5 secs. from the command " Go " until No. 2 presses the trigger.	As for Test 4.
8. *Strip* correctly filled—so as not to cause a stoppage.	1 min. 10 secs. from the command " Go ' until loader says " Up."	Normally dummy ammunition will be used for this Test but live ammunition may be used provided the test is carried out on the range and the precautions taken to prevent live ammunition getting mixed with dummy ammunition.
9. Same as Test 5.	17 secs.	—
10. Immediate action performed correctly by both Nos. 1 and 2. No. 2's aim should be checked as he presses the *trigger* on completing the I.A.	5 secs. from the command " Gun stops " until No. 2 completes the Immediate Action, *i.e.,* presses the trigger.	3 out of 4 tries to be correct.
11. On the command " Cease firing," No. 2 unloads correctly and No. 1 replaces the *strips* in the *carrier.* Both numbers move back 5 yds. and lie down.	12 secs. from the command " Cease firing" until Nos. 1 and 2 are in the " Cease firing " position.	—

Test	Kit required.	Conditions before Test.
12. Reloading.	Same as for Test 5.	Nos. 1 and 2 in the correct firing position, *Breech block* held back by the *feed piece* as if the last round of a strip had been fired. Empty *strip* not completely thrown out of the gun. Word of command to be " Change."
13. Remedying a stoppage due to filings.	As for Test 5. D.P. gun must be used.	Nos. 1 and 2 in the correct firing positions, *Breech block* forward. The instructor gives the command "Gun stops" and when No. 2 has applied the "immediate action," "Gun does not fire."
14. Changing the *barrel.*	As for Test 5. D.P. gun must be used.	Nos. 1 and 2 in the correct firing positions. Gun loaded but *breech block* back. The spare *barrel*, in its *case.*
15. "Action"	*Pack,* complete with gun, spare *barrel*, in its *case — Drill ammunition —* Equipment, Battle order.	The detachment will be mounted in their correct formation. The gun will be in its cover on the pack. The detachment will move forward at "The Trot." The instructor will indicate beforehand the fire position— Range and Target, and when the detachment is within about 30 yards of the fire position will give the command "For action Dismount."

Manipulation Tested.	Standard Time.	Remarks.
12. On the command "Change," No. 2 presses up the *feed piece*, keeping the *butt* in the shoulder. No. 1 reloads with a fresh *strip* and No. 2 relays his aim.	3 secs. from the command "Change" until No. 2 is ready to fire again.	To pass in 3 out of 4 tries.
13. On the command "Gun does not fire," No. 2 clears the gun correctly, strips down to the *fermeture nut*, and cleans the *breech block* and *fermeture nut*; reassembles the gun, reloads and fires.	1 min. 20 secs. from the command "Gun does not fire" until the gun is again firing.	No. 1 may assist No. 2 in any way. The correct sequence of stripping need not be followed, but damage to the gun in stripping and assembling must be avoided.
14. On the command "Change the *barrel*," No. 2, assisted by No. 1, unloads and changes the *barrel* correctly, reloads and fires.	30 secs. from the command "Change" until No. 2 fires again.	The *barrel* to be changed must not be touched by the hands of either No. 1 or 2.
15, On the command "For Action Dismount," Nos. 1 and 2 dismount, hand over their horses to No. 3, take the gun, spare *barrel* and one *ammunition carrier* off the pack, double forward to the fire position, mount the gun correctly in the position indicated, load, adjust the *sights* and aim at the target given.	1 min. 20 secs. from the command "For action dismount" until No. 2 is ready to fire.	—

Test.	Kit required.	Conditions before Test.
16. " Cease firing."	As for Test 15.	No. 1 and 2 in the correct firing positions. Gun loaded but *breech block* back. The led horses to be 25 yds. away from the gun position.
17. " A.A. Action."	Gun—*Spare parts* — A.A. *sights* — A.A. *mounting* — Target aeroplane —*Strips* and *Drill ammunition.*	Nos. 1, 2 and 3 perform the same duties as they do before reporting " Ready " in A.A elementary handling. No. 1 reports " Ready."

"L"—*continued.*

Manipulation Tested.	Standard Time.	Remarks.
16. On the command "Mount," No. 2, assisted by No. 1, unloads, No. 1 replaces the strips in the *carrier.* Both Nos. double to the *pack*; No. 2 puts the gun on the pack and mounts; No. 1 replaces the spare barrel and *ammunition* carrier on the *pack,* fastens the *straps* and mounts.	1 min. 30 secs. from the word of command until both numbers are mounted.	—
17. On the command "Aircraft Action" the 3 numbers perform the necessary duties as laid down in A.A. elementary handling. No. 2 fires as soon as he has taken the correct aim on his target	14 secs. from the command "Aircraft Action" until No. 2 presses the *trigger.*	The instructor will check the aim by means of the *aim corrector.*

(B 27/7)Q 14009—4980/728 100M 5/24 H & S Ltd. **Gp.27** Gs. 295.

www.ingramcontent.com/pod-product-compliance
Lightning Source LLC
Chambersburg PA
CBHW031937080426
42735CB00007B/169